Edward Carroll

Principles and Practice of Finance

A Practical Guide for Bankers, Merchants and Lawyers

Edward Carroll

Principles and Practice of Finance
A Practical Guide for Bankers, Merchants and Lawyers

ISBN/EAN: 9783743404618

Manufactured in Europe, USA, Canada, Australia, Japa

Cover: Foto ©Suzi / pixelio.de

Manufactured and distributed by brebook publishing software (www.brebook.com)

Edward Carroll

Principles and Practice of Finance

PRINCIPLES AND PRACTICE OF FINANCE

A PRACTICAL GUIDE FOR BANKERS, MERCHANTS, AND LAWYERS. TOGETHER WITH A SUMMARY OF THE NATIONAL AND STATE BANKING LAWS, AND THE LEGAL RATES OF INTEREST, TABLES OF FOREIGN COINS, AND A GLOSSARY OF COMMERCIAL AND FINANCIAL TERMS.

BY

EDWARD CARROLL, JR.

G. P. PUTNAM'S SONS

NEW YORK　　　　　　　　　LONDON
27 WEST TWENTY-THIRD STREET　　24 BEDFORD STREET, STRAND

The Knickerbocker Press

1897

PREFACE.

WHILE there are many books treating of the principles of money and some which discuss the operations of finance, to the writer's knowledge there is no one work combining both a treatment of principles and a discussion of practices. This apparent want the writer has sought to supply in the present work, and he hopes that the practical information contained herein will be sufficient reason for its issue. This book is intended to be a practical one, from which a person can obtain data on the subjects treated, rather than an exhaustive exposition of the theory of money. The Principles of Finance are discussed only to that extent deemed necessary to enable the reader, uneducated in the principles of money; to clearly understand the Practice of Finance.

The book is divided into two parts. The first which deals only with the Principles of Finance, and the second which is confined to the practical application of those principles through the machinery of finance and commerce.

The principles of finance are discussed in the first two chapters in as short space as is compatible with a sufficiently comprehensive treatment to make them clear.

The remainder of the book is devoted to the Practice of Finance, and, while it is necessarily not exhaustive, it has been sought to discuss those parts of finance, a knowledge of which is most necessary.

The writer, fully realizing the practical impossibility of any one individual possessing sufficient information of the various subjects discussed to treat of them authoritatively, has freely availed himself of information obtainable by him, and desires here to acknowledge his indebtedness to many bankers and business men for their kind interest in his work and the valuable data afforded him.

The entire manuscript, involving as it necessarily does many legal questions, has been submitted to Messrs. Redfield & Redfield, whom the writer desires especially to thank for their painstaking work. The author's thanks are also due to Mr. D. D. Sherman for his able advice as to many legal questions; to Mr. Frank H. Edmunds for information in regard to the presentation and protest of negotiable paper; to Mr. I. L. Carroll for valuable data in relation to stocks and bonds; and particularly to Mr. Maurice L. Muhleman, of the United States Sub-Treasury at New York, for his uniform courtesy in supplying the writer with statistical information, and especially in regard to the United States Sub-Treasury; and to Mr. William Sherer, the present manager of the New York Clearing House, for information in relation to that institution.

No one realizes more fully than the writer the liability to error in a work covering so large a field, the information for which must be drawn from many sources; and while he cannot even hope, despite his efforts to render his work as free from error as possible, a complete immunity therefrom, he asks for a fair consideration of the work in its entirety.

CONTENTS.

PART I.

PRINCIPLES OF FINANCE.

CHAPTER I.

                                                                    PAGE
Introductory — Barter — Value — Barter — Money — Bullion — Metal Money — Fiat Money — Paper Money — Government Regulation of Money and Currency 1

CHAPTER II.

Capital — Credit — Interest — Exchange — Price 27

PART II.

PRACTICE OF FINANCE.

CHAPTER I.

Money and Currency of the United States — The New York Sub-Treasury 60

CHAPTER II.

Banks — National Bank Act . . 68

CHAPTER III.

State Banks — New York State Banks of Deposit, and Banking Laws . 90

CONTENTS.

CHAPTER IV.

Methods of Business of Banks—Loans—Mutual Assistance—Over-Certification—Reclamation—Management—Board of Directors—Officers and Employés 110

CHAPTER V.

New York Clearing House 132

CHAPTER VI.

Savings Banks 138

CHAPTER VII.

Trust Companies 150

CHAPTER VIII.

Safe Deposit Companies—Building and Mutual Loan Associations—Co-operative Loan Associations—Mortgage and Debenture Companies 163

CHAPTER IX.

Private Bankers—Brokers—Stock Brokers—Note Brokers—Puts and Calls 178

CHAPTER X.

Exchanges—New York Stock Exchange 194

CHAPTER XI.

Corporations, Officers, Etc. 200

CHAPTER XII.

Stocks, Bonds, Interest Warrants, and Receivers' Certificates . . 209

CHAPTER XIII.

Commercial Houses—Commercial Agencies . . . 230

CHAPTER XIV.

Transmission and Remittance of Money—Money Orders—Cheque Banks—Commercial Bills—Cable and Telegraph Transfers . . 237

CHAPTER XV.

Notes—Endorsements—Drafts—Bills of Exchange—Notary Presentation—Protest—Notice of Protest—Checks—Course of Check through a Bank—Cashiers' Checks—Certificates of Deposit—Letters of Credit—Table Showing U. S. Treasurer's Valuation of Foreign Coins—Table Giving Weight of Alloyed and Pure Metal of Units of Value of Principal Countries 246

CHAPTER XVI.

Interest—Grace—Legal Holidays 268

GLOSSARY 277

INDEX 305

PRINCIPLES AND PRACTICE OF FINANCE.

PART I.

PRINCIPLES OF FINANCE.

CHAPTER I.

Introductory—Barter—Value—Barter—Money—Bullion—Metal Money—Fiat Money—Paper Money—Government Regulation of Money and Currency.

IN order that the subject of this work "Finance," should be clearly presented and intelligently read, it is deemed necessary to point out, if but briefly, the natural development of its different principles; and after the development of those principles has been indicated, their application to business and financial methods and systems will be discussed.

The various articles on the principles of Finance are not intended to be exhaustive, but simply to lay a groundwork for the proper understanding of those principles in their application to the business of Finance.

First. As to the development of principles; which it is well to trace from their birth.

In the earliest stage of human existence, when primitive man secured or accumulated by effort or by accident something which was either useful to or which was desired by others, and for the possession of which they were willing to part with some possession, such thing became valuable, and the principle of value was established.

So soon as an exchange was effected of one thing for another, that minute the principle of barter came into being. It was not possible however that the possessor of a particular commodity in excess of his immediate needs should be able to exchange that commodity for all the other commodities or things which he desired; resort was therefore had to the conversion of such surplus into some intermediate commodity which the owner could use at his pleasure in procuring what he wished, and upon the exchange of such surplus for this intermediate value or commodity, the third great principle of finance and the first and chief function of true money was established. Necessarily this intermediate value must be one of as nearly as possible staple and indestructible value and hence naturally would become not only an intermediate value, but also the agent of divisibility of value, and by reason of its possession of these qualities it naturally became the measure of the value of other commodities and the fourth principle, a measure of value, arose.

So soon as this surplus product could be converted into value of a permanent character, and thus made available for future use, an accumulation of value or capital became a fact.

Credit was surely created when the possessor of one value delivered that value to another, receiving at the time of the delivery a promise that at some future time an equivalent in value would be given.

The first charge made for the use of capital or credit was "Interest."

The money-changers were probably the earliest bankers.

They not only changed money, but kept it for others, and loaned it at interest.

The simplest example of what has since developed into exchange, is where A having a claim against B, and owing a similar amount to C, directs B to pay to C, which being done both debts are cancelled.

The assumption by early kings of the sole right to issue coins and to compel their circulation, whether possessed of the value stamped on them or not, was the beginning of fiat money, and out of this assumption naturally grew governmental control of both metal and paper money, bankers and banks.

The money value of things is termed "Price," and "Price" has existed ever since money has been used as a means of expressing values.

The above constitutes all the real principles of Finance, and on them, singly or combined, every transaction must rest; and to one or more of them every financial proposition is deducible.

We shall now discuss these principles somewhat in detail.

Barter.—The simultaneous and direct exchange of one commodity, thing, or value, for another commodity, thing, or value, without the intervention of an intermediate commodity, such as money, or the promise of some other value or commodity, as credit.

Barter presupposes a recognition of property rights, as a person would not be likely to make an exchange with another except for what he believed and admitted to be the property of that person. This recognition of property rights marks the first step in the moral development of man from the plane of the lower animals, where, without regard to, or recognition of, the rights of others, he took that which his wishes or necessities dictated, peaceably, stealthily, or forcibly, as occasion required or his mood suggested. When, however, owing to climatic conditions or the danger of destruction from other animals more powerful and ferocious than himself, he found it necessary for his protection and preservation to live with other men, then a community of interest was created, the very corner-stone of which was individual effort; but individual effort, in order to be put forth, must be sure of its reward; this reward must be recognized and accorded by others to be fully enjoyed, *i. e.*, property rights (value).

Value.—Before proceeding further with the discussion of barter we must define Value, the existence of which must be anterior to barter, although barter may be the act which frequently fixes the value of a thing.

Value—the amount of other commodities for which a thing can be exchanged in open market, the ratio in which one thing exchanges against others, the command which one commodity has over others in traffic,—in political economy distinguished from " price," which is worth estimated in money, while "value" is worth estimated in commodities in general,—the quantity of labor, or of the product of labor, which will exchange for a given quantity of some other product thereof.

Hence, while value is in the first instance the creation of labor—and nothing which Nature supplies in such abundance as to require no labor on the part of man to adapt to his use has any exchangeable value,—yet labor is not the only element in determining the exchangeable worth or value of a thing, but supply and demand are also factors. As a broad proposition, however, the amount of labor expended or required in the procuring or production of a given article, and therefore the amount of labor for which that article can be exchanged, indicates its value. While values are created by labor, it does not follow that all labor creates values, consequently only labor producing some commodity or conferring some good for which man is willing to part with some other commodity or service need be considered.

Limitation of quantity and capability of measurement are two essential elements in order that a thing may possess value. Another requisite is that the commodity have in itself some quality or substance useful or agreeable to man or necessary to the maintenance of other life on which his depends, and by a selection fostered by necessity and ranging over the period of human life these intrinsic qualities of things have been discovered and adapted to man's needs, and the possession of these qualities in any substance constitutes, if not the greatest, at any rate, a large portion of their value.

Barter—Resumed.—While transactions in barter are perhaps fewer as civilization progresses, yet it is the real basis of all trade and commerce, and the relative values of commodities to each other, as fixed by barter, are what govern now just as much as they ever did, and although the merchant sells his wheat or cotton for so much in money, that amount is regulated after all by how much manufactured product or other commodities the wheat or cotton, for example, will exchange for.

In order that even Barter should be practised, it immediately became necessary that the respective persons to the trade should agree upon some measure of the value of the respective thing or things which they desired to exchange. The ultimate measure of this value was necessarily the amount of effort put forth in the production or procuring of the things to be exchanged,—in other words, the labor.

As long as barter was confined to individuals of the same tribe, probably the article of most general use in the tribe was accepted as such measure. Thus, among pastoral people, the sheep, horse, or cow was the measure of value; whereas, among agricultural people, a given quantity of some cereal was doubtless used for this purpose. As long as this barter did not go beyond the confines of trade—which, in its more restricted and technical meaning, is the dealing between individuals of the same community,—a local measure of value was sufficient; but the moment it grew into commerce—or the dealing between communities or countries, or the individuals of different countries or tribes,—that moment another and more generally accepted standard became absolutely necessary.

We have now come to the consideration of one of the functions of money which will be treated more in detail under the head of money. We have neither the time nor the inclination to trace the different standards of value, nor do we believe that it could be here done to advantage.

Metals, being the first commodities of general use by all peoples by natural selection, became the measure of value.

In this connection we naturally inquire why metals should have been selected, as we know there must have been good reasons, first why they were selected, and secondly why their use should have continued.

We answer: First, because of their value—the large amount of value compressed into a small compass. Second, their portability—the ease with which they can be taken from place to place. Third, their comparative indestructibility, metals being the least destructible of all substances capable of receiving an impress marking their value. Fourth, their homogeneity—a given weight of a particular metal being, or capable of being, made of equal value. Fifth, divisibility—the quality of being divided into larger or smaller proportions without disproportionate accretion or loss. Sixth, their stability of value—*i. e.*, the ratio in which they exchange for other values; and seventh, cognizibility, impressibility, or coinability—meaning not only a general recognition of their commodity value, but also the ability to impress or stamp letters or characters.

These conditions are essential, and the metal possessing

most of these characteristics will by a law as certain as that of gravitation, be chosen as the measure of value. Mankind has found that gold possesses in a larger degree than any other metal these essentials, hence its almost universal choice among civilized nations as the measure of value.

Barter necessitates immediate exchange, but it is not always either possible or desirable to immediately deliver or receive the article or articles, service or advantage given or sought. Hence we naturally seek to convert the product of our labor into some commodity of stable, indestructible, and well recognized value, with which we may at our convenience secure what portion we desire of other commodities or services. This brings us to the consideration of the divisibility of value, and on this question it is well to be somewhat explicit.

It is often erroneously asserted that money is necessary for the purpose of divisibility, especially where the division is effected at a time remote from that of the original transaction. The following illustration will show that such is not the case:

A farmer takes to market say a thousand bushels of wheat. This he desires to exchange for other commodities. Should he receive in exchange for his wheat, at the time of delivery, one particular commodity of equal value, the barter would be completed then and there; but the probabilities are that he would not need only one thing, but many, some of which would not be possessed by the person with whom he dealt, hence he would have to act as his own distributing agent, making many transactions in order to secure the different commodities for which he was desirous of exchanging his wheat, and probably not getting what he wanted at once or when he wanted it.

To avoid these numerous exchanges, and to economize not only the farmer's time, but the time of those with whom he deals, the merchant or distributing agent has arisen. To the merchant the farmer sells his wheat, and from him receives either money—an intermediate value, exchangeable at any time for any of the many values which he desires in exchange for such wheat—or a credit —improperly called, in reality an obligation of the merchant,—which he can use as his necessities or wishes dictate in the purchase of those commodities which he desires. Or credit may have been extended to the farmer in anticipation, or the value of the wheat may have been advanced him in various other values before the wheat was delivered.

This certainly is the method by which a large majority of the country stores throughout the States are conducted; and while the intervention of credit or money as a medium of exchange and divisibility would technically destroy the character of the transaction as one in simple barter, as a matter of fact it only facilitates the disposal of values and avoids the necessity of the immediate consummation of the final exchange, rendering it possible for the parties thereto to receive such commodities at such times as they desire.

Inasmuch as the agricultural products of the world, while produced during different months in various countries, are still, generally speaking, only produced in each country during about six months of the year, and as all men must subsist upon that which has been produced, it follows that man must make provision during those six months for his subsistence and maintenance during the other six months, and the surplus then produced must be so exchanged as to provide him with a credit from the ending of such season till the produce of the next season is marketable. Hence credits occupy so important a position in commercial life. It may be said, broadly speaking, that, the world over, man lives twelve months on the product of six months' labor, and that in these six months he must provide for the twelve months which are to follow. This, perhaps, is not true to the same extent of the peoples engaged in manufactures and distribution, which after all are but auxiliary industries dependent for their life upon those creative industries, of which agriculture, fisheries, and mining are the principal,— these industries creating values, whereas manufactures and distribution simply change the form of, and add to, the value of the raw material. Although what has just been said belongs more particularly to credit than to barter, still, as credit is but the outcome of barter and dependent upon barter, it has been thought best to here insert it.

The business of the world is done strictly on the basis of barter, and the vast credits which are extended are but the representatives of the enormous transactions in barter; money, on account of its insignificant proportion to the exchanges consummated annually, forming but a relatively small item to credit in the commercial transactions of the globe.

While a comparatively small percentage of the business of the world is done by direct and immediate exchange of one or more commodities or values for one or more other commodities or values, money or credits nearly always intervening as a medium for the purposes stated, yet inasmuch as all commerce is regulated by barter, money, which does not and cannot in any broad sense either diminish or increase values, and is but a temporary medium in their exchange, must adjust itself to the conditions of barter.

Having heretofore shown rather incidentally the relation of money to barter, we now proceed to a more specific consideration of the subject.

Money.—Webster defines money as:

First—" A piece of metal, as gold, silver, copper, etc., coined or stamped, and issued by the sovereign authority as a medium of exchange in financial transactions between citizens and with the government ; also, any number of such pieces ; coin."

Second—"Any general or stamped promise, certificate, or order, as a government note, bank note, a certificate of deposit, etc., which is payable in standard coined money, and is lawfully current in lieu thereof ; in a comprehensive sense, any currency usually and lawfully employed in buying and selling."

Money is, first, a thing possessing a universally recognized intrinsic value, but not necessarily of a universally exchangeable power ; and, secondly, money based upon credit, *i. e.*, promises to redeem in some commodity, usually gold or silver. For the purposes of convenience, gold and silver and other metals, all possessing universally recognized values, have been accepted as the money of civilization, and all paper money (credits) or promises to pay are payable in some one or more of these metals. It may be well to remark parenthetically that while money is currency, currency is not necessarily money.

All true money being itself a commodity, possessed of an intrinsic value, used as a means to facilitate barter or the exchange of one value for another, and being always of a smaller aggregate value than the combined value of the numerous commodities or values, the exchange of which it is called upon to facilitate, must adjust itself to this greater combined value, rather than that the greater value of all other commodities should adjust itself to money ; although money, being the standard of value, the price of other commodities, as measured by money, changes, and not the price of money. The purchasing power of money in the markets of the world is governed by its commodity value.

Hence it follows, should the ratio of increase of money be greater than the ratio of increase of other values, or should a given amount of labor produce a larger quantity of bullion, then the purchasing or exchangeable power of money becomes less, and other values, which are measured by it, greater, as was illustrated by the discovery of gold in California, when, owing to the vast supply of gold and the comparatively small output of labor required to secure it, the relation between it and other commodities was disturbed, and its exchangeable value became very much less, and the relative value of the other commodities to it very much greater. Should the ratio of increase of money be less than the ratio of increase of other commodities, then the relative value of money becomes greater and the value of all other commodities, compared with this particular commodity (money), less; but should the other commodities maintain their relative value to each other, the holders of other commodities are not sufferers thereby, as their relative value to each other is not disturbed, and the holder of money is certainly just as much entitled to receive the benefit of its enhancement in value as he is liable to suffer the loss of its depreciation.

Paper money, or promises to pay, secured by a mortgage of either the income of a government or a compulsory deposit or retention by an individual or corporation of a certain percentage of bullion, is not and cannot in any sense be considered true money, but should be designated as currency, as it passes current in lieu of money, and as it lacks the universality of value and exchangeable quality which all true money does possess. Its usfulness as a means of facilitating exchange or barter is measured by the knowledge of the acceptor of such currency of the ability of the issuer to redeem it in coin; thus gold and silver, possessing as they do a universally known intrinsic value, are receivable in every portion of the world, civilized and uncivilized; but a legal-tender note of the United States, or a Bank of England note, would not be received in exchange for values by people ignorant of the ability of the respective issuers or obligors to redeem such promises, or to give for such notes an exchangeable value proportionate to the value of the commodity transferred.

Paper money is nothing more than a promisory note payable on demand in a particular commodity (money). Should either the government or the individual promising to pay fail so to do the note would simply be a piece of writing, obligating the issuer to the payment of that value, and nothing more, and its value is therefore dependent upon the ability of the issuer to pay.

One of the chief uses of money is as the measure of value, and in the treatment of this aspect of the question it is impossible to avoid some discussion of whether there should be one or more measures of value, and whether it be necessary that all money should be a measure of value, rather than some particular kind of money. It does not deprive a particular kind of money of its utility that it is not the universally accepted measure of value, but only deprives it of one function and makes it subsidiary in one respect, as a measure of value, to the money which is such measure; nor does it deprive it of its intrinsic value, which still remains, and is recognized in different proportions by different peoples; but for the convenience of commerce it is not only best, but absolutely necessary, that some particular form of money should be the accepted measure; and that form which possesses in itself the greatest intrinsic value, maintains the most uniform relative value, and is the most convenient for use, will of necessity become the standard of value, and other moneys will have their value regulated by it, exactly the same as every other commodity.

There can be but one standard of value, and that standard is fixed not by the laws of a particular country or even a number of countries acting together, but by the general consensus of opinion of sellers and buyers. Values are fixed not in the districts where commodities are produced, but in the large distributing centres, cities, where they are fetched for exchange, and the values there agreed upon are everywhere accepted. The value of a commodity is fixed not by its entire mass, the larger portion of which is consumed by its producers, but rather by the surplus which is exchanged. Thus the value of wheat and cotton in the United States is fixed by the price of the surplus sold abroad. In other words, that portion of a commodity or product which seeks exchange in the markets of the world for other commodities fixes the value of that larger portion which does not. Practically all of the great consuming countries, England, France, and Germany, employ the gold standard as the measure of value. In fact, over 80 per cent. of international commerce is directly figured on a gold standard of value, hence gold may be said to be the practically universal standard ; and even in countries on a silver basis, domestic prices being fixed and regulated by the export prices, the silver coin is accepted as representing so much gold value. To repeat,—values are fixed by the exchangeable worth of the surplus of products in the markets of the world. Gold is the standard employed in those markets, consequently the universal measure of value; and while silver, some other metal, currency, or other forms of credit may be used as gold's representative, still gold is the standard of value in all countries having any foreign trade, even though that metal may be practically unknown to its citizens.

Before discussing true money more in detail it is necessary to say a few words about *bullion*, of which all true money is composed. The definition usually given " gold or silver in the bar or lump, coined or uncoined," while inexact, and not one which could be accepted without considerable limitation, is perhaps sufficiently near the correct definition for our present purpose.

Bullion is bought and sold the same as any other commodity, the price thereof being governed by : 1, the demand ; 2, the supply ; 3, weight ; and 4, fineness. The price of gold being always stationary, as it is the measure of value, its actual value is determined by its purchasing power of other commodities, while the price of silver, and other less valuable metals used for coin, is determined by their relative value to gold. In the case of every metal it is bought where it commands the least value and sold where it commands the greatest.

The close relation between the shipment of bullion, and a high rate of exchange on the point to which the bullion is sent leads many to suppose that it is sent to such points to pay a balance of trade against the country from which it is shipped. This is not necessarily the case; but when, for any reason, the rate of exchange to the point of destination reaches the cost of the shipment of bullion, obviously there is no object in purchasing exchange, and as bullion may be sent at such times more advantageously, and as most foreign houses at that time buy, it is then shipped in greater quantities than when exchange is simply at par, or in favor of the country shipping; and while this condition of exchange is looked upon as favorable to its shipment, bullion may be shipped at any time.

From the above it is evident that under ordinary conditions the rate of exchange can never be greater than the cost of the actual transportation of bullion, as it would be shipped in such event.

The business in bullion is almost entirely carried on in this country by private bankers, who are known as dealers in bullion. Most of the houses engaged in this business have agents in Europe, to whom they ship from here, or who ship to them from Europe.

The scope of this work does not warrant us in treating money from an historical standpoint further than is necessary to emphasize certain fundamental principles. Consequently, without any attempt to trace its gradual evolution into its present forms, we will consider the subject as it presents itself to us at the present day and shall therefore confine our observations almost exclusively to the money of the United States.

Our money, like that of many civilized nations, is now divided into metal money (coins) and paper money (promissory notes payable on demand). Both metal money and paper money may be partly or practically wholly fiat money.

Metal Money or Coins.—It is not necessary here to repeat the observations previously made as to the peculiar adaptability of certain metals for use as money, and the advantages of some metals over others for this purpose, so we will proceed directly to the general consideration of this subject. In order to consider which intelligently we must understand the laws governing the coining of metals.

Previous to the art of coinage, metals were used by weight and fineness for money, which made it necessary for the merchant to have at his command scales and often crucibles to ascertain the same. The inconvenience of this system was such as to demand some change, and the rational solution was the division of metals into small pieces of convenient size and uniform value, with such value attested by some well known and responsible power, and no power so fully met these requirements as the government. Hence, the early history of coins clearly establishes the fact that coinage was invariably regarded as a prerogative belonging solely to and exercised only by the sovereign power or government.

The art of coinage certainly does not date back farther than the ninth century B.C., and the Lydians are supposed to have been the first people to have used coin money.

For various reasons the power to coin money should only be reposed in the person or body of most widely known power, solvency, and integrity, and this is necessarily the state. There never has been any attempt at lawful individual issue of coin. It required the government to properly regulate the weight and fineness and vouch for the integrity of the coins put in circulation.

At first coins were very rude and easily counterfeited and it was necessary to inflict severe penalties to guard against this danger, but even these penalties failed to deter the counterfeiting, mutilation, and clipping of coins, which was made very easy by the practical absence of all protecting devices and designs, which at the present day tend to make the simulation of a well minted coin so difficult and expensive as to deprive it of any profit.

One of the commonest and best known laws governing coins is that in order to keep a coin in circulation the bullion value of that coin should be a little less than the face value, in fact enough less, that no probable fluctuation in the market price of the metal of which it is composed will render the commodity value of the coin greater than its face value; otherwise as soon as it becomes so, it is immediately profitable to put the coin into the melting pot and convert it again into bullion.

Another principle is, that a superior coin will not circulate side by side with an inferior one. The superior coin being of greater value is either hoarded up and retired from circulation, or, on account of the inferior coin becoming the real measure of value, is converted into bullion. The reason of this is very plain, as no debtor will pay his creditor in a better or more valuable coin when he can legally pay him in an inferior and less valuable one. Used as money the value of the superior coin is no greater than that of the inferior coin, whereas it is greater when used as bullion. This principle is known as Gresham's law and furnishes an explanation of the difficulty we have had during the last few years in keeping gold in circulation side by side with silver.

The working of this principle had been previously illustrated in this country quite as clearly at the time of the discovery of gold in California, when, owing to the enormously increased production of gold, its relative value to other commodities was diminished, and the prescribed ratio between gold and silver fixed by the government remaining unchanged, silver, the production of which had remained practically stationary, was undervalued. Many of our citizens who at that time possessed silver coin exported it or had it melted up and converted into household articles; and silver coins went practically out of circulation.

It must, however, be borne in mind that while an inferior coin if sufficient in quantity will drive the superior out of circulation, it will only circulate at about its real value, unless the difference between its face value and its real value is guaranteed by some responsible government.

Fiat Money.—This is money issued by a state with presumable power to enforce its acceptance as a legal tender in payment of obligations.

In this sense, of course, all money issued by the state is fiat money, but in the more restricted view only money possessed of no intrinsic value, or of a less intrinsic value than its face value, is fiat money. And as a large quota of money is not possessed of intrinsic value to the amount of its face value, the difference between the two values is fiat money. Paper money issued by a government is wholly fiat money, whether secured by a deposit of securities or of bullion.

The issue of banks, unless made legal tender by the government, is not fiat money.

Paper Money.—While this subject should be properly treated under the head of "Credit," yet for the purpose of convenience, and because as currency it acts in lieu of real money, it has been decided best to discuss it here.

Until within the last few hundred years, a comparatively recent date in the history of money, paper money was not used in Europe, although the Chinese are supposed to have used it even before the Christian era.

Unlike coined money, the issue of paper money or credits was never held to be a sovereign prerogative, nor did governments arrogate to themselves the sole power of the issue of credits in this form and the consequent restriction of its use by their subjects.

In the early European history of paper money its issue seems to have been exercised almost exclusively by individuals and corporations.

If individuals and corporations could issue their promises to pay and exchange the same for marketable values, why could not a government do the same? Many of the European governments, on account of the frequent wars in which their rulers were engaged, the incidental depletion of their treasuries, and the necessity of raising money with which to support large armies and procure supplies, and having exhausted practically all other resources, were compelled sooner or later to resort to this as a last relief, although most have since funded such issues of paper money in the shape of bonds.

The necessities of the European states, which compelled the making or rather forcing of frequent loans from their bankers, gradually created the device of the governments issuing paper money; but even yet governments did not deem it necessary to restrict the issue by their subjects of credits in this form, and it is only as an extreme measure that any civilized government has ever issued or compelled the acceptance of this paper money as legal tender, thereby making a forced loan and compelling the persons accepting such loans to part with a value without receiving any interest for its use.

All of the great European nations, with a few exceptions, while reserving to themselves this right, in case of extreme necessity, as a great war, do not at present exercise it, but have practically done no more than to restrict its use to certain corporations complying with conditions prescribed by them.

In this country the early issues of paper money by the colonies previous to and by the confederated colonies during the War of Independence were attended with such disastrous results that the Federal power issued no paper money of its own until the early part of the late Civil War.

Up to the enactment of the National Banking Act in 1863, with the exception of the time during which the United States Bank existed, all of our paper money was issued by State banks, the different States delegating the power of issue to banks complying with certain conditions, generally the maintenance of a certain percentage in bullion to the notes issued, etc.

In every representative government it must be borne in mind that this right of issue of credits is one inherent in the individual, and which he, through his representatives, has delegated to the state or national government for various purposes, chief among which is the securing of greater uniformity of value and regularity of issue, under conditions sought to make the acceptor of such credits as safe as possible in receiving them.

After an experience of some seventy years it was proven that even States, owing to lack of uniformity of requirements and conditions imposed by them upon the banks within their borders, could not ensure a uniform and sound currency. Not but that many of the State laws were models in themselves, but they lacked uniformity. And while some were admirable and furnished an excellent groundwork for the National Bank Act, yet others were very illy conceived and even worse enforced; some States allowing their banks to issue circulating notes against real estate and various personal and other kinds of security.

It did not take long to establish the fact that land was not a proper security for paper money; for the reason that all issues of paper, in order to circulate freely, must purport on their face to be redeemable in coin, and while the land might be of ample value to secure the notes, yet it could not always be immediately converted into coin. This fact was so generally recognized that all of the more conservative and successful State systems required the maintenance of a metal reserve and a thorough State supervision of banks issuing circulating notes (see State Banks).

Paper money to be of any value must be secured by some value, and when so secured it is a mortgage on that value, and thereby restricts its use, and takes from the channels of trade the amount of the particular commodity by which it is secured, whether it be metal, some other commodity, or real estate.

As the amount of paper money must be greatly in excess of the metal reserve by which it is secured, to make its issue of any use, if proper safeguards are thrown around such issue, on account of the increase in volume (if needed), it may greatly facilitate commerce and trade; but while the currency has increased in volume it has deteriorated in quality, and no more value has been created; and the question narrows itself down to whether it is better to have $100,000,000 in metal in active circulation, or to tie that amount of metal up as a reserve to secure the issue of say $300,000,000 of paper.

The theory of course on which paper money, secured by a deposit of metal, is made to circulate, is that all its holders will not wish its redemption in coin at the same time.

Additional value and security are given to such money when a government agrees to accept it in payment of a certain class, or of all debts and dues to it; and this additional value and security is necessarily measured by the proportion the entire issue bears to the amount receivable in payment of such debts, and the ability of the government to continue to receive such money in this way.

As yet we have only considered paper money payable in coin on demand. Now we must consider inconvertible paper money issued by a government, or paper which is simply a promise to pay, without any or a very small metal reserve to secure it.

To this kind of money there are many objections. The most potent of which is that a practically insolvent government—if it were not insolvent it would not need to issue this form of money—mortgages its future revenues to redeem notes issued to provide for its present indebtedness or for advances made presumably for immediate uses. Next the great incentive to over-issue, and the necessarily diminishing value of the notes. The placing in the market of a large volume of government credits unsettles values, disturbs commerce, and is certain first to beget over-sanguineness and later on the inevitable depression which follows.

The issuing of demand obligations payable at the option of the holder, the first notice of which option the government receives when the notes are presented for payment, cannot but be dangerous to that government's credit; as it is almost certain that so long as the government is amply able to meet its notes their payment will not be demanded, but the very moment its inability is suspected,—the time when it most needs its available assets,—then the note holders demand payment. The issue of government notes is generally effected only by either the actual restriction of the issue of individuals, or the practical restriction by making such issue unprofitable.

Again, the want of elasticity of such a currency; the issue of which is regulated by the necessity of the government and not by the needs of commerce; and no government is in that close touch with commercial life which enables it to increase such issue when necessary and to contract the amount thereof when not needed. In fact the necessities of a government generally prevent its acting solely with a view to the interests of commerce.

Indeed, it seems a preposterous contention that the debt of a government should measure the volume of the people's currency, and that debt remain unpaid because it might restrict the amount of currency in circulation.

The fact is that the very existence of such a currency is a discrimination against the non-governmental issue of credits, and a restriction of the power of the utilization by banks and others of their credits, the United States Government requiring, in order to make a place for its own notes and bonds, banks to deposit in its Treasury United States registered bonds selling at say 117 in order to secure 90 per cent. of their par value in notes, on which issue they must pay the government taxes annually, making the issue of notes of so little profit that few banks will now issue them, and in reality depriving banks of the use of one of their most profitable rights, the use of their credit as currency, and absolutely prohibiting the exercise of credits in this form by individuals.

Only banks or bankers and men who are in daily contact with business life can be in a position to know the demands of trade, and the regulation of the amount of paper credits in the shape of money is best left under certain restrictions in their hands. They should be given the power upon the deposit of a certain percentage of bullion with some central bank or banks or depositary under the supervision and partial control of the government to issue paper money when needed, and at their option to retire such issue and reclaim the bullion deposited.

In this connection it is earnestly suggested that no good reason can be shown why a paper currency should not be regulated by that same law of supply and demand which governs all business transactions; nor why the government should take from the persons who are the interpreters of that law in all other business relations the interpretation of the law when applied to currency.

To recur to the subject of an inconvertible paper currency. If such can be made a legal tender in the payment of the government's obligations to individuals, in order to protect the receiver it is necessary that he should be able to compel his creditor to accept it in payment of his debt to that creditor, and to the same extent that the first individual has been deprived by the government of his rights to that extent can he lawfully deprive his creditor of such creditor's rights against him. And it is in order to prevent just this contingency arising, as well as for other reasons, that many contracts are made payable in gold coin of a certain weight and fineness.

Postage-stamps, while in no sense credits or obligations to pay, but simply evidences of pre-payment of a service to be rendered, yet as they always can command that service, and as it is a service in which the public stands in constant need, are frequently used to remit small amounts.

Various forms of credit such as checks, drafts, notes, bills of exchange, letters of credit, certificates of deposit, cashiers' checks, etc., greatly assist, if they do not actually, in many instances, take the place of currency.

In Queensland checks to bearer are used almost entirely in place of money and form the general currency of the people. This is an example however that we are happily not called upon to emulate.

Government Regulation of Money.—The regulation of metal and token money has always reposed in the sovereign power for reasons before stated.

The regulation of coinage and its issuance by the mints of the various countries follow naturally from the exercise of similar powers in earlier times, as does the issuance of, or the restriction of the issue of paper money by the governments of the present day the issue of token money by the ancients.

First we will consider how the government obtains the metal which it coins, and secondly, how that metal becomes distributed among the people.

Any possessor of gold may deposit the same with the government and have it converted into coin and returned to him minus a small charge for refining where the gold is less than $\tfrac{9}{10}$ fine. This is practically an unlimited or free coinage of that metal.

The government does not only coin metal belonging to others, but also the bullion which it receives in payment of obligations due it, which it, in course of time, distributes through its disbursing officers, banks, etc., in payment of its debts, the government paying out annually in coin and currency over $125,000,000 in pensions alone.

The coinage of silver at different times in the history of this country has been unlimited, except for the seigniorage charge, which at present consists of the difference between the commercial value of the silver in the coin and the face value. Under the Sherman law, now repealed, the government bought about $50,000,000 of silver yearly at the market rates per ounce, and coined it at a ratio to gold established years ago. The difference between the two is generally spoken of as the seigniorage. At other times the coinage of silver has been, and is now, limited in amount, whereas the coinage of gold has always been unlimited.

The possessor of gold bullion can, and always since the formation of our government could, have it coined; and there has been no limit to the quantity, while the contrary is the case with silver, the government only coining its own silver in such quantities as it needs.

Next we must consider the government's issue of paper money and its restriction of the issue of such money by others. This money when issued by the government reaches the channels of trade in just the same way that coin owned by the government does—that is, it is paid out in discharge of the government's obligations, frequently in payment of bullion or coin furnished the government by others and by them paid out to their creditors or in purchase of commodities or values.

That portion of paper money issued by others and the extent of which issue is restricted by the government is first printed and issued by the government to the banks on a deposit by the banks with the government of United States bonds, as is more fully described in the condensation of the National Banking Act. These bills are then, by the banks, loaned or used in the payment of their obligations, or the extension of their credits, and thus become disseminated among the people.

Neither the Federal or State government nor any corporation or individual can remain solvent and part with money except it or he receive for the money an equivalent value. It is true a corporation or an individual may lend its issue to others on promises of payment, and State, municipal, and county governments have at times issued their bonds in support of, or have guaranteed, semi-public and semi-private enterprises; and even the United States Government has guaranteed and paid the interest on the bonds of certain railroads, but they have never gone so far as to issue their money except in payment of their own debts already incurred, or in the purchase of values. Nor is the government guarantee of the payment of national bank notes a violation of this rule, as at first glance it might appear to be, because the government not only secured by the institution of national banks a safe means of placing its bonds on the market, but by compelling a deposit of those bonds to secure these national bank notes, as well as by the imposition of a tax on their circulation, amply protected and at the same time compensated itself for the risk assumed. In other words, it made that part of its debt, which it compelled national banks to purchase and deposit with it as a condition precedent to operation, the security of the circulating notes of these banks.

The government can neither give away money (pensions are considered a debt) nor loan it, and if it did either to any great extent the issue would become so large as to render the small security in the shape of bullion and the revenues available for the redemption of such issues practically valueless, and the issue worthless. The government should receive equivalent value in some shape for every dollar put into circulation by it.

It has been suggested that the government might make advances to certain classes, on different kinds of produce, etc.—in other words, go into the business of loaning money on commercial paper and warehouse receipts. Bankers, merchants, and warehousemen will do this now, on good security. Certainly the government could not long continue to do it on any lesser security than the bankers, merchants, and others are willing to accept. And if it did, would soon be in a position where it could make no further advances. And if one class is entitled to borrow money from the government, why not all classes?

Capital is not and cannot be created by printing "greenbacks," paper money, neither by a government nor by an individual, and the usefulness of paper money is measured by the ability of the issuer to redeem such promissory notes upon demand. Should the issuer part with them without receiving an equivalent value, he places himself in a position where whatever security exists for their payment must soon be exhausted, and where there is no income to provide for the unpaid issue.

The necessity of government supervision and control of the issuance of both coin and currency in the shape of money has previously been commented upon in the article on "Money," and need not be here repeated.

As the financial operations of the government with business life are usually consummated not through the Treasury at Washington, but rather through its sub-treasuries and fiscal agencies (national banks, generally), outside of mentioning the amount of money in the Treasury, it has been thought best to describe the operations of a sub-treasury, in preference to those of the main Treasury. As that in New York is the largest and most important, as well as fairly typical of the others, that has been chosen.

CHAPTER II.

Capital—Credit—Interest—Exchange—Price.

Capital.—In order to arrive at any true understanding of the meaning of this much-used word, we will have to consider it, first, in the broader definition accorded it in political economy, and secondly, in the more restricted sense in which it is used in commerce.

In political economy capital is that part of the product of industry not needed for immediate consumption, and which may be used for the support and maintenance of life during a subsequent period of productivity. Capital is the surplus beyond the present necessities: in the case of an individual, of that individual; in the case of a community or state, of that community or state. Capital is the accumulated product of past labor upon natural objects, over and above the immediate needs of mankind and the animal or mechanical labor which he calls to his aid, and which may be used at a future time. The real capital of either a man or a community is that portion of his property on which he may subsist during some future period, or that which he may exchange for such subsistence. Wheat, corn, rye, rice, and other cereals, cattle, hogs, sheep, etc., wool, cotton, and the skins of wild animals are practically the only forms of capital whose value is always real, and not, as in the case of precious stones and many other things, almost wholly dependent upon their exchangeable value for the above-named necessities. Few circumstances could arise where these things would not be of value, whereas under many circumstances metals or precious stones would be of no value to the possessor. In fact they derive their only value from a surplus of the necessities of life, the exchange of which they are largely used to facilitate, and as that surplus is greater or less their value increases or diminishes.

Capital is often described as a moving force, and the fact that it is the surplus which makes possible the continued use and development of wealth and property by providing food, raiment, and other necessities, as well as luxuries of life during this time, is one of its distinguishing features from property, or wealth, or value. And yet capital is property, capital is wealth, but it is only that part of property or that part of wealth which, by affording man and his agents subsistence during the period of the development and maturing of the labor expended upon wealth or property, makes that development possible. Capital as the support of labor is the active force, acting on property the passive object.

Capital is subject to the same laws which govern the whole universe; it is created, matures, and passes away. Only the most insignificant portion is of a character which renders its disuse without loss possible. Practically the whole of capital, being composed of the articles and commodities necessary for the maintenance of life, and therefore of a nature not admitting of permanent preservation, must needs be used in order to supply labor with the power to re-create more capital.

While an individual may add to his capital by disposing of a portion of his property, the relative amount of capital to property in a community or state cannot be affected by any such transfer unless the capital is furnished by some other community or state; such transfers between its own citizens cannot alter the relation of capital to property, but if beneficial to both persons it may afterwards result in increased productivity.

It cannot be too strenuously insisted that land is not capital, but that its whole value is dependent upon its adaptability to the use of capital upon it.

Secondly, in its restricted, commercial use, capital is either money or what may readily be converted into money without subtracting from the earning capacity of the industry in which it is invested. Thus the net earnings of a factory after the payment of all charges, or the funds or securities, things or values which may be used without diminishing its plant, is capital, but the sale of its fixtures or machinery would not be in any sense capital, especially if they were necessary to its proper conduct. This interpretation is so generally accepted that the results of all sales of machinery, fixtures, or equipment are invariably recorded in the books of all properly managed companies as belonging to their respective accounts and forming no part of capital.

We will then assume capital to be the fund used in the actual conduct of a business, the place or plant and the fixtures or machinery necessary thereto having been paid for previously or provided for out of other property.

While by many stock in trade is regarded as capital, which in the broader definition given the word by political economists it certainly is, yet when used commercially, and considered as the surplus fund by which the business is conducted during the interval between the purchase and sale of this stock, such a treatment, while theoretically correct, is unwise and inexpedient.

What ratio should capital bear to the business transacted? This is a question which nearly every business man has at some time asked. So much has to be taken into consideration in attempting an answer that most men, appalled at the task, do not attempt it. Certainly only the most general rules can be suggested, so much depends upon the nature of the business, the conditions of purchase of stock and the sale of product, the time given the purchaser, and the time he in turn extends to those purchasing from him; the variations in the price of both the raw material and the manufactured product, the rate of interest which capital commands in the open market, the condition of the country, and a hundred other things have to be taken into consideration in answering this question as to any particular industry. Of course, less capital is required to conduct a commission business than a business where the goods are purchased outright and sold again, but even here there must be sufficient capital to conduct the business until commissions are earned and received, to make necessary advances, etc.

In most trades or businesses there is some ratio which careful men consider necessary to maintain under even the most auspicious circumstances. There should certainly be enough capital in a manufacturing business to run the business, pay all expenses, labor, etc., and leave a moderate reserve fund on hand, from the time of the purchase of a stock until that stock is made up, sold, and paid for. Where the time consumed is short, less capital is required than where it is long. By way of illustration we will take a factory whose annual output is $1,000,000, ten per cent. of which, or $100,000, is profit. $500,000 represents the cost of raw material, and $400,000 of labor, taxes, insurance, etc., and which is divided into four purchases of stock, of four periods of three months each. The cost of running the factory for three months would thus be $225,000, or $900,000 annually. It would seem that $225,000 would be the smallest sum with which such a factory could be safely and comfortably run; and this would involve turning over the whole capital four times in a year to reach the figures given. A great many factories, however, are not run on this cash basis, but on a credit basis, in which event the owners must, of necessity, pay for the use of the capital of others during the interval between the purchase of the raw material and the sale of the manufactured product.

In the case of a store carrying a stock of say $100,000, the amount of capital is dependent upon the length of time required to consummate a sale of the stock. In most retail businesses the goods are sold before the wholesale merchant is paid, when the money received from their sale is used to pay the wholesaler, in which case a comparatively small capital is required. The ratio is further affected by the amount of bills payable and bills receivable. Capital should always be sufficient to allow for a 20 per cent. depreciation in the value of the stock.

Capital to be available need not be kept uninvested, because good investments are readily converted into money at a profit; hence the large holdings by business men of bonds and stocks which have a ready market.

Capital, if insufficient for the accomplishment of the object aimed at, is often lost, sometimes only partially, other times wholly. The most fruitful source of bankruptcy is the undertaking of too great enterprises with insufficient capital. Especially is this true where the enterprise is away from the large money centres. On the other hand must be borne in mind the danger of allowing capital to remain inactive, which is attended in the aggregate with almost as serious results, although perhaps not so apparent in individual cases.

Unemployed capital enforces idleness, which means a decreased production of values, consequently a diminished demand for other values. Active employment of capital on safe lines means just the reverse.

Credit.—Credit is the belief, founded upon a promise—that is, contract, expressed or implied—by which the possessor of a given value surrenders it to another, without at the time of such transfer himself receiving an actual equivalent, but instead thereof a promise, expressed or implied, to deliver a stated value at a future time. Credit is trust, confidence; it is a reliance upon a written or implied obligation on the part of another—a trust in man's honesty.

The very first element of credit would seem to be the conviction that the person to whom a credit is extended is and will be in a position to fulfil the promise on which such credit is based, as no sane man would extend credit to a person whom he knew to be incapable of meeting the obligation incurred; this would not be credit, but benevolence or foolishness, as the case may be.

The importance of credit and its proper regulation in financial matters can hardly be too strongly dwelt upon. It is the corner-stone of all financial systems; and no matter how much money there is in a country, there can never be enough to take the place of credit. Hence any impairment of credit causes more disturbance in commerce and finance than the locking up or taking out of circulation of hundreds of millions of bullion or other values.

Credit is equal in amount to nearly 90 per cent. of the aggregate of all marketable values, for the reason, speaking broadly, that credit will be extended to that amount, with the pledge of the values as security, and money is only called upon to do what credit cannot. Money (coin) is only equal in volume in the United States—that is, that portion of it in circulation—to about 3 per cent. of annual marketable values. The statements frequently made to show the rapidity of the circulation of money, the most common of which is that the annual clearings of the clearing houses of the country aggregate about $62,000,000,000, would seem to indicate that each dollar (the amount in circulation being little more than one and a half billions, one third of which is currency) had changed hands about forty-five times; but when it is remembered that clearing houses are simply creations of banks—themselves emporiums of credit—for the purpose of facilitating their methods of setting off credits against debits, and debits against credits, it will be perceived that it does not at all show the rapidity of the circulation of money, but rather, as compared with credit, what an insignificant part money plays in the business of the nation. The only function money performs in the clearing-house business is the settlement of balances, which average in New York less than 3 per cent. of the clearings, and it is probable that a ratio of one to twenty is maintained throughout other business operations, as that is the relation money bears to credit, and there is no good reason to believe that money circulates any faster than does credit, especially if we bear in mind what a large part of our money (see Paper Money) is simply credit.

In commerce, money as an intermediate value is used largely as the auxiliary of credit, or, to use a bookkeeping term, "to make the petty cash disbursements," and to make change between values; and no matter how rapidly it might be made to circulate, as its circulation to be of most use must be largely at those seasons of the year when practically the whole agricultural interests of a country are debtors, and debtors to an amount greatly in excess of the whole currency of the country, it is evident that then it can only assist credit.

To illustrate the credit system of the country:

The planter or farmer obtains his supplies during the growing of his crops from the factor, on credit, pledging the crops as security. These supplies the factor has purchased from various merchants, on credit, securing such advances or credit by his paper (notes). The merchant obtained the same from the wholesale dealer, on credit, securing such credit by a transfer of the factor's notes. The wholesale dealer bought the same from the producer or manufacturer, on credit, either his own or his bank's, depositing with the seller his paper, or that of others in his possession,—in each instance the credit being based primarily on the crop to be produced by the farmer.

When the crop is grown and about to be harvested, then the large money centres advance the local banks, on a rediscount of paper, the sums necessary to harvest such crops, which sums the local banks advance to the farmers, and the farmers pay to the laborers, who in turn pay it to the local tradesmen, who reimburse the wholesaler, and so on until it reaches the original holder of the commodity which the laborer purchased, and for which he has been paid in money; but this is but a small item in the general transaction.

Transportation companies now bring the crops to market; the factor gives the company his check, which it deposits in its bank, a large part of which is consumed, perhaps, to take up advances made by the bank during the summer months. The crop is sold by the factor, who draws upon the purchaser; the factor deposits his draft to his credit in his bank, and after deducting from the proceeds of the sale his advances, interest charges, insurance, etc., remits the planter the balance to his credit, often in a check. The factor gives the merchant his check, which he in turn deposits, and draws his own against in favor of the persons to whom he is indebted, and so on until the persons who first extended the credit are repaid, and then not in money, but in credits, or in the ownership of a value, their credits when obtained being largely used to enable them to purchase other values, which they again transfer on credit. The laborers and small tradesmen are practically the only persons paid in money.

Careful financiers and good business men rarely extend credit secured by anything less than a real value of greater amount than the credit given, the exception to this rule being in the case of corporations, whose continuance is a matter of considerable certainty, and whose earnings are capable of close estimate. The earning capacity of an individual is not a proper basis for credit, for it may cease at any moment.

Purchases of bonds are simply credits to corporations, secured by their plant, franchises, and a first interest on their net earnings.

Credit being, next to value itself, the most important thing a person can possess, cannot be too carefully guarded. Its worth is so well recognized that men are anxious to purchase the credit of others whose credit is widely known, and banks, corporations, and individuals sell their credit to those whose credit is not so good or generally recognized. In fact, the largest source of revenue of many private bankers is a sale of their credit in various forms, such as letters of credit and bills of exchange.

Interest.—Interest is the charge made by the lender to the borrower for the use or opportunity to use capital, money, or credit, and is stated in terms of money. This charge when paid at the time the loan is made is deducted from the amount of the loan and is known technically as "discount." The rate of either interest or discount charged is called "per cent." The sum on which the charge is made, the amount of the loan, is the "principal."

Interest is charged not only on loans but on debts overdue, whether converted into the form of a loan by the consent of the creditor to their payment at a future date, or when, without such consent, a debt remains unpaid after it is due.

Interest due on debts, in the absence of an agreement expressed or implied by the custom of trade, is collectible at the prescribed legal rate, and no higher rate can be collected.

The distinction between the current or market rate of interest and the legal rate must be borne in mind. The legal rate is an arbitrary one fixed by law, whereas the market rate is governed by the conditions and principles about to be explained.

The market rate of interest is not necessarily governed by the quantity of money available in a particular community, because interest is not only a charge for the use of money, which bears a comparatively small ratio to capital, but is the charge for the use of capital itself, as well as credit, and capital and credit may be plentiful in the same community in which money is scarce. For this reason the total amount of money per capita in a given country is a very slight factor in determining the interest rate.

The rate of interest or the price charged for the use of capital or credit or money is governed by the earning capacity of money, capital, or credit when employed not in any one particular industry, but in all. Although it must be borne in mind that the whole earning capacity of capital, and in this relation when the word capital is used it is meant to include capital, money, and credit, must be greater than the rate of interest charged, otherwise there would be no object in the borrower employing capital and paying out to the lender the entire profit of its employment. Consequently the earning capacity not only of capital but of man must be taken into consideration. For instance, A, who by the employment of $100,000 could make a profit of $10,000, would doubtless be willing to pay 5 per cent. for the use of that $100,000 if he were content with $5000 in payment of his services in the employment of that capital; but C, who could by its employment make a profit in his particular business of not more than $5000, would certainly be unwilling to pay the whole amount of the earnings of that capital plus his own labor for its employment. And C's refusal to pay so high a price for its use would tend to lessen the rate of interest.

Where capital is plentiful and the wage of labor is small, interest charges are low. Where capital is scarce and the earning capacity of man great, interest charges are high. The truth of this proposition is borne out by the rates of interest prevailing in older countries and in the newer countries, and even in different sections of our own country; on the Atlantic seaboard, especially in the Northern and Eastern States, the market rate being comparatively low, while in the Southern and Western States it is high.

The rate of interest is further regulated by the risk incurred, and the greater the risk necessarily the higher the rate of interest. Competition is also an important element in determining the rate, as is evidenced by the fact that in communities where practically the whole available capital is reposed in few hands the rate is higher, because of their monopoly of capital; while in communities where that capital is held by many, all anxious to lend and coming into competition with each other, it is necessarily lower. In other words, the law of supply and demand is here as potent as in regard to any commodity.

Another, if not one of the chief factors in determining the rate of interest, is the cost of the transportation of values, the transmission of money and credits, and the ease and rapidity with which they can be made, and this is certainly meant to include exchange between different countries. The more highly perfected and instantaneous communication between different countries, cities, and parts of the same country becomes, the more uniform must be the rate of interest. For under these conditions of practically unrestricted movement, capital immediately seeks the place where it can command the best price, and this inflow necessarily tends to equalize that rate with the rate prevailing elsewhere where the risks are proportionately the same.

If the rate of exchange or the cost of the transfer of money or credits is a factor in determining the rate of interest, it is equally true that the rates of interest prevailing in different places, when very disproportionate, causing a rapid transfer of credits or money, also affect the rates of exchange.

In relation to the legal rate of interest, the principles before stated apply with modified force on account of governmental interference with their natural operation, and while it is true that in many States there are no laws prohibiting the collection of any agreed rate of interest between borrower and lender, and that the legal rate is usually fixed not to interfere with private contracts, but to protect debtors against unfair exactions on the part of their creditors, yet in other States even the collection of an agreed rate of interest beyond the legal limit is prohibited, and the lender exacting such an illegal rate pays the penalty by the forfeiture of double the amount of his interest.

Banks, insurance companies, and other corporations deriving their powers from Federal or State governments are generally restricted by those governments as to the rate they may charge.

But this is hardly the place to enter into a discussion of the legal rate of interest prevailing in our different States, the laws in regard to which as well as the prescribed rates differing very widely.

(See Interest Rates of States,—end of book.)

Exchange.—Exchange is one of the most difficult terms in finance to accurately and yet comprehensively define, but in a general way it may be said to be that operation by which, through the setting off of credit against debit and debit against credit, the actual transfer of so much coin, bullion, or currency is avoided.

Exchange is divided into Domestic Exchange, that between different portions of the same country, and Foreign Exchange, that between a city of one country and a city of some other country, the principles being exactly the same in either case.

As an illustration of a transaction in simple foreign exchange:

Suppose A in New York owes B in London $1000, and C in London owes D in New York $1000, then there is $1000 owing in London to New York and $1000 owing in New York to London. Upon A in New York paying to D in New York $1000, and C paying to B in London $1000, A of New York has by this transfer paid his obligation to B in London, and C in London has at the same time paid his obligation to D in New York; but A in New York would have no means of knowing that C in London owed D in New York a like sum, nor would C in London know that A in New York was in debt to B in London in a like amount. A in New York goes to a dealer in exchange (a banker) and buys a bill of exchange on London to pay his indebtedness to B. Meanwhile, C in London buys a bill of exchange (for the purpose of this example, from the same house, which has offices in both cities), to pay his debt to D in New York. The dealer in exchange, upon comparison, finds that his New York house has to remit to his London house $1000, and his London house to his New York house a like amount to effect the payments for which the bills were purchased; but instead of doing this, he simply pays at his New York house to D the money which A has paid in for his bill of exchange to pay B, D having in the meantime received from London a bill of exchange from C payable at the New York house. The London branch, in like manner, pays out to B, upon presentation of his bill of exchange purchased by A in New York, the money paid in by C in London to secure his exchange in favor of D in New York, the whole transaction being accomplished without the transmission of one dollar across the Atlantic.

The principle here laid down applies with equal force whether the amount of the indebtedness of A to B is the same as the indebtedness of C to D, the only difference being that should the amount owing to London be greater than that owing to New York, then New York deducts from the actual transmission of money, the entire amount which London owes her, and remits the balance, and vice versa in the case of New York.

No matter how many debtors in New York remit to creditors in London, nor how many debtors in London remit to creditors in New York, the amount of New York's credits against London's debits are offset against New York's debits to London's credits, and London's credits against New York are offset against her debits, and only the difference between London's debits less her credits, the former of necessity being greater than the latter if London is called upon to remit, is sent to New York, and just the reverse in the case of New York—that is, the city whose debits are greater than her credits being the one which must remit to the other.

As these debits and credits are constantly changing, being at one time in favor of one city or country and at another in favor of the other, and there being no specified date of settlement of all houses or dealers in exchange, it naturally follows that the actual transmission of money merely to pay balances is resorted to with little regularity. In fact, herein comes the element of premium and discount of exchange, so termed ; it being always regulated by the debtors' available supply of bullion, with which to pay balances, the cost of the transportation of that bullion from one place to the other, and by the rates of interest prevailing in the two places.

As business men are constantly incurring obligations due in the respective cities, as soon as exchange sells at a discount in New York the New Yorkers buy in anticipation of their wants, and when exchange is at a discount in London the Londoner buys for the same reason. This tends to equalize and steady the price of exchange. Of course, some men simply buy exchange as a speculation, purchasing at a discount and holding it against the time when it can be used at a premium. Nor is this an absolute tying up of that amount of money, as bills of exchange can be used as collateral.

Exchange between cities in the same country is governed by the same principles, and needs no further explanation than to say that the forms of the bills are not usually the same as those used in foreign exchange, often being simply a cashier's check on his bank, payable at some correspondent institution, or a letter introducing a depositor to a correspondent and certifying to the amount of his balance, drafts against which such correspondent pays and charges against the writer of such letter.

While these are the principles upon which exchange is based, the complexity of our relations is such that commercial usage has so far outgrown these primitive principles as to almost entirely obscure them; in fact, they are rarely remembered, and to-day in the money centres a man can buy a bill of exchange from dealers payable in almost any city in the world, however remote, despite the absence of credits as offsets to such bill; but if that city has no commercial relations with the city of issue, or with another city having relations with the first city, which is a very rare thing, it is not in any sense a matter of exchange, but simply the transmission of so much money, of which the bill of exchange is simply a forerunner, the banker in the city of presentation paying the same, and in due course receiving the amount of the bill plus his charges in coin or bullion.

This naturally leads to a discussion and explanation of what for a better name might be called "complex exchange," as contradistinguished from simple exchange— that is, an exchange which is not effected between city and city, but between one place and another through the intervention of one or more other places. Take, for instance, New York, which effects most of her exchange on Rio Janeiro through London, which is accomplished in the following way:

A in New York owing B in Rio Janeiro $1000, buys a bill via London; C in Rio Janeiro, owing D in New York $100, buys a bill on New York via London; while E in Rio Janeiro, owing F $900 in London, buys a bill on London; and G in London, owing H in New York $900, buys a bill on New York. Upon the London house paying F in London $900, the Rio Janeiro house paying B in Rio Janeiro $1000, the New York house paying to D $100 and $900 to H, the debts of all these persons to each other have been paid. In other words, Rio Janeiro uses the $1000 to her credit in London, payable from New York, in payment of her debt of $100 to New York and $900 to London, while London uses the $1000 so paid by Rio Janeiro in payment of Rio Janeiro's $100 debt to New York, which she has purchased, and her own $900.

The same laws that govern simple or direct exchange also apply to complex exchange, and need not be repeated, except to say that our credits in London are applied against our indebtedness to Rio Janeiro, and her debits to London are settled by her claims against us.

Domestic exchange is figured in one currency, and is consequently simpler than foreign exchange, which has to be calculated in two currencies, that of the country of the purchaser and that of the country of the purchasee, and in the case of complex exchange in three currencies, first the currency of the place of purchase, which must be converted into the currency of the place where such exchange is payable. All foreign exchange is calculated on a gold bullion basis, *i. e.*, that an ounce or a part thereof of gold of a given fineness possesses exactly the same value in all parts of the world.

The relative value of the currency of each country to such gold bullion must be first ascertained before such conversion from one currency to another can be made, and this is rendered doubly necessary from the fact that the bullion value of coin is generally less than its face value. Thus in remitting $1000 United States money by means of exchange to Mexico, assuming the transaction to be one in simple foreign exchange between this country and Mexico, Mexico's currency being on a silver basis and ours on a gold basis, it would be necessary first to determine the relative value of the Mexican silver dollar to our gold coin; how many Mexican dollars are the equivalent in value of a thousand dollars United States money. This having been determined, the "par of exchange" between the two countries has been ascertained. Next is calculated the exchange premium or discount, as the case may be, existing in favor of the one or the other country, which, in the case of a discount, would be subtracted from the cost of such exchange, and in the case of a premium added, and vice versa in the case of Mexico remitting to the United States. Should, however, this transaction be effected by way of London, it would be necessary first, on the same gold bullion basis, to convert $1000 United States money into pounds, shillings, and pence, adding the premium or subtracting the discount, then to convert the pounds, shillings, and pence into Mexican money with the discount from London to Mexico subtracted, or the premium added, the invariable rule being that the purchaser receives the benefit of the discount when the exchange is favorable to him, and pays the premium when it is against him.

Owing to causes and conditions too numerous to detail, the relative value of one currency to another is constantly changing, and obviously it would result in great confusion and wrong to allow this relative value to be fixed by a few dealers in exchange. To avoid this confusion, lack of uniformity, and possible wrong, as well as to protect both the buyer and the purchaser, houses known as "arbitrage houses," which are the principal banking houses doing an international business, daily agree upon such relative values, and the values set by them are accepted by both purchasers and sellers.

Foreign exchange is calculated and sold in the currency of the country where purchased and paid in that of the country in which it is payable.

The same rule applies in the case of all foreign exchange. It is calculated in the unit of value of the country where purchased, and remitted in the unit of value of the country where payable. In Germany it is calculated in marks, in France and Antwerp in francs, in Amsterdam in guilders. The relative value of the coins of the principal commercial countries will be found in table "Relative Values of Moneys."

The premium on, or discount off, foreign exchange is not, as in the case of domestic exchange, stated in per cent., but in an addition, in the case of a premium to, and a subtraction, in the case of a discount from, the relative value of the respective currencies, viz.: $4.86¾ being the par of sterling exchange, when exchange sells at $4.85 it is at a discount, and in like manner when it sells at $4.88, it is at a premium.

Selling Exchange.—So far only the buying of exchange by persons wishing to remit in discharge of obligations has been treated of, but clearly if banks will purchase or advance money on drafts, why should not dealers in exchange purchase the claims of persons holding demands against others residing elsewhere, instead of waiting for these persons to remit? They do, and this is termed Selling Exchange.

The volume of business done in this way is probably greater than that done in the buying of exchange, as comparatively few creditors now wait for their debtors to remit, but instead, by the selling of their demands in the shape of exchange, payable, as the case may be, on presentation, or at thirty, sixty, or ninety days, they realize the amount owing by such debtor at once instead of having it tied up in the shape of bills receivable.

Necessarily the same system of offsets of credits against debits and debits against credits above explained in regard to buying, applies in regard to selling, the only difference being that the dealer purchasing the exchange occupies the position of the person from whom it was purchased, and presents the same through his London agents, when due, for payment to the person against whom it is drawn.

Foreign exchange, payable at a future date, can only be sold to a dealer at a discount, as such dealer must obviously receive interest on the amount of the transaction from the date of purchase to the date of payment, else he is deprived of the use of that amount of money and the same is used by another without any compensation; he has also incurred the risk of being unable to collect his bill of exchange when presented for payment, which risk ought not to be assumed without his receiving therefor a premium sufficient, considering the financial standing of the payee, to compensate him. It is true that he is usually protected by the bills of lading of the goods against which such exchange is drawn, and of which bills he becomes the owner, but in the case of a thirty- or sixty-days bill of exchange this cannot apply, as the goods may have been delivered and used before the exchange is presented for payment.

Further, there must be taken into account the probable condition of the exchange market at the time such bill becomes due, which, owing to the general uniformity of balances for or against certain countries at a given period of the year, can generally be closely approximated. If at the time of the maturity of such bill it is probable that exchange against such country will be at a premium, then clearly the amount of this probable premium must make such exchange still more valuable and necessitate a still further premium, but should it be probable that exchange at said time will be at a discount, then the amount of such discount should subtract that much from the price of said bill.

Prime exchange is that issued by houses of known solvency, whose bills are everywhere accepted, and the character of whose credit is beyond question.

A large business is done in the buying of bills of exchange payable at a future date, sometimes as long as ninety days, in anticipation of obligations then falling due, in consideration of the fact that exchange may be at a discount at the time of purchase, and possibly will be at a premium at the time the obligations become due; and the fact that most dealers are willing to allow the purchaser as much interest for the money from the date of purchase to that of the maturity of the bill as the money commands in the market, avoids the loss incident to tying up that amount of money.

"Exchange," while originally and technically limited to the definition given in the opening of this chapter, at the present time in commercial parlance includes bills of exchange, transfers by cable, and, in fact, the transmission of demands of all kinds by which money or an order for its payment is made payable at a place other than the place of issuance of such demand.

The prevalent impression that a particular country at more or less regular periods settles in gold the balance due in favor of some other particular creditor country is unwarranted by the very principles which govern exchange as well as by all the facts deducible from the statistics of the money world. The reason why such settlements between country and country are not so effected is seldom thoughtfully considered. The fact that the debits and credits of the entire commerce of the world must equal each other, and that it is impossible that either can be in excess of the other, is generally lost sight of. It is axiomatic to say that debits and credits must agree. The entire amount of exports and imports of the world's commerce must be the same, from the fact that one country must of necessity export what another country imports.

To maintain that the total amount of debits and credits could vary, or that exports and imports could differ, would be equivalent to saying that the debtor and creditor sides of an accurately kept double-entry ledger would not be the same.

In the settlement of the balance of trade between nations that balance is rarely, if ever, settled between nation and nation, but only the final balance on the gross exports and imports of the entire commerce of a country is settled, and ultimately only by those countries which are the final debtor countries paying such balance to those countries which are the final creditor countries. The excess of our entire credits over our entire debits, taking our country for the purpose of illustration, as a rule being due from the three principal debtor nations of the world, England, Germany, and France, must, in the absence of some credit, equivalent to their own and assumed debit to us, be remitted to us in gold. But, as a matter of fact, this final credit to us, due from our excess of exports over imports, is more than balanced by the large holdings of interest-bearing American securities held by these countries, and which often more than offset our credit on exports over imports, and occasion, in addition, the exportation of large amounts of gold from this country yearly, to pay the balance which is finally in their favor. It is not intended to assert that there may not be times when one of these countries on the total of all transactions, including holdings of American securities, is in this country's debt, but to assert that, taking the three collectively, such is not generally the case.

The shipment of bullion does not necessarily, nor even generally, indicate the location of the balance of trade. Because while the balance of trade may be largely in favor of some young country, that balance may be, as explained in the previous paragraph, more than offset by the payments of interest to countries commercially debtor and financially creditor, which excess of sums due for return of securities must be remitted in bullion. It may be more truly said that the shipment of bullion is an indication of the excess of the entire credits of all countries against the entire credits of one particular country; but even this is not always true, because bullion is largely purchased simply as a commodity, the same as wheat or cotton, the purchase usually being made when the relative value of bullion to other commodities is less than usual, and being sold when that relative value is greater.

The assumption is that the value of gold never changes. This assumption is not absolutely accurate, because while the prices of other commodities adjust themselves to the value of gold, instead of the price of gold adjusting itself to the value of other commodities; yet it is perfectly clear that when the relative value of numerous other commodities is greater relatively to the value of gold than at another given time, then the buying power of gold is reduced, and when the relative value of other commodities is less, as compared with the buying power of gold, then the value of gold is greater. The real value of gold is adjusted by the enormously greater value of other commodities; and when the value of other commodities to the value of gold is greater, then gold which has really depreciated will be purchased for export, because at that time certain commodities will buy more gold than when the relative value of these commodities to gold is less.

Price.—Price is the money measure of a commodity, service, or thing—that is, the amount of money for which it will exchange. Value is the relation a thing bears to all other things, while price is the relation a particular commodity, service, or thing bears to money, and money only. In other words, price is the value of a thing expressed in money. The same principles which govern value also in a somewhat modified degree fix price.

Before discussing the price of commodities and things, it is necessary to make a few brief remarks with regard to the price of labor, which is governed by much the same factors that control the price of commodities, inasmuch as the value of the bulk of labor is measured by its productivity of commodities. There is, however, a class engaged in the rendering of services of a professional and personal character, whose price is fixed almost solely by their reputation, skill, or ability, and the demand for their services. The price of labor is fixed not only by supply and demand, its productivity, and the interest charged for capital, the wages received in a particular industry, vocation, calling, or profession, but to a considerable extent by the wages received in all. The effect of this is to equalize the rewards of labor of a like character.

While the wage of labor is measured in time and money, the real wage is the value received for the effort expended, and at no time in the history of the world has labor received such substantial rewards as it does at the present day. The wages of workmen, the incomes of business and professional men, are greater now than ever before. The reason for this is not far to seek. The forces of nature, through the application of machinery, have become powerful auxiliaries to man, and much that previously required the expenditure of manual force is now accomplished by machinery. The result has been to enormously increase the productivity of labor, and thereby augment the fund out of which it is rewarded. As this fund accumulates the laborer becomes more independent, industry more profitable, and the demand for his services, and the price, greater.

The statements in relation to price apply entirely to wholesale prices, such as are found in current price-lists, exchange quotations, etc., and have no application to the prices of the retailer, which are governed by so many conditions as to render the principles stated often inapplicable.

The retail price of a particular article is often governed largely by the reputation of the maker or producer, and the ability of the purchaser to pay the price demanded, rather than by well defined laws, hence the apparently unreasonable variations in the retail prices of various articles, such as clothing, hats, shoes, jewelry, etc.

Price presupposes, first, the possession by certain persons of a surplus of some article, commodity, service, or thing, beyond their needs, and which they desire to exchange; second, the existence of some generally accepted measure of value, money; without this exchangeable surplus, and this measure of value, price is an impossibility.

Those products necessary to the support of life are of the most certain and universally accepted value; they are the only things that man cannot do without, and in case of necessity he sacrifices any other form of wealth to procure food and clothing; consequently gold, silver, precious stones, works of art, and other commodities or things on which a large amount of labor may be expended, and which form the principal means of preserving the values of the surplus of agriculture and pastoral production, depend largely for their value upon the existence of a surplus of the necessities of life.

Until a people or country has reached a degree of progress in which they have accumulated a certain surplus of food and clothing products, that is, necessaries of life, there is but little use for preservative commodities, therefore among such peoples their relatively insignificant value, value being dependent upon usefulness. As soon as a substantial surplus has been accumulated, so soon do preservative commodities possess an increased price; consequently in the older countries, where wealth and values in the shape of improved real estate and many of the comforts of life have been accumulated, rendering unnecessary the expenditure of human energy for this part of wealth, and allowing thereby a larger expenditure of energy for production, the surplus of food and clothing products would yearly become greater than in the younger countries, where a larger part of labor must be expended for the procuring of shelter, furniture, etc.

To minimize this yearly increasing surplus of necessaries in older countries, recourse is had to diversity of industry—a larger number of individuals are employed in the production of works of art and the manufacture of articles of personal adornment and the rendering of various services for which there is no need, and no surplus to pay for, in more primitive communities.

The progress of mankind means the accumulation not only of a surplus which may be expended for his mental and moral elevation, but also a decrease in the amount of labor necessary to make provision for the purely bodily and material wants, hence the price of what may be termed necessities of life must decrease in price. As the surplus of the necessities of life, which are practically all of a perishable nature, increases, the necessity of means for converting that surplus likewise increases, and prices of the commodities or things best adapted for this purpose are necessarily enhanced, while prices must necessarily continue to decrease for those products the surplus of which is yearly growing greater, as long as this disproportionate increase between the different classes of commodities continues in its present ratio. This continued disproportion however seems improbable in view of the well known economic law that both capital and labor will naturally seek the more and leave the less remunerative fields. This rush of capital and labor to very profitable enterprises soon creates a surplus of the thing or service which previously commanded a high price on account of its limited supply, and by the withdrawal of capital and labor from the hitherto unprofitable employments, the volume of those products is reduced, and the demand correspondingly increased. This system of economic adjustment is going on constantly, and tends to the preservation of fair relative values and prices.

The following factors control the price of articles and commodities: first, cost of production, which includes labor, capital, and interest; second, transportation and distribution; third, supply and demand; fourth, competition and combination; fifth, artificial restraints of trade.

1. Cost of Production. The cost of production is measured, first, by the amount of capital necessarily employed in the production of a given product. It makes no difference whether the capital be owned by the producer or is borrowed. If possessed, its usefulness is measured by the rate of interest it could produce otherwise invested. If borrowed, its cost is measured by the charge made for its use. The wage of labor, taxes, insurance, and compensation of employer are likewise elements of cost.

The more perfect and general becomes the use of machinery, the more certain and speedy the means of transportation—in other words, the greater becomes the supply, or the less effort required to secure it, the lower prices must go. The whole aim and trend of civilization for the last two hundred years has been in this direction.

2. Transportation or Procurability. Price is further governed or modified by means of transportation and distribution, which practically tend to the procurability of the article or commodity, and no matter how limited the supply or great the demand, if a particular commodity or thing is produced at a place in excess of the local demand for it, and no means of transportation are provided for its carriage to points of demand where the supply is inadequate, the price of sale is fixed at the place in which it can be sold. There can be no question that corn and wheat, prior to the opening of the Erie Canal or to the

establishment of our interoceanic lines of railway, possessed all the food values they now do, but in the absence of means of transportation, being produced greatly in excess of the needs of their local consumers, the surplus was a practical waste, owing to the prohibitory transportation charges incident to the carriage of this surplus by the primitive means afforded by wagons and pack-horses. The cost of transportation must necessarily be deducted from the price. Thus wheat sells at Omaha less its carrying charges to Chicago, in Chicago less its carrying charges to New York, in New York less its carrying charges to Liverpool. This statement is based on the assumption that there is a surplus of wheat in Omaha over Chicago, a surplus in Chicago over New York, and a surplus in New York over Liverpool. If through excessive purchases Liverpool should acquire this surplus, and some of the other cities a deficiency, then the conditions would be altered and the price in the city suffering from the deficiency would be plus that of the city enjoying a surplus. In other words, the price of wheat in the place where there is an insufficient supply is the price in the city where there is a surplus, plus the carrying charges between the two places.

The building of railways, the opening of canals, the establishment of lines of ocean steamers, putting the whole world in communication, and opening the markets of the old world to the produce of the new, and the markets of the new to the manufactures of the old, have all tended to increase the supply where needed of both food and clothing products, and to reduce their price in the markets of the world.

Distribution is a necessary part of the cost of transportation, in fact distribution itself is one element of transportation; consequently the charges of factors, merchants, middlemen, brokers, insurance companies, and others, all of whom render services incident to the transportation or distribution of commodities, become an inherent part of their cost and an element in fixing the ultimate market price.

3. Supply and Demand. These terms are so intimately connected as to be practically inseparable. By supply is meant only the available supply, and not the total mass of a given product, a large part of which under certain conditions may be unavailable; thus, if some country should have a surplus of wheat, and that surplus could not be brought into the markets of the world, it would not be available and would not affect the market price of the available supply. By demand is meant the effective demand; that is, the demand of persons in a position to give an exchangeable value for the value they desire to possess.

Supply is the measure of quantity; demand is the measure of effective desire. Generally speaking, where the supply is large the relative demand is reduced and the price of the product is consequently lowered, but even though the supply should be larger than formerly, should the demand increase in like ratio the price is maintained; again, while ordinarily a decrease in supply would mean an increase in price, this is only true where there is a corresponding increase in demand. It may, and often does, happen that a decreased supply going hand in hand with a decreased demand means a stationary or even falling price. This is especially true of articles dependent for their sale upon the taste or caprice of the purchasing public, such as textile fabrics of particular patterns. The desire to possess them having decreased, even though their supply may have diminished in greater ratio, they become practically unsalable or command but little price.

Low prices for food and clothing products show beyond dispute that they are plentiful, and that it is desired to preserve the value of their surplus production. Plenty is surely cause for congratulation, perhaps not to the producer of these commodities, who may be compelled to take a low price for them, but if he will insist upon producing what the world already has a full supply of, he has only himself to blame for a waste of effort.

High prices for food and clothing are an infallible indication of scarcity, and show that there is but little surplus to be converted into more permanent forms of value, and while this condition may be cause for rejoicing to the food and clothing producers, it is cause for apprehension and discomfort to all others.

Where the price of a product is insufficient to pay the producer a fair rate of interest on the capital invested and a reasonable wage for his labor, it is evident that there is either little demand for his product, or, what to him is equally bad, an excessive supply; because the rewards of labor, whether they be to the employer or employee, tend practically to the same level in all industries, of course measured by the productivity, skill, dexterity, and rarity of the labor employed.

4. Competition and Combination. As civilization advances and population becomes more dense, competition increases owing to the larger number of producers. This increased production necessarily decreases the price of the product, and owing to the very large number of small proprietors engaged in certain classes of industry, principally food and clothing products, renders combination between such producers limiting production practically impossible. In many products competition has become so fierce as to leave but little profit to either the producer or the distributing agent.

Combination, which is the antithesis of competition, when applied to articles and commodities is known as trusts; when designed to limit the supply and to increase the wages of labor, it takes the form of trades unions and other labor organizations.

When applied to commodities, combination or monopoly

is generally practicable only in relation to articles requiring for their production a large amount of capital in the hands of a comparatively few corporations or individuals, who may readily combine to limit the output of its different members; hence these trusts, monopolies, or combinations are generally confined to manufactured articles, and in this country are rendered doubly effective by the large import duties imposed on many manufactured articles, thereby giving a practical monopoly of the domestic market to the home manufacturers; but in the absence of such import duties a combination to be effective would have to embrace all the manufacturers of the world producing that article.

Competition necessarily reduces prices; combination is designed to increase them. The law-makers of the Federal Government and of the States have considered combinations so inimical to the general welfare as to pass most stringent laws against agreements or contracts in restraint of trade, and to refuse to enforce them.

5. Artificial Restraints of Trade, by which is meant interference either by governments or individuals with the natural laws and conduct of trade, necessarily affect the price of the article upon which that interference is exercised. Governmental restraints, whether they consist of the licenses which a city requires the vendors of various kinds of merchandise to purchase, the internal revenue taxes levied by the Federal Government, or the import duties imposed by the same power, add to the price of the article on which they are imposed, and this additional price must be paid by each subsequent purchaser. In the case of imported commodities on which there is an import duty, the import price is the price of the country of export plus the duty. In some classes of manufactured articles where the profit is great, it is sometimes the custom of merchants to make one price to their home buyers and another to their foreign purchasers, in order to reach

a market from which the duty would exclude their goods. Obviously, however, this reduced price for export goods can enable goods to reach the desired market only where the profit is large enough to admit of great reduction from the home price and where the duty is comparatively small. In the case of such staple commodities as food products, and the great bulk of clothing products, especially the cheaper grades, if there is any difference between the home and export price it is so slight as to amount to practically nothing, and the cost to the importer is nearly always the price prevailing in the country of export plus import duties, transportation, and insurance. Sometimes foreign merchants in order to dispose of their surplus or old stock, will sell to foreign buyers at a much lower price than to domestic, sooner than reduce the selling price of their products in the home market.

Individual restraints of trade usually consist of the purchasing by one or a number of men, of a quantity of a given product largely in excess of their legitimate wants or expectations of exchange. In common parlance this is known as a "corner." One or more men purchase the available supply of a particular commodity and thereby are able to demand whatever price they choose from buyers. While this may effect a temporary rise in the price of the product "cornered," it is impossible that it can permanently affect either its value or its price, because its only worth to the possessors is an exchangeable one, they possessing an amount largely in excess of their own needs, and of necessity being compelled to soon dispose of their holdings.

Effect of Standard of Value on Price. By many it is contended that what they term the demonetization of silver and the consequent making of gold the single standard of value has led to a decrease in the price of commodities and a consequent increase in the price of gold.

In order to sustain this contention it is necessary to show that gold has not been practically the sole universal standard of value for the last hundred years, and that the alleged demonetization of silver had resulted not only in the restriction of its legal-tender quality, but had likewise deprived it of its value as a commodity, and had been the sole cause of its relative decrease in value. This will probably not be attempted. It would be further necessary to prove that the available ratio of gold to the commerce of the world had not been maintained, or that the demand for gold as a circulating medium had increased out of proportion to its production, because as a standard it simply bears an abstract relation to other commodities. It could only as a measure of value itself increase in value and the things measured by it decrease as it became the preservative of value, not the measure of it. Again must be considered the fact that even if the proportion of gold to other commodities has not been maintained, this fact has been more than offset by the various devices brought into operation by governments, bankers, and financiers, by means of which the representatives of gold in the shape of paper money, credits, bills of exchange, etc., have been greatly augmented and the use of the metal itself as an actual medium of exchange has been minimized. It would be further necessary to show that other preservative values had decreased in amount and that a greater burden and therefore a larger demand for gold as a preservative commodity, which is its most restricted use, had ensued. This in the face of the obvious accumulation of wealth in other preservative forms it is impossible to prove. We may therefore conclude that whether there be one or more standards of value (it is in this work contended that there can be but one standard of value) the relative value of commodities to each other is not thereby changed.

In this relation it should be remembered that the tendency of finance during the last century at least has been toward the restricted circulation of metals as the media of exchange, and in the direction of the storing of those metals and the issuing against them of currency or credits in excess of the bullion value of the metals, and the securing of the deficiency in amount between the market value of the metal and the face value of the currency by the deposit of other credits, principally government, state, and municipal obligations. In other words, these last-named obligations have come to the assistance of the metals as a basis for the media of exchange, and have tended to minimize the actual use of metals, whose money use in most civilized countries is now principally as one of the bases of currency.

While gold, in common with other preservative commodities, has increased in relative value to food and clothing products, as the surplus of these products became yearly greater, its increase has not been so great as that of other preservative values. The price of government, state, municipal, corporate, and individual credits has increased in a much greater ratio, bonds bearing a rate of interest which enabled their makers to dispose of them at par fifty years ago would now sell at over 200. Capital generally is so plentiful that nearly all states and countries have reduced the legal rate of interest, and have been enabled repeatedly to fund their interest-bearing securities in others bearing a lower rate. This increase is not confined to securities and credits, but pertains to practically every commodity or article by which value can be preserved. The obvious reason for this enhanced value of preservative commodities, credits, and securities is the enormously increased supply of the necessities of life, owing largely to the rapid development of new areas and the greatly reduced cost of production.

PART II.

PRACTICE OF FINANCE.

CHAPTER I.

Money and Currency of the United States—The New York Sub-Treasury.

Practice.—In the succeeding articles the application of the principles previously described, it is assumed, will be readily determined by the reader, without the writer pointing out the particular principles involved in each kind of business discussed.

Money of the United States.—The money of the United States consists of gold and silver coin. Nickel and copper are used for the minor subsidiary coin.

Gold, the coinage of which is unlimited, is legal tender for a period of twenty years from the date of coinage to any amount, when not reduced in weight more than one half of one per cent.

The coins now minted are the quarter eagles ($2.50), $64\frac{1}{2}$ grains; the half eagle ($5.00), 129 grains; the eagle ($10), 258 grains; and the double eagle ($20), 516 grains, all $\frac{900}{1000}$ths fine, or nine-tenths pure gold and one-tenth alloy.

Silver. The coinage of this metal is now practically confined to minor coins, and the purchase of silver bullion since the repeal in 1893 of the purchasing clause of the Sherman Act has ceased.

Silver in dollar pieces of full weight is legal tender for all purposes and to any amount in the absence of a contract to the contrary. The smaller silver coins are only legal tender to the amount of ten dollars.

Coins of the following nominal value, $\frac{900}{1000}$ths fine, are now outstanding: Dollar, value $1.00, weight $412\frac{1}{2}$ grains; half dollar, $0.50, weight $192\frac{9}{10}$ grains; quarter, $0.25, weight $96\frac{45}{100}$ grains; and dime, $0.10, weight $38\frac{58}{100}$ grains.

At various times other silver coins have been issued; thus the Trade Dollar, weighing 420 grains, and by implication a legal tender to the amount of $5.00, coined under the Act of 1873, circulated for about five years, when its coinage was discontinued, and provision made for its redemption at its face value, and for recoinage; the twenty-cent piece, coined from 1873 to 1878; the Columbian half-dollar to the amount of $2,500,000, and the Columbian quarter-dollar to the amount of $10,000, issued in 1892. Three-cent pieces and a half-dime were also coined.

It will be observed that while about $423,000,000 silver dollars have been coined, that less than $54,000,000 were in circulation and over $369,000,000 on deposit in the United States Treasury on April 1, 1895. The reason for this is that the silver coins being too bulky and heavy for extensive use in large amounts, it became necessary for the government to receive them on deposit and to issue in their place silver certificates.

Nickel and Copper. These metals are used entirely for minor coins which are only legal tender to the amount of 25 cents and which are redeemable by the United States in lawful money in sums of not less than twenty dollars. While at various times half-cents of copper, nickel cents, bronze cents, and two- and three-cent pieces of nickel have been coined; at present only the copper cent, weight 48 grains, and the five-cent piece nickel, weight $77\frac{16}{100}$ grains, are coined. Some of the other coins, however, are still occasionally seen.

Only the one-cent piece (copper) and five-cent piece (nickel) are now coined.

Currency of the United States.—In addition to the gold and silver which are legal tender as before stated, a large part of the country's currency is also legal tender, and that fact will be indicated in speaking of the particular notes.

As previously explained, the currency of the country, excepting gold and silver certificates, is secured by the government's credit and its metal reserve. Of course the metal on deposit with the government against which certificates have been issued, is held exclusively for the redemption of those certificates and is not applicable to any other purpose. The national bank notes are secured by the pledge of the government strengthened by the lawful money reserve required to be kept by the banks of issue and by the United States bonds and the 5 % redemption fund deposited by such banks with the Treasurer of the United States to insure their redemption.

United States Notes or "Greenbacks." These notes constitute the balance of the unredeemed forced paper currency issued during the late Civil War, of which a fixed amount, $346,681,006, is outstanding. They are legal tender for all debts, public and private, except duties on imports and interest on the public debt, but being redeemable upon demand in coin, the latter limitation of their legal-tender quality is of little effect; in fact, by a regulation of the Secretary of the Treasury they are received in payment of customs and other duties. These notes when received by the government may be re-issued and of course constitute a constant claim upon the government's lawful money.

United States Treasury Notes. Under the Act of 1890, commonly known as the Sherman bill, these notes were issued in payment of purchases of silver, and are legal tender for all debts, public and private, except where otherwise stipulated in the contract between the parties. They are redeemable in gold or silver coin at the discretion of the Secretary of the Treasury. In order to maintain a nominal parity of silver and gold, it has been found necessary during the last few years to redeem these notes when demanded by the holder in gold. There are now outstanding $155,000,000 of United States Treasury notes.

Gold Certificates are issued in denominations of not less than $20 by the Secretary of the Treasury against deposits of gold coin, which coin shall be retained in the Treasury exclusively for their redemption upon demand. Gold certificates are receivable for customs, taxes, and all public dues, although not legal tender.

Silver Certificates, in $1, $2, $5, and $10, and higher denominations, are issued against standard silver dollars deposited in the Treasury. They are not legal tender, but are receivable for public dues. As explained in the remarks on silver, these certificates circulate largely in place of the coin and form a large proportion of our currency.

Currency Certificates (not legal tender) are issued by the United States in denominations of $5000 and upwards upon deposits of currency with the United States Treasury.

National Bank Notes are issued by the Comptroller of the Currency to national banks upon deposit by them of United States bonds with the Treasurer of the United States. The conditions of the issue of these notes and the security by which they are protected are so fully stated in the article on National Banks as to make any repetition of it here superfluous.

The following table contains a statement of the kinds and amounts of money of the United States and the banks of issue on April 1, 1895:

Kinds.	Total.	In Treasury.	In Circulation.
Gold..............	$567,592,416	$88,098,517	$479,493,899
Silver dollars [1]......	422,927,039	369,009,182	53,917,857
Subsidiary silver, copper, and nickel....	76,450,557	16,577,511	59,873,046
U. S. notes.........	346,681,016	89,745,257	256,935,759
U. S. Treasury notes	150,330,089	28,872,489	121,457,600
National bank notes.	207,541,211	4,449,893	203,091,318
	$1,771,522,328	$596,752,849	$1,174,769,479

Besides the above, there was gold bullion to the amount of $51,387,979, and silver bullion of the nominal value of $124,673,187 in the Treasury on April 1, 1895.

Gold certificates, silver certificates, and currency certificates are not included in the above table, for the obvious reason that they are only issued against metal or currency as previously explained, and of course constitute no addition to the lawful money supply.

The amount of silver and gold certificates in circulation, however, while it constitutes a demand claim upon the government's metal holdings against which these certificates are issued, increases the circulating medium.

NEW YORK SUB-TREASURY.

The Sub-Treasury, situated at the corner of Wall and Nassau Streets, which bound it on the south and west, while Pine Street is on the north and the Assay Office a part of the Sub-Treasury, is on the east, occupies the site of the old City Hall of New York, which, at a later period, was known as "Federal Hall." Here Washington was inaugurated as the first President of the United States of America, and took the oath of office on the spot now

---

[1] The currency is augmented by the issue of $331,121,504 of silver certificates of various denominations issued against silver dollars. $7,374,748 of these certificates were in the Treasury, and $323,746,756 in circulation on April 1, 1895.

marked by the imposing bronze statue, of which J. Q. A. Ward is the sculptor.

This building is conspicuous among the loftier buildings surrounding it, particularly for its pure architecture and its adaptability for its present use. Its solid and substantial form, its doors, guarded with steel gratings, its massive safes, immense vaults, and its uniformed guards and attendant policemen, as well as the fire-proof character of the building, suggest it as a proper place for the safe storing of the millions of gold and silver which are always within its walls. From the time of its completion in 1842, down to 1862, it was used as a Custom House, since which time it has been devoted to its present use.

In the basement are the vaults where the gold and silver, after being received through the Pine Street entrance, are stored. Besides the vaults in the basement, there are large safes on the main floor, in which a lesser amount of silver and gold is kept.

The main entrance to the Sub-Treasury on Wall Street leads to a large and well lighted rotunda, surmounted by a beautiful dome. The office of the Assistant U. S. Treasurer is on the left of the main entrance. The coin division is in the Pine Street end of the building. On one side of the hall is the division where the larger denominations of coin are received and paid out, while across the hall is the minor-coin division. The upper floors are devoted to the accounting offices and files.

This Sub-Treasury is only second in importance to the United States Treasury in Washington in the amount of business transacted, which exceeds the aggregate of all the other sub-treasuries in the country, two thirds of the government revenues and disbursements being here received and disbursed; due principally to the fact that it only costs about $1.01 per million to handle money in this office, whereas the cost of handling in the other subtreasuries averages $2.47 a million.

The average daily balance of cash (by which is meant Treasury certificates, gold certificates, silver certificates, National Bank Notes, greenbacks, gold and silver bullion, gold and silver coin, subsidiary coins of copper and nickel) is very difficult to state with any exactness, inasmuch as it varies daily not in thousands of dollars or hundreds of thousands or even millions, but often in tens of millions. Within the last year ending December, 1894, the average daily balance has been about $110,000,000.

The receipts consist mainly of duties received at the Custom House, which are daily paid in, internal-revenue taxes, deposits of postmasters, remittances from banks acting as national depositories, and deposits of banks or individuals throughout the country of bullion. Here gold certificates payable in coin or in bullion, all forms of paper money, save silver certificates, are redeemed in coin upon presentation.

Silver and gold coin and bullion in large amounts are deposited by banks and private individuals on receipt. These deposits form no part of the real available assets of the Sub-Treasury, which, for the time being, is simply used as a storehouse for their safekeeping.

The principal payments and disbursements are those made to the disbursing officers of the army and navy, against which payments deposits have been previously made from the main Treasury in Washington. Other disbursements are the regular Treasury payments on appropriations for public buildings, improvements, the construction of public works, and the payment of pensions, about $90,000,000 being paid out annually by this Sub-Treasury for this account alone. In addition to these disbursements the interest charges on government bonds falling due are here paid to the holders.

Several times when its financial condition warranted, the government has, in order to relieve the stringency of the money market, anticipated the payment of its bonds, the necessary disbursements for which were made principally through this Sub-Treasury.

The Sub-Treasury is a member by courtesy of "The New York Clearing-House Association," as it has daily to pay large balances to the different banks, and it thereby saves itself and them the trouble of making payments to each, instead paying the amount due all to the Clearing House, which distributes it.

The Assay Office, immediately to the right and adjoining the Sub-Treasury, of which it forms a necessary part, is interesting principally as the storehouse of the Sub-Treasury and from the fact that millions of coin and bullion are here stored. A comparatively small part of the gold and silver here in store is in the shape of coin, that being generally kept at the Sub-Treasury. But here may be seen bricks, as they are termed, of gold bullion, little larger than a watch charm, square in shape, and worth about $130, according to the fineness of the metal, to larger bricks worth $6000.

Bullion is received in this office through the Sub-Treasury from all parts of the republic, and requisitions are made by the various mints of the country on it for such bullion as they need for coinage.

CHAPTER II.

Banks—National Bank Act.

THE function of a bank is to issue, receive on deposit, and loan money, to economize its use, and to receive, extend, and facilitate the interchange of credits; and to banks is largely due the extension and the development of the system of domestic and foreign exchange, which is an extension of the system of banking itself.

To appreciate fully the extent of the exchanges effected by banks, we must bear in mind that while the active currency of our country is about $1,600,000,000 the total annual clearances of the Clearing Houses of the country are $62,000,000,000.

These associations are formed by banks for the purpose of avoiding actual payment, in money, of their obligations to each other (see Clearing House). Nor does this amount include transfers between depositors of the same banks effected on the books of those banks.

Banks are divided into six different kinds, the first and most important being those organized under the National Banking Act of 1863, and the amendments which have from time to time been made thereto, and called *National Banks*. *Trust Companies* which are organized under the laws of the various States in which they are located, *State banks, savings banks, National Gold Banks*, and *private banks*.

The present national banking system came into existence under the Act of 1863; this Act, however, was repealed and superseded by that of 1864, previous to which the banks of issue were organized under the laws of the different States in which they were located. These laws were not uniform, some being far more stringent than others. The banking laws of some States, however, were almost models of their kind, and provided ample security for the protection of the holders of the bank notes as well as of the depositors.

The banking laws of several of the States furnish excellent object-lessons, in the difference between sound principles and their application to finance, and dangerous experiments in the attempt to create money out of nothing, or, at most, out of values insufficient to secure the face value of the paper money issued against it, and which value could not be readily converted into good money.

In considering the question of banking laws, the natural and political conditions of a country must always be taken into consideration, and it is not fair to assume, because at a certain stage of a country's development a law has been unsuccessful, at a later period, when the conditions have been entirely changed, the result would be the same. Unquestionably, if the present national banking system had been tried in the earlier days of our republic, or, in fact, at any period sooner than it was, it must have met with nearly the same result as attended State legislation, or at best have been but little more successful than the average. It would, undoubtedly, however, have secured uniformity in the price of circulating notes—that is, the notes of every bank would be of the same value as that of every other, which is something unattainable under State laws.

The National Bank Act provides for the incorporation of National Banks, and prescribes that such banks shall include as a part of their title the word "National," and prohibits all other banks from using the word "National" as a part of their name. Under this law are also organized and operated, principally on the Pacific Coast, what are termed "National Gold Banks," In the District of Columbia there is a National Savings Bank, authorized by this act. State banks are organized under the laws of the States in which they are located. Trust companies are also formed under the State laws.

Savings banks are organized under the laws of the various States in which they are located, and are subject to many restrictions in regard to the character of their investments and of the collateral on which they may loan, also the proportion of currency to deposits which must be kept on hand, and other matters which will be more fully explained under "Savings Banks."

Private banks and bankers, *i.e.*, one or more individuals engaged in the business of banking but not incorporated as a company, are subject to State supervision, the same as State banks, only when they issue circulating notes, which they are permitted to do under the laws of New York, on the same conditions imposed upon State banks, but which they have found unprofitable on account of the Federal tax of ten per cent. on the issue of all but national banks.

In order to convey a clear idea of the powers of, and the differences between the several kinds of banks, it has been found necessary to give a synopsis of the laws under which they exist, and to which they are amenable.

NATIONAL BANKS.

The National Banking Act of the United States was first passed in the year 1863, repealed and a new act substituted in 1864, which has been amended from time to time since. Below is the act as it at present stands.

To thoroughly establish the national banking system, it became necessary for the Federal Government to impose a tax of ten per cent. upon the circulating notes of all other than national banks. By many, this tax is considered if not unconstitutional, an abuse of the Federal taxing power, but had the desired effect of making the "National" the prevailing banking system of the country.

Condensation National Bank Act.—The first provision of the national banking act as now in force provides for the establishment of the Bureau of the Comptroller of the Currency, to whom all matters relating to national banks are referred, with power to grant certificates to such banks to commence business, on being convinced that the conditions of the act are complied with, or in his discretion to withhold such certificates; and through bank examiners to make examinations whenever he may deem it necessary.

Organization and Powers.—The first provision of the law proper is in regard to the organization and powers of national banks, and prescribes that not less than five natural persons—and by natural persons is meant individuals and not corporations, executors, administrators, etc.—may associate themselves together to organize a national bank.

They must make an organization certificate specifying the object of the formation of such association, and this certificate, which must be properly signed and forwarded to the Comptroller of the Currency, shall state: first, the name of such association; second, the town or city and State where its operations are to be conducted; the amount of capital stock; the number of shares into which it is to be divided; the names and places of residence of the shareholders, and the number of shares, held by each of them. It must be acknowledged before a judge of some court of record or a notary public, whose seal must be attached thereto.

From the date of filing the articles of association, after approval of their application by the Comptroller of the Currency, the associates become a body corporate, and as such are vested with the power to use a corporate seal and to have for twenty years the use and enjoyment of the privileges of this act, subject to its restrictions, limitations, and obligations, although this incorporation may be sooner dissolved, according to the provisions of its articles of association, by the vote, in value, of two thirds of the shareholders. The franchise may be forfeited through violation of the law.

It shall have power to make contracts.

Such association may sue or be sued in the same manner as natural persons; can elect or appoint directors, and such directors may appoint or elect a president, vice-president, cashier, and other officers necessary to carry on its business, and may dismiss these and appoint others to fill their places.

Its Board of Directors may adopt by-laws not inconsistent with law. Through its Board of Directors and officers it may exercise such powers as shall be necessary to carry on the business of banking, in its various forms.

May issue circulating notes as is further on fully stated, and may exercise such incidental powers as shall be necessary to carry on the business of banking: by discounting and negotiating promissory notes, drafts, bills of exchange, and other evidences of debt; by receiving deposits; by buying and selling exchange, coin, and bullion; by loaning money on personal security; and by obtaining, issuing, and circulating notes according to the provisions of this title.

May purchase, hold, and convey real estate, but only as much as shall be necessary for its immediate accommodation in the transaction of its business, and such as shall be mortgaged or conveyed to it in good faith as security for or satisfaction of debts previously contracted, and it may hold for the space of five years the possession of real estate under mortgage or the title and possession of such real estate as may be purchased to secure a previously incurred debt, at the expiration of which time such real estate must be sold.

No national bank may be organized having a capital of less than $50,000, in a town whose population is less than six thousand inhabitants; $100,000 in a city of less than fifty thousand; or $200,000 in a city of more than fifty thousand inhabitants.

Its capital stock shall be divided into shares of one hundred dollars each, and be deemed personal property, transferable on its books as prescribed in the by-laws or articles of association; a person becoming a shareholder by transfer having the rights and incurring the obligations of the original shareholder.

At least fifty per cent. of the capital stock of such association shall be paid in before it is authorized to commence business, and the remainder to be paid in equal monthly instalments of ten per cent. each.

The first payment of fifty per cent. and each subsequent payment must be certified by the President or Cashier of such association to the Comptroller of the Currency.

Upon the failure of a shareholder to pay any instalment on the stock subscribed to by him, such association may sell the stock of such delinquent shareholder at public auction, after three weeks' public notice thereof published in a newspaper of general circulation in the city or county where the association is located, or in the city or county nearest the location of such association, to the person paying the highest price therefor, which price shall not be less than the amount then due, together with the expenses of advertising and sale. In case of failure to sell, the amount previously paid by such shareholder shall be forfeited to the association, and the stock shall again, within six months after due notice as above provided, be offered for sale, when, if not then sold, it may be cancelled.

Upon the certificate of payment of the fifty per cent. of the capital stock being sent to the Comptroller, he may make such examination as he thinks necessary to determine whether such association is entitled to commence business, and if such examination proves it is, he must then issue such certificate ; but if such examination proves unsatisfactory, he may withold the same. Such association shall cause the certificate so issued by the Comptroller to be published, in the manner before stated, for at least sixty days.

Before any bank is permitted to begin business, however, it is required to transfer and deliver to the Treasurer of the United States, United States registered interest-bearing bonds, to an amount of not less than thirty thousand dollars and not less than one third of the capital stock of such bank, except in the case of banks having a capital of one hundred and fifty thousand dollars or less, which shall be only required to transfer United States bonds to the extent of one fourth of their capital. Such bonds shall be received by the Treasurer on deposit, and shall be kept safely in his office until otherwise disposed of under the provisions of this act.

All transfers of bonds made by any bank to the Treasurer under this act are made in trust for the association, and a memorandum to that effect should be written or printed on each bond and signed by the Cashier or some other officer of the bank, for which bonds the Comptroller or a clerk will issue a receipt, stating that the bond is held in trust for the bank and as security for the redemption and payment of any circulating notes that have been or may be delivered to such bank. No assignment or transfer of any such bond by the Treasurer shall be deemed valid unless countersigned by the Comptroller, who shall keep in his office a book in which shall be entered, immediately upon his counter-signing it, every transfer or assignment by the Treasurer of any bonds belonging to a national bank, which entry shall state the name of the bank from whose account the transfer is made, the name of the party to whom made, and the par value of the bonds transferred ; notice of which transfer shall be immediately given to the bank by the Comptroller.

The Comptroller is given access to the books of the Treasurer of the United States, for the purpose of ascertaining the correctness of any such transfer or assignment, and also to the bonds to ascertain their amount and condition. Like access is given the Treasurer to the books of the Comptroller for the same purpose.

Each bank is required at least once a year, through some officer or representative, to compare the bonds pledged by it, with the books of the Comptroller, and if found correct to execute to the Treasurer a certificate setting forth the different kinds and the amounts thereof, and that the same are in the possession and custody of the Treasurer, a duplicate of which, signed by the Treasurer, shall be retained by the bank.

The bonds transferred to and deposited with the Treasurer of the United States by any bank, for the security of its circulating notes, shall be held exclusively for that purpose, until such notes are redeemed. The Comptroller of the Currency shall give to any such bank powers of attorney to receive and appropriate to its own use the interest on the bonds which it has so transferred to the Treasurer ; but such powers shall become inoperative whenever such association fails to redeem its circulating notes. Whenever the market or cash value of any bonds thus deposited with the Treasurer is reduced below the amount of the circulation issued for the same, the Comptroller may demand and receive the amount of such depreciation in other United States bonds at cash value, or in money, from the association, to be deposited with the Treasurer as long as such depreciation continues. And the Comptroller, upon the terms prescribed by the Secretary of the Treasury, may permit an exchange to be made of any of the bonds deposited with the Treasurer by any association for other bonds of the United States authorized to be received as security for circulating notes, if he is of opinion that such an exchange can be made without prejudice to the United States; and he may direct the return of any bonds to the bank which transferred the same, in sums of not less than one thousand dollars, upon the surrender to him and the cancellation of a proportionate amount of such circulating notes.

The association making a deposit of bonds as herein provided shall be entitled to receive from the Comptroller of the Currency circulating notes of different denominations, in blank, registered and countersigned as provided by law, equal in amount to ninety per centum of the current market value, not exceeding par, of the United States bonds so transferred and delivered.

" In order to furnish suitable notes for circulation, the Comptroller of the Currency shall, under the direction of the Secretary of the Treasury, cause plates and dies to be engraved, in the best manner to guard against counterfeiting and fraudulent alterations, and shall have printed therefrom, and numbered, such quantity of circulating notes, in blank, of the denominations of one dollar, two dollars, three dollars, five dollars, ten dollars, twenty dollars, fifty dollars, one hundred dollars, five hundred dollars, and one thousand dollars, as may be required to supply the associations entitled to receive the same. Such notes shall express upon their face that they are secured by United States bonds, deposited with the Treasurer of the United States, by the written or engraved signatures of the Treasurer and Register, and by the imprint of the seal of the Treasury; and shall also express upon their face the promise of the association receiving the same to pay on demand, attested by the signatures of the president or vice-president and cashier; and shall bear such devices and such other statements, and shall be in such form, as the Secretary of the Treasury shall, by regulation, direct."

The expenses of the issuance of such notes shall be paid from the taxes assessed on the circulation of the banks to which they are issued.

The Comptroller of the Currency shall cause to be examined each year, the plates, dies, butt-pieces (bed-pieces), and other material from which the national-bank circulation is printed, and file in his office annually a correct list of the same.

Such material as shall have been used in the printing of the notes of associations which are in liquidation, or have closed business, shall be destroyed under such regulations as shall be prescribed by the Comptroller of the Currency and approved by the Secretary of the Treasury. The expenses of any such examination or destruction shall be paid out of any appropriation made by Congress for the special examination of national banks and bank-note plates.

National banks can only issue notes furnished by the Federal Government. Since specie payments have been resumed no association has been furnished with notes of a less denomination than five dollars.

It may increase or decrease its stock on a two-thirds vote in value of its stockholders, and after notice, subject to the following conditions: In the case of increasing its stock, it must also increase its transfer of bonds to the Treasurer of the United States, so that there may always be in the hands of the Comptroller bonds to the amount of twenty-five per cent. of the capital of such association. In the case of a decrease of capital, it can, after providing for the payment of its outstanding circulating notes, decrease its deposit of bonds with the Comptroller, but never below twenty-five per cent. of its capital.

It may elect directors at its annual meeting, or in the case of a failure then to elect, at some subsequent meeting, of which due notice shall be given. Its affairs shall be managed by not less than five directors, elected by the shareholders, each director being required to be a bona-fide owner of at least ten shares of unpledged stock. Every director must, during his whole term of service, be a citizen of the United States, and at least three fourths of the directors must at the time, and for at least a year previous, have resided in the State, territory, or district, in which the association is located.

Directors are required to take an oath as to their diligent and honest administration of the affairs of the association, and transmit the same to the Comptroller of the Currency, to be filed. The Directors may fill any vacancy occurring in their Board until the next election.

" The shareholders of a national bank are held individually responsible, equally and ratably and not for one another, for all contracts, debts, and engagements of such association to the extent of the amount of their stock therein, at the par value thereof, in addition to the amount invested in such shares ; except that shareholders of any banking association now existing under State laws, having not less than five milllions of dollars of capital actually paid in, and a surplus of twenty per centum on hand, both to be determined by the Comptroller of the Currency, shall be liable only to the amount invested in their shares ; and such surplus of twenty per centum shall be kept undiminished and be in addition to the surplus provided for in this title ; and if at any time there is a deficiency of twenty per centum in such surplus, such association shall not pay any dividends to its shareholders until the deficiency is made good ; and in case of such deficiency, the Comptroller may compel the association to close its business and wind up its affairs. . . ."

Executors, administrators, guardians, or trustees holding stock are not personally subject to any liabilities as stockholders, but the estates which they represent are.

A national bank may, upon a further deposit of government bonds with the Secretary of the Treasury, be designated, and act as a depository of public moneys and as the financial agent of the government, and every association so designated as a receiver and depository of public money shall take and receive at par all national currency bills by whatever association issued, which have been paid into the government for internal revenue or for loans or stocks.

A State bank may reorganize under the provisions of this Act and may retain and keep in operation its branches.

Associations may be organized under the National Banking Act for the purpose of issuing notes payable in gold upon the deposit of any United States bonds bearing interest payable in gold, with the Treasurer of the United States, but none of a smaller denomination than $5, nor can they issue notes in excess of eighty per cent. of the par value of the bonds so deposited.

"Gold Banks," as these are termed, are required to keep on hand twenty-five per cent. of their outstanding circulation in gold and silver coin of the United States, and to receive, at par, in the payment of debts, the gold notes of every other like association which, at the time of such payment, is redeeming its circulating notes in gold coin of the United States.

The words "lawful money" are construed to mean "gold or silver" coin of the United States.

A fine of one hundred dollars is imposed for use of any National Bank bill as a means of advertising, either by writing or printing the name and business thereon, or by sending out an advertisement in the shape of a copy of any such bill. There is also a fine of fifty dollars for defacing or mutilating these bills.

The cities in which national banks are located are divided into three classes: first, ordinary; second, reserve; and third, central reserve cities.

Ordinary cities comprise the great number of cities, neither reserve nor central reserve, in which national banks are required to maintain a reserve of fifteen per cent. of the amount on deposit with them, three fifths of which reserve may be deposited by them in reserve or central reserve banks.

In reserve cities, which are divided into four groups, at

this date (1895) comprising the following cities: Group 1, Boston, Albany, Brooklyn, Philadelphia, and Pittsburg. Group 2, Baltimore, Washington, New Orleans, and Louisville. Group 3, Cincinnati, Cleveland, Detroit, Milwaukee, Des Moines, and Minneapolis. Group 4, Kansas City, St. Joseph, Lincoln, Omaha, and San Francisco. National banks must keep on hand twenty-five per cent. of the amount on deposit with them, one half of which may consist of amounts on deposit to their credit in central reserve banks.

Central reserve cities, consisting in 1895 of New York, Chicago, and St. Louis. In these cities national banks must maintain a reserve of twenty-five per cent. and may act as the depositories of a portion of the reserve of ordinary and reserve city banks. Any city of more than two hundred thousand population may, upon written application to and approval of the Comptroller, signed by three fourths of the national banks, become a "Central Reserve City." Upon like application, any city with a population of fifty thousand or more may be added to the list of reserve cities.

All national banks are required to deposit with the Comptroller a fund equal to five per cent. of their circulating notes, which fund shall be held exclusively for that purpose, but may be considered as a part of their lawful money reserve.

"Clearing-house certificates, representing specie and lawful money specially deposited for the purpose of any clearing-house association, shall also be deemed to be lawful money in the possession of any association belonging to such clearing house."

When the reserve of any bank falls below the respective percentages above given, such bank shall not increase its liabilities by making new loans or discounts otherwise than by discounting or purchasing bills of exchange payable at sight, nor declare or pay any dividend on its profits, until such reserve is made good. If within thirty days after notice from the Comptroller to make such reserve good the same is not done, the Comptroller, with the concurrence of the Secretary of the Treasury, may appoint a receiver to wind up the affairs of such bank.

The reserve required to be kept by National Gold Banks is not only a percentage on its deposits, as in the case of national banks, but on its circulation as well.

Each national bank in any of the reserve cities shall, with the approval of the Comptroller, select a national bank in a central reserve city, at which it may redeem its circulating notes at par, and may keep one half of its lawful money reserve in cash deposits in such central reserve city, but this does not apply to National Gold Banks.

Every national bank must receive and take at par, for any debt or liability to it, the notes or bills of any other national bank, except the notes of associations organized for the purpose of issuing notes payable in gold.

The rate of interest which may be charged is the legal rate prevailing in the State where such bank is located, or the same as that which State banks of issue are permitted by State law to charge.

Where no rate is fixed, seven per centum; but the premium on a bill of exchange payable at some other place, is not considered interest.

The penalty for usury is the recovery of twice the amount of interest received, by an action commenced within two years from the time of the transaction.

The Directors may, semi-annually, declare a dividend of so much of the net profits as they shall judge expedient, but before the declaration of such dividend, each bank shall carry one tenth of its net earnings of the preceding half year to its surplus fund until the same shall amount to twenty per cent. of its capital stock.

Not more than ten per cent. of the capital paid in shall

be loaned to any individual corporation or firm, or the different members thereof, but this does not prohibit the discount of bills of exchange drawn against existing values, or of commercial paper owned by the person negotiating the same.

No loan or discount may be made on the security of the stock of such bank, nor shall a bank become the purchaser or holder of such shares except as security for a previously contracted debt, and such stock shall within six months be disposed of, on notice, at public sale, on failure to do which a receiver may be appointed.

The liabilities of a bank shall at no time exceed its capital stock paid in and undiminished, except on demands of the following nature:

1st. Notes of circulation.

2d. Moneys deposited with or collected by the association.

3d. Bills of exchange or drafts drawn against money actually on deposit to the credit of the association, or due thereto.

4th. Liabilities to the stockholders of the association for dividends and reserve profits. Its circulating notes shall not be pledged or hypothecated to procure money to be paid in on, or to increase its capital.

No portion of its capital, either in the form of dividends or otherwise, shall be withdrawn by the association or any member.

No dividends shall be declared in excess of the net profits of the bank, after deducting all losses sustained and bad debts contracted. Debts on which interest is due and unpaid for six months, unless well secured and in process of collection, shall be considered "bad debts."

"Every association which shall have failed to pay up its capital stock, as required by law, and every association whose capital stock shall have become impaired by losses or otherwise, shall, within three months after receiving notice thereof from the Comptroller of the Currency, pay the deficiency in the capital stock, by assessment upon the shareholders pro rata for the amount of capital stock held by each; and the Treasurer of the United States shall withhold the interest upon all bonds held by him in trust for such association upon notification from the Comptroller of the Currency, until otherwise notified by him.

"And provided. That if any shareholder or shareholders of such bank shall neglect or refuse, after three months' notice, to pay the assessment, as provided in this section, it shall be the duty of the board of directors to cause a sufficient amount of the capital stock of such shareholder or shareholders to be sold at public auction (after thirty days' notice shall be given by posting such notice of sale in the office of the bank, and by publishing such notice in a newspaper of the city or town in which the bank is located, or in a newspaper published nearest thereto), to make good the deficiency; and the balance, if any, shall be returned to such delinquent shareholder or shareholders."

No bank shall pay out or put in circulation the notes of any other bank which are not receivable and redeemable at par by such bank.

Over-certification of checks is strictly prohibited, rendering officers or clerks liable to imprisonment for not less than five years nor more than ten, and giving the Comptroller power to appoint a receiver.

A list of the shareholders shall be kept by the President and Cashier, containing the names and residences of the shareholders and the number of shares of stock held by each, which list shall be subject to inspection by the shareholders of the banks, creditors, and State officers authorized to assess taxes, and on the first Monday of July a copy of such list sworn to by the President or Cashier shall be mailed to the Comptroller.

Five reports a year shall be mailed by each bank to the Comptroller, verified under oath by the President and Cashier and attested by at least three directors, giving in detail under proper headings the resources and liabilities of the bank at the close of business of any past day by him specified, and shall be mailed to the Comptroller within five days after a request for same, and in the form in which mailed to the Comptroller shall be published in a newspaper, as heretofore described, and proof of such publication sent the Comptroller. The Comptroller may also, whenever he deems it desirable, call for special reports.

Each bank must, within ten days after declaring any dividend, report to the Comptroller the amount of such dividend, also the amount of the net earnings, of such bank in excess of such dividend, which report shall be attested by the oath of the President or the Cashier.

A penalty of one hundred dollars a day for each day's delay after the periods named in the last two paragraphs is imposed for failure to make and transmit the reports therein mentioned, which penalty, upon delay or refusal to pay by the association after it has been assessed, may be retained by the United States Treasurer, upon the order of the Comptroller, out of the interest, as it may become due, on the bonds deposited by said association to secure circulation. All penalties collected under this section shall be paid into the Treasury of the United States.

The following taxes are payable, on the average amount of its circulating notes, in January and July of each year one half of one per cent.

Semi-annually on the *average deposits one fourth* of *one per cent.* and a *like per cent.* on the *average* amount of its *capital stock beyond the sum invested* in *United States bonds.*

It is required to report, within ten days from the first days of January and July yearly, to the Treasurer the average amount of its notes in circulation, of its deposits, and of its capital beyond the amount invested in United States bonds for the preceding half year. The penalty provided for a failure to so report is two hundred dollars, to be collected as above, or by suit.

The Comptroller upon the failure of any bank to make such report shall assess the tax on circulation, on the amount of notes delivered to such bank, and upon the highest amount of its capital and deposits. These taxes are collected out of the interest on the bonds to the credit of the bank. Over-payments of taxes are refunded.

The National taxes just recited do not prevent the imposition of State taxes, except that such taxes shall not be of a discriminating nature.

Examiners may be appointed by the Comptroller with the approval of the United States Treasurer to make an examination into all the affairs of any national bank, and report thereon. They shall have the power to examine officers or clerks under oath, and call for the production of any books and papers belonging to the bank which they may deem necessary. The fees of such examiner or examiners, for the examination of banks not located in the redemption cities or in the States of Oregon, California, Nevada, or the Territories, shall be, for banks having a capital of less than $100,000, $20; $100,000–$300,000, $25; $300,000 and less than $400,000, $35; $400,000 but less than $500,000, $40; $500,000–$600,000, $50; $600,000 and over, $75.

These charges shall be assessed by the Comptroller upon, and paid by the banks so examined.

The fees charged for the examination of banks in the redemption cities[1] and in the States of Oregon, California, or Nevada, or any of the Territories, shall be fixed by the Secretary of the Treasury upon the recommendation of the Comptroller. No person shall be appointed to examine the affairs of any bank of which he is a director or other officer.

Any national bank may go into liquidation and be

---

[1] There are now no redemption cities.

closed by the vote of shareholders owning two thirds of its stock, of which vote it shall be the duty of the directors to cause notice, certified under seal by the President and Cashier, to be sent the Comptroller, and have the same published for two months, in a newspaper published in the city of New York, and in a local paper as provided in the case of other notices. The notice shall state that the association is closing up its affairs, and shall notify the holders of its notes and other creditors to present their notes or claims for payment. Such association shall within six months after such vote deposit with the Treasurer of the United States lawful money of the United States sufficient to redeem all its outstanding circulating notes, which money shall be placed to its credit upon "redemption account" and duly receipted for by the Treasurer.

An association which is in good faith winding up its business for the purpose of consolidating with another association, shall not be required to deposit lawful money for its outstanding circulation; but its assets and liabilities shall be reported by the association with which it is in process of consolidation.

Upon the deposit of sufficient lawful money to redeem its outstanding circulating notes, the United States bonds transferred by such association to the Treasurer of the United States shall be re-assigned to it, and its shareholders are discharged of all liability upon such notes, which shall be redeemed at the Treasury of the United States; but should such association fail within thirty days after the expiration of the time specified to make said deposit, and take up its bonds, the Comptroller may sell the same at public auction in the city of New York, and after providing for the redemption and cancellation of its circulating notes, and expenses of sale, he shall pay over any balance remaining to the bank or its legal representatives.

Redeemed notes shall be destroyed.

Upon the failure of a bank to redeem its circulating notes either at its place of business or designated place of redemption, the holder may cause the same to be protested in one package by a notary public, unless such protest is waived by the President or Cashier of such bank, and he delivers to the party making such demand an admission in writing stating the time of the demand, the amount demanded, and the fact of the non-payment thereof. The notary shall forward such protest or admission to the Comptroller, retaining a copy thereof. If, however, satisfactory proof is produced to the notary public that the payment of the notes demanded is restrained by order of any Court of competent jurisdiction, he shall not protest the same. The holder can recover for only one protest fee on the same day.

Upon such notice of protest of the notes of a bank, the Comptroller may order an examination of such bank by a special agent, and if satisfied by his report, that it has refused to redeem its notes, and is in default, may, within thirty days after the reception of such notice of such failure, declare the bonds deposited by such association forfeited to the United States.

After failure to pay any of its circulating notes, except by order or injunction of Court, such bank is forbidden to continue its business.

Notice shall be given to the holders of the notes of such defaulting bank by the Comptroller to present them for payment at the United States Treasury, and he may cancel an amount of bonds deposited by said bank equal at current market rates, not exceeding par, to the notes paid.

The United States has a first lien upon the assets of all national banks until it has been reimbursed for the amount of any payments made by it on account of the circulating notes of said defaulting association.

The bonds on deposit may be sold at public or private sale by the Comptroller to redeem the circulating notes of any delinquent bank, but at no price less than par or less than the market value at the time of sale.

The Comptroller shall, upon becoming satisfied of the refusal of any national bank to redeem its notes, or of its insolvency, or its violations of those provisions of the National Banking Act, which authorize the appointment of a receiver for a non-compliance, therewith appoint a receiver with the usual powers, and require of him a bond in such sum as he shall deem necessary. The receiver so appointed shall pay over all moneys collected by him to the Treasurer of the United States, subject to the order of the Comptroller. The Comptroller shall, upon the appointment of a receiver, give three months' notice to creditors to present claims against such bank.

It is necessary to say but little more of that part of the national banking law which relates to the dissolution of banks and the placing of them in the hands of receivers, as the law in regard to receiverships, etc., is not wholly covered by the National Banking Act, but is to a large extent that laid down in the Revised Statutes and the Civil Codes of the several States in reference to receiverships in general.

While the statute law on the subject is very strict and rigorous in its dealings with all violators of its commands, or failures to comply with its provisions, yet the extreme penalties provided are not always enforced, as great interests would often be seriously damaged by a rigid enforcement of those provisions which are meant not for the oppression of banks but rather for the protection of the general public. These are considerations which always weigh with the bank examiners and the officials who act upon their reports.

In cases of great money stringency or panics, it is seldom that some of the banks do not violate one or more of the injunctions of the national banking law; but it would be obviously ruinous, not only to the interests of the community in which such bank is situated, but oftentimes to the country at large, to forfeit the charter of a bank for some minor offence. And while it is not intended that bank officials should be allowed to violate or fail to comply with the law, still it may be remembered that all the actions of the bank examiners and others are or should be tempered by that good sense which is allowed them under the expansive expression, "in the discretion of the Comptroller," and it is wise for all interests that a competent and honest Comptroller should have the right to exercise his discretion.

Upon the putting of a bank into the hands of a receiver, it is then in the hands of the Courts, the same as any other receivership, and is therefore subject to the laws governing receiverships, with the single exception that the circulating notes of such bank, being secured by a deposit of United States bonds, are redeemed by the Government, and the bonds held as collateral sold; the surplus resulting from such sale, after the incidental expenses are paid, is turned over to the receiver and paid out by him by way of dividends on obligations of the bank. Should a surplus still remain, it is paid over to the shareholders.

All other claims against a defunct national bank are collected in the manner like claims are recovered against any other corporation insolvent or in liquidation.

CHAPTER III.

State Banks—New York State Banks of Deposit, and Banking Law.

State Banks.—State Banks are organized under and exist subject to the laws of the State in which they are located, and inasmuch as we are now the proud possessors of forty-four States, even if some have not yet reached the stage of maturity where they can rejoice in a banking law better than all the others, still there are too many State banking laws to admit of even a digest of them here. It is necessary, however, that the salient features of the banking laws of the State of New York, recognized as one of the best, should be given.

No attempt will be made to explain the cause of the failure of many of the State banking laws prior to 1862, beyond the fact that, in a majority of cases, they imposed insufficient restrictions in relation to the issue of circulating notes, allowing notes to be issued against railroad bonds, and in some instances against real estate; permitting loans on real estate (which is always considered poor policy for a bank of deposit, as real estate is not readily convertible into cash), imposed no extra liability on directors, and permitted the banks' own stock, to be pledged as security for loans; but most important of all, they provided for no given percentage of coin or bullion, or, at any rate, an insufficient percentage for the redemption of circulating notes. The banks, not being required to keep a certain percentage of gold and silver on hand in the shape of a redemption fund, did not do so, and when the crisis came there was comparatively little "lawful money" to be had; what little there was at once commanded a large premium, and, owing to the then lack of telegraph and transportation facilities, it was not possible to have London or New York come to the rescue, as it is to-day. In other words, whatever the object may have been, the effect of this lack of provision for a sufficient specie redemption fund was to greatly increase the amount of circulating notes without increasing the supply of the only thing in which they could be redeemed. Nor were these banks, for the reason just given, in any better position to redeem the notes of any other bank, no matter how solvent, than their own; and the moment it was desired to use these notes outside of the State in which they were issued, it could only be done at a discount proportionate to the cost of transportation to their bank of issue, the shipment back of the coin or bullion therefor, and the risk of the notes not being paid. These were the principal causes of the variations in the price of paper money issued by State banks.

What was a possible condition in the West between 1820 and 1860, a period when State government was, to say the least, in a formative stage, when banking was simply being experimented with, when what are now large cities were little more than villages of a few hundred inhabitants and these widely separated, when the only means of communication between town and town was that furnished by the country roads or the steamers plying on our rivers, is not possible to-day, with the instant means of communication afforded by the telegraph, and the reliable information obtainable from mercantile agencies, who have the financial rating of every institution and firm in the country. In other words, what was possible in a state of chaos and general irresponsibility, is not possible where order prevails, and the fullest information is instantly obtainable. Hence it is not fair to assume that, because the issue of State bank-notes in the West was unsuccessful then, it would necessarily be so now. In speaking of State banks, there has been a general disposition to term the systems of all States, without discrimination, "wild-cat" and "yellow-dog" banking, and to speak of the circulating notes of all State banks in these decidedly inelegant but generally understood terms.

These words, however, when applied to the bank-notes or banking systems prevailing in Indiana from 1834 down to 1850, that of Ohio from 1845 to 1854, that of Louisiana from 1842 till the capture of New Orleans by the Federal forces in the late Civil War, and that of Massachusetts, commonly known as the Suffolk Bank system, and also that of New York, which largely served as a model for the present National Bank Act, are absolutely misleading and false.

These systems were all based on sound principles, many of them very scientific, and they would doubtless, if not, so far as the issue of notes is concerned, rendered inoperative by the practically prohibitory tax levied by the Federal Government on the circulating notes of State banks, have continued to the present day showing satisfactory results.

While some of the State banking laws were good and calculated to insure all possible safety in the redemption of circulating notes and other obligations, it must be said that even at most, if modelled on the National Banking Act and the State guaranteeing their notes, they could only offer the guaranty of that particular State, and that could never be as generally acceptable a guaranty as that of the Federal Government.

New York State Banking Laws. In speaking of the banking laws of the State of New York it may be said parenthetically that these laws do not relate exclusively to banks of deposit, but relate also to savings banks, trust companies, building and mutual loan associations, co-operative loan associations, mortgage, loan, and investment corporations, and safe-deposit companies, all of which are rightly considered as belonging to banking. But we will only at present discuss that portion of the law which relates to banks of deposits.

The law defines " Bank " as follows :

" Any moneyed corporation authorized by law to issue bills, or notes, or other evidences of debt for circulation as money, or to receive deposits of money and commercial paper, and to make loans thereon, and to discount bills, notes, or other commercial paper, and to buy and sell gold and silver bullion or foreign coins, or bills of exchange."

The act continues the State Banking Department, under the direction of a superintendent, who is appointed by the Governor for the term of three years and given power to appoint a deputy, clerks, and examiners. The expenses of his office are defrayed by the corporations and individuals required by the act to report to him.

The power of the Superintendent over the State banks is practically the same as the power of the Comptroller over the national banks, and no bank may transact any business without his approval and a certificate from him that it has complied with the law and is authorized to do business. He is required through some representative to examine each banking corporation, other than savings banks, at least once a year, and each savings bank once in two years, and oftener if he deem it expedient so to do.

No examiner shall be appointed as the receiver of the corporation which he examines.

The president or cashier of every banking corporation, under the State laws, is required at least once a year to make a comparison of securities deposited in the office of the Superintendent with the books of the Banking Department.

As in the case of the national banks, no bank, nor individual banker, who issues circulating notes, is permitted to commence business until the receipt of a certificate from the Bank Department authorizing such commencement, which certificate is only issued after examination as to the financial standing of such bank or banker, satisfactory to such department, and a deposit with such department of securities to the amount of 10 per cent. of its paid-up capital, but in no case less than the following: In cities containing 500,000 or more inhabitants, $100,000; 100,000 to 500,000 inhabitants, $50,000; 25,000 to 100,000 inhabitants, $30,000; and in cities of less population, $25,000; and the approval of such securities by such department. Nor shall such bank commence business until its president and cashier, or treasurer, or secretary, or its two principal officers, shall have made an affidavit stating that the whole of its capital stock, or such portion thereof as by law shall be required to be paid or secured before the commencement of its operations, has been actually paid or secured to be paid according to law, and such bank shall cease to be a corporation if such affidavit is not filed within a year from the time its charter is granted.

In Section 14 is found the principal difference between the State and the National banking systems in regard to the class of securities allowed to be deposited with the respective banking departments:

"And every such corporation thereafter proposing to engage in such business [*i.e.*, the banking business] in this State, shall before engaging in such business transfer and assign to the Superintendent registered public stocks or bonds of the United States, or of *this State*, or of *any city, county, town, village, or free school district in this State* authorized by the Legislature to be issued, to the amount in value, and to be at all times so maintained by the corporation, of 10 per cent. on its paid-up capital stock; but no less in any case than $100,000 in cities the population of which exceeds 500,000 inhabitants, $50,000 in cities of 100,000 inhabitants, and not less than $30,000 in cities containing more than 25,000 inhabitants. Such stocks must be registered in the name of the Superintendent."

Foreign banking corporations doing business in the State of New York are required to make the same deposit as State banks, and on failure to do so the State may restrain them from the transaction of their business therein.

Securities deposited may be exchanged for other securities by the consent and with the approval of the Superintendent, and any excess thereof beyond the amount required may be refunded.

Bonds and mortgages on real estate may also be deposited, with the approval of the Superintendent, as part of the collateral for the issue of circulating notes, but in such case the president or authorized agent of every corporation depositing the same shall annex to every such mortgage his affidavit that the mortgage was made and taken in good faith for money loaned by the corporation which he represents, to the amount therein named, and that he has reason to believe that the premises thereby mortgaged are worth at least 75 per cent. more than the amount of the mortgage. In the discretion of the Superintendent the report of any bank examiner shall be published in the State paper, and in at least one daily newspaper in the city of New York, and also a paper in the county where the principal place of business of such corporation or individual is located.

Section 17 is similar in its purport to the provision of the National Banking law in regard to the impairment of the capital, but instead of giving the Superintendent power, if such impairment is not made good, to place the bank in the hands of a receiver, it directs the Attorney-General to institute proceedings for the closing of such corporation or bank.

In case banks or private bankers refuse to give such information as may be demanded by the Superintendent or his agent, or submit their books to examination, the Superintendent is not allowed to take such heroic measures as is the Comptroller of the United States, but the Attorney-General must institute proceedings.

Creditors of, or shareholders in, any State banking corporation whose debts or shares shall amount to $1000 or more, may apply to the Supreme Court for an order permitting and directing an examination of the affairs of such corporation, and the Court may order such examination to be made by a referee, to ascertain the safety of the investments and the prudence of the management of the corporation; the result of which examination, with the opinion of the referee, may be published as directed by the Court. There is no similar provision in the National Bank Act.

Every corporation subject to the banking laws of this State shall make a written report to the Superintendent of Banks in form prescribed by him; in the case of a bank of deposit at least once in three months, on a day to be designated by the Superintendent.

The law imposes a forfeiture of $100 by any bank, and of $10 by any other corporation, subject to the banking law for each day intervening between the time such report should have been filed and the day when it actually is filed, and also that any corporation failing to make two successive reports as required in Section 21, shall forfeit its privileges as such bank and its business shall be closed.

A summary of each report other than those of savings banks shall be published by the Superintendent, within thirty days after the same shall have been filed, in a paper at Albany, in which notices of State officers are required by law to be published, and the separate report of each corporation shall be published by it in at least one newspaper in the place where its business is located; or if there be no newspaper in such place, in the nearest place in which a newspaper is published.

The Superintendent is required to render an annual report to the Legislature at the commencement of its first session similar to that required of the Comptroller of the Currency.

No corporation shall make any loan or discount to any person, company, corporation, or firm, or upon paper upon which any such persons, company, corporation, or firm may be liable, to an amount exceeding the one fifth part of its capital stock actually paid in, and surplus. Under the national banking laws no bank is allowed to make a loan to any such person in excess of 10 per cent. of its capital, but under both laws the discount of bills of exchange drawn in good faith against actually existing values or commercial or business paper actually negotiated by the person issuing the same shall not be considered as a part of any such loan or discount.

"No such corporation nor any of its directors, officers, agents, or servants shall directly or indirectly purchase or be interested in the purchase of any promissory note or other evidence of debt issued by it for a less sum than shall appear on the face thereof to be due. Every person violating the provisions of this subdivision shall forfeit three times the nominal amount of the note or other evidence of debt or purchase."

This provision is entirely lacking in the national banking law, for what reason is not apparent.

The surplus profits, from which alone a dividend can be made, is ascertained by charging in the account of profit and loss, and deducting from the actual profits, all expenses paid, interest on debts, and all losses sustained. Interest unpaid, although due or accrued on debts owing to the corporation, should not be included in the calculation of its profits previous to a dividend. Losses in excess of its undivided profits should be charged against principal, and no dividend should be made until such deficit of capital be made good.

Any bank may, after notice of its intention so to do, make application signed by its two principal officers to the Superintendent for leave to change its place of business to another in the same or an adjoining county, but such notice must be upon the vote of a majority of the Board of Directors, accompanied by the written assent of two thirds in amount of the stockholders.

In the case of foreign corporations it is necessary for them to secure the written permission of the Superintendent and a written certificate from him stating that such corporation has complied with all of the provisions of the banking law applicable to it before it is authorized to transact its business within this State. Such permission and certificate continues in force but one year from its date, but may be renewed from time to time for a like period.

Foreign corporations must execute and file with the Superintendent of Banks a written instrument appointing him their true and lawful attorney, upon whom process may be served in any legal action or proceeding. Upon the service of such process upon the Superintendent as the attorney he shall forward a copy thereof to such foreign corporation.

" If it is made to appear upon application of any creditor or shareholder in any such corporation, company, or association, residing in this State, that the funds on deposit with the Superintendent of Banks are insufficient to pay in full the creditors and shareholders residing in this State, or that it is insolvent, or has suspended business, or that insolvency or bankruptcy proceedings have been taken against it either voluntarily or involuntarily, the Supreme Court may, upon due notice to the corporation, company, or association, as the court shall prescribe, appoint a receiver of such funds ; and pending such application, the court or judge thereof may enjoin the commencement or prosecution of any other action or proceeding against such corporation, company, or association. Upon the qualifications of such receiver, the Superintendent of Banks shall pay over to him the funds remaining in his hands less any charges which he may have against the same, and the receiver shall distribute such funds among the creditors and shareholders of the corporation, company, or association residing in this State in the manner prescribed by law for the payment of creditors in the case of voluntary dissolution of a corporation."

Article 2 of the State law prescribes more in detail the privileges, functions, duties, and requirements of banks.

Section 40 provides that five or more persons may become a bank by making, acknowledging, and filing in the office of the clerk of the county where such bank is to be located and in the office of the Superintendent of Banks a certificate in duplicate, which shall state, first, the name by which such bank is to be known; second, the city, town, or village where its business is to be conducted; third, the amount of its capital stock, and the number of shares into which the same shall be divided; fourth, the names and places of residence of the stockholders and the number of shares held by each; fifth, the dates at which such corporation shall commence and terminate; sixth, the number of directors of the bank (not less than five), and the names of the stockholders who shall be directors for the first year of its incorporation.

This certificate must be recorded by the county clerk and by the Superintendent of Banks in books kept by them respectively for that purpose.

Provision may be made in such certificate for an increase of the capital stock, for the manner in which the stock of the corporation may be transferred, the number of directors necessary to constitute a quorum, and for the time when the annual election of directors shall be held.

Any change in any of the matters enumerated in such certificate shall only become valid upon the execution of a certificate thereof filed and recorded in like manner as the certificate of incorporation.

An individual banker desiring to transact business under the State banking laws must file a certificate similar to the above, and for failure so to do is subject to a forfeit of $1000 to the people of the State for each neglect. Since the enactment of the National Banking Act there has been no inducement to private bankers to avail themselves of the provisions of the State law, and as none now issue circulating notes, they prefer to conduct their business without State interference.

Section 43 enumerates the general powers granted.

"In addition to the powers conferred by the general and stock corporation laws every bank shall have power:

"1. To exercise by its board of directors, or duly authorized officers or agents, subject to law, all such incidental powers as shall be necessary to carry on the business of banking; by discounting and negotiating promissory notes, drafts, bills of exchange, and other evidences of debt; by receiving deposits; by buying and selling exchange, coin, and bullion; by loaning money on personal security; and by obtaining, issuing, and circulating notes according to the provisions of this chapter.

"2. To take and become the owner of any stock or bonds or interest-bearing obligations of the United States, or of the State of New York, or of any city, county, town, or village of this State, the interest on which is not in arrears.

"3. To purchase, hold, and convey real property for the following purposes:

"(*a*) Such as shall be necessary for its immediate accommodation in the convenient transaction of its business.

"(*b*) Such as shall be mortgaged to it in good faith, by way of security for loans made by, or moneys due to, such corporation.

"(*c*) Such as shall be conveyed to it in satisfaction of debts previously contracted in the course of its dealings.

"(*d*) Such as it shall purchase at sales under judgments, decrees, or mortgages held by it.

"No such corporation shall purchase, hold, or convey real property in any other case or for any other purpose, and all conveyances of real property shall be made to it directly and by name.

"All such corporations and all individual bankers shall be banks of discount and deposit as well as of circulation, and the usual business of banking of such corporations or individual bankers shall be transacted at the place where such corporations or individual bankers shall be located, agreeably to the location specified in the certificates required by law to be made by them respectively, and filed in the office of the Superintendent of Banks, and not elsewhere, except as otherwise provided in this chapter in relation to the redemption of circulating notes by agents."

By Section 44 every bank or individual banker is required at all times to have on hand in "lawful money" of the United States, when such bank or banker transacts its or his business in a city of more than eight hundred thousand inhabitants, at least 15 per cent. of the aggregate amount of its or his deposits, and at least 10 per cent. of such deposits if such business is transacted elsewhere in the State. This amount shall be called its "Lawful Money Reserve."

One half of such reserve may consist of moneys on deposit, subject to call, with any bank or trust company in this State having a capital of not less than $200,000, and approved by the Superindendent of Banks as a depository of "Lawful Money Reserve."

If the "Lawful Money Reserve" of any bank or individual banker shall be less than the amount above stated, then such bank or banker shall not increase his liabilities by making any new loans or discounts "otherwise than by discounting bills of exchange payable on sight," nor shall it or he declare dividends or profits until such lawful money reserve has been restored.

The Superintendent of Banks may require such bank

or banker to make good such money reserve, and if it or he shall fail for thirty days so to do such bank or individual banker shall be deemed insolvent and may be proceeded against as an insolvent moneyed corporation.

The act of April 23, 1895, which repeals sections forty-five, forty-six, forty-seven, and forty-eight of the banking law, and which went into effect immediately, provides, that any two or more corporations, except savings banks, organized under the banking law or any section thereof, are authorized to consolidate upon compliance with the following conditions: The boards of directors of the respective corporations may enter into an agreement of merger under their respective corporate seals, which agreement shall be subject to the approval of the Superintendent of Banks, and which shall be submitted to the stockholders of each of such corporations, at a meeting, called upon at least two weeks' notice, and published for at least two successive weeks in a newspaper in the counties in which such corporations are located, and which agreement shall be approved at each of such meetings of the respective stockholders separately by stockholders owning at least two thirds of the stock; such agreement and verified copies in duplicate of the proceedings of the stockholders of the respective corporations shall be filed with the Superintendent of Banks, and with the clerk of the county of the domicil of the corporation into which the other is merged. Upon which the merger is deemed consummated, and the consolidated corporation may call in the stock of the old corporations, and issue new stock.

Any stockholder not voting in favor of such merger, may at such meeting or within twenty days thereafter object to such merger and demand payment for his stock.

The consolidated corporation shall have all the rights, powers, and privileges of the old companies, and be responsible for their debts and obligations.

At least 50 per cent. of the capital stock of every bank

shall be paid in before it shall commence business, and the remainder of its capital stock shall be paid in instalments of at least 10 per cent. each on the whole amount of the capital, as frequently as one instalment at the end of each succeeding month from the time it shall be authorized by the Superintendent of Banks to commence business, and the payment of each instalment shall be certified to the Superintendent under oath by the president or cashier of the corporation.

Only citizens of the United States are eligible as directors, and at least three fourths of the directors must be citizens of the State, and in case of a bank having a capital of $50,000 or over, each director must own in his own right stock of the bank equal in value to $1000, and in case of a bank having a less capital than $50,000 must be a stockholder in his own right to an amount equal to at least $500, such directorship to terminate upon his ceasing to possess such amount of stock. Directors shall hold office for one year and until their successors are elected and have qualified. The president is to be chosen from among the Board of Directors.

Each director, when appointed or elected, shall take an oath that he will, so far as the duty devolves on him, diligently and honestly administer the affairs of such corporation, and will not knowingly violate, or willingly permit to be violated, any of the provisions of law applicable to such corporation, and that he is the owner in good faith and in his own right of the number of shares of stock required by this chapter, subscribed by him or standing in his name on the books of the corporation, and that the same is not hypothecated, or in any way pledged as security for any loan or debt. Such oath shall be subscribed by the director making it, and certified by the officer before whom it is taken, and shall be immediately transmitted to the Superintendent of Banks, and filed and preserved in his office.

"Except as prescribed in the stock corporation law, the stockholders of every such corporation shall be individually responsible, equally and ratably, and not one for another, for all contracts, debts, and engagements of such corporation to the extent of the amount of their stock therein at the par value thereof, in addition to the amount invested in such shares.

"The term 'stockholder,' when used in this chapter, shall apply not only to such persons as appear by the books of the corporation to be stockholders, but also to every owner of stock, legal or equitable, although the same may be on such books in the name of another person, but not a person who may hold the stock as collateral security for the payment of a debt."

A stockholder who in good faith and without intent to evade his liability as a stockholder transfers his stock on the books of the corporation, when such corporation is solvent, to any resident of this State of full age, is relieved of the responsibility of a stockholder, and such responsibility devolves upon the person to whom the stock is transferred.

All contracts and all notes and bills issued by it and put in circulation as money shall be signed by the president or vice-president and cashier.

The rate of interest permitted to be charged is 6 per cent., which interest may be taken in advance, reckoning the days for which the evidence of debt has to run.

Knowingly taking, receiving, reserving, or charging a greater rate of interest forfeits the entire interest which the note, bill, or other evidence of debt carries with it, or which has been agreed to be paid thereon, and the person paying the same may recover back twice the amount of interest thus paid, provided such action is brought within two years from the time such excessive interest is taken, but the discount of a bill of exchange, note, or other evidence of debt payable at some other place than the place of purchase, discount, or sale, at not more than the current rate of exchange for sight drafts, or a reasonable charge for the collection of the same in addition to the interest, shall not be considered as taking or receiving a greater rate of interest than 6 per cent. per annum.

The avowed object of this section is to place and maintain State banks on an equality in this particular with national banks.

An exception is made to the above rule in the case of advances of money repayable on demand to an amount of not less than $5000 upon warehouse receipts, bills of lading, certificates of stock, certificates of deposit, bills of exchange, bonds, or other negotiable instruments pledged as collateral, when the banks and the borrower may agree upon any rate of interest they choose.

In addition to securities deposited as collateral to its circulating notes, each bank or banker before commencing business shall place and keep on deposit with the Superintendent of Banks, stocks of this State or of the United States bearing interest to the amount of $1000, to be held as a pledge of good faith and a guaranty of compliance with the banking laws of the State on the part of such bank or individual banker, out of which interest the Superintendent may retain any assessments or penalties imposed upon such bank or individual banker after the institution of proper legal proceedings.

Section 50 makes provision for the change of a State to a National bank. This is already detailed in the chapter on National Banks.

Incorporation as a National bank is deemed a surrender of its charter as a State bank, and it shall cease to be a corporation under the laws of the State, except that for the term of three years thereafter its corporate existence shall be deemed to continue for the purpose of prosecuting and defending suits by and against it and of enabling it to close its concerns and to dispose of and convey its property. Such change, however, shall not release any bank from its obligation to pay and discharge all the liabilities created by law, or incurred by it before such change.

Upon such change the plates and dies of any such bank in the Banking Department shall be forthwith so obliterated as to prevent all future use of the same.

Section 63 : "Whenever any banking corporation, organized and doing business under the laws of the United States, shall under the provisions of any act of Congress be authorized to dissolve its organization as such national bank corporation, and shall have taken the action required to effect such dissolution, a majority of the directors of such dissolved corporation may, upon the authority in writing of the owners of two thirds of its capital stock, execute the certificate of incorporation required by Section 40 of this chapter.

" Upon the execution and proof of acknowledgment of such certificate, which shall also set forth the authority in writing of the stockholders as required by this section, and upon filing a copy thereof in the office of the Superintendent of Banks, with proof that the original is duly recorded in the office of the clerk of the county where any office of such corporation shall be located, such corporation shall be held and regarded as an incorporated bank under and in pursuance of the laws of this State, and shall be entitled to all the privileges and be subject to all the liabilities of banks so incorporated ; and thereupon all the property of the dissolved national bank corporation shall immediately by act of law and without any conveyance or transfer be vested in and become the property of such State bank. The directors of the dissolved corporation at the time of such dissolution shall be the directors of the bank created in pursuance hereof until the first annual election of directors thereafter, and shall have power to take all necessary measures to perfect its organization, and to adopt such regulations concerning its business and management as may be proper and just and not inconsistent with law."

The section relating to *Circulating notes, plates, etc.*, will be here omitted, as State banks no longer issue circulating notes, only one bank having out an issue of about $2400. The sections relating to the issue of notes, deposit of securities to insure their payment, and other matters connected therewith are consequently omitted.

Section 76. After the application of the proceeds of such security to the redemption of the circulating notes presented within the time prescribed by Section 73, the residue of such proceeds shall be deposited in the Treasury and applied toward paying the ordinary expenses of the Banking Department.

Notices required to be given to creditors of insolvent banks shall be published at least six weeks in one or more newspapers selected by the Superintendent.

Section 79. Any bank or its receiver or agents and any individual banker or his legal representative or successor may give notice to the superintendent of their or his intention to close business.

After the payment of all lawful claims and demands against such bank or banker they or he may divide the remaining property of the bank or banker among the stockholders or their personal representatives.

Section 82 prohibits the circulation of foreign bank notes, by which is meant the notes of any bank situated outside of the State of New York.

Section 83 provides that no bank shall pay out for paper discounted or purchased any circulating note not received by such bank at par.

No bank or individual banker shall issue or put in circulation any bill or note of such bank or banker unless the same shall be made payable on demand and without interest, except bills of exchange on foreign countries or places beyond the limits or the jurisdiction of the United States, which bills may be made payable at or within the customary usance, or at or within ninety-days' sight, and, except certificates of deposit payable on presentation, with or without interest, to bearer or to the order of a person named therein; but no such certificate of deposit shall be issued except as representing money actually on deposit.

"All checks, bills of exchange, or drafts appearing on their face to have been drawn upon any bank or individual banker carrying on banking business under the laws of this State, which are on their face payable on any specified day or in any number of days after date or sight thereof, shall be due and payable on the day mentioned for the payment of the same, without any days of grace being allowed, and it shall not be necessary to protest the same for non-acceptance."

By the Act of May 9, 1894, "on all notes, drafts, checks, acceptances, bills of exchange, bonds, or other evidences of indebtedness made, drawn, or accepted by any person or corporation after this act shall take effect and in which there is no expressed stipulation to the contrary, no grace, according to the custom of merchants, shall be allowed, but the same shall be due and payable, as therein expressed, without grace.

"This act shall take effect and be in force on the 1st day of January, 1895."

Section 88.—"No foreign corporation, other than a national bank, shall keep any office for the purpose of receiving deposits, or discounting notes or bills, or issuing any evidence of debt to be loaned or put in circulation as money within this State."

Section 89.—"No bank in this State or any officer or director thereof, shall open or keep an office of deposit or discount other than at its usual place of business.

"Every such officer or director violating the provisions of this section shall forfeit to the people of the State the sum of $1000 for every such violation."

Section 90.—"No person shall pay, give, or receive in payment, or in any way circulate or attempt to circulate any bank bill or any promissory note, bill, check, draft, or other evidence of debt, issued by any bank or individual banker, which shall be made payable otherwise than in lawful money of the United States.

"Every person violating this provision shall forfeit to the people of the State the face amount or value of such bill, note, or other evidence of debt so given, paid, received, circulated, or offered, to any person who will sue for the same sixty days after the commission of the offence."

Section 91.—"All bills, notes, or other instruments which shall be issued by any bank or individual banker purporting to be received in payment of debts due to it, shall be deemed and taken to be promissory notes for the payment on demand of the sum or value expressed in such instrument, and such sum shall be recoverable by the holder or bearer of such instrument, in like manner as if the same were a promissory note."

Section 92.—"No person engaged in the business of banking in this State, not subject to the supervision of the superintendent and not required to report to him by the provisions of this chapter, shall make use of any office sign at the place where such business is transacted, having thereon any artificial or corporate name, or other words indicating that such place or office is the place or office of a bank; nor shall such person or persons make use of or circulate any letter-heads, bill-heads, blank notes, blank receipts, certificates, circulars, or any written or printed or partly written and partly printed paper whatever, having thereon any artificial or corporate name, or other word or words, indicating that such business is the business of a bank.

"Every person violating this provision shall forfeit the sum of $1000. But this section shall not apply to any person or persons engaged in the business of banking prior to October, 1892."

CHAPTER IV.

Methods of Business of Banks—Loans—Mutual Assistance—Over-Certification—Reclamation—Management—Board of Directors—Officers and Employés.

Methods of Business.—The method of conducting business is in a general way the same in all banks, whether national, State, savings, or private. They all receive money from their depositors, on which savings banks and some private banks allow interest, but State and national banks generally do not. This money is again loaned at a higher rate of interest than that paid to the depositors; the difference in rate between the interest paid and the interest received constituting the entire income of savings banks and forming the principal income of all banks.

Of course, in the different banks the loans made by them assume a different form, the law prescribing that banks of deposit may negotiate loans on commercial paper and personal securities, the National law forbidding banks organized under it to loan on real estate. Consequently, the bulk of all loans made by banks of deposit must be on commercial paper and personal security.

The laws of the State of New York forbid savings banks loaning on commercial paper, and specify, with great particularity, the kind of collateral on which they may make loans, including in that collateral first mortgages on real estate,—hence, a very large portion of their loans are made on real estate.

Banks of deposit, at one time, received a large income from acting as the fiscal agent of corporations, but this business has been almost entirely absorbed by trust companies and private bankers, which, on account of their fewer governmental restrictions, can offer greater accommodations to the companies for which they act when such companies are in need of assistance.

Another source of revenue was in acting as the agent of the Federal Government for the sale and registration of United States bonds. This, however, no longer exists.

Although loans of banks of deposit, other than the discount of commercial paper, are based generally on stocks, shares, warehouse receipts, bills of lading, or certificates representing the ownership of some commodity, as a broad proposition it may be said that anything which possesses a real tangible value is dealt in and money can be obtained upon it.

Domestic exchange is also a source of large revenue to both national and State banks of deposit.

Mutual Assistance of Banks.—Any careful study of the capital, surplus, amount of loans, etc., of the banks of any large city in this country, and more particularly of New York, cannot fail to convince one of the necessity of banks extending to each other assistance. This assistance is rendered only on a business basis, but could nevertheless be seldom dispensed with, and certainly not during a stringency of money, when it is necessary that all our banks should stand shoulder to shoulder, the stronger assisting the weaker. A good illustration of this was the acceptance, by all the bank members of the Clearing House, of its certificates in payment of their daily balances in 1875, 1884, during the threatened panic following the embarrassment of the Barings, and again in 1893. The ordinary form of assistance is that rendered by the re-discount of paper, *i. e.*, where one bank has more paper than it can conveniently carry, it re-discounts a portion thereof with one or more banks. This aid is being constantly extended by the banks in the larger cities to those in the smaller cities and towns.

Over-Certification.—At one time, the over-certification of the checks of private bankers and brokers became such a common matter, and one or two banks were so badly crippled by the failure to make good these over-certified checks, that the Comptroller of the Currency found it necessary to threaten to enforce the provision in the National Banking Act in relation thereto, which is placing the bank in the hands of a receiver.

This inability to over-certify would have so seriously interfered with the business of some few banks that they resigned their National Bank charters and reorganized under the State law, which is more liberal. Of course, this over-certification can be easily avoided by the teller stating he will pay the check in money, which cannot be refused.

Reclamations.—Reclamations of improperly or irregularly drawn or endorsed checks, or checks which are not good for the amounts called for, take place daily between the various banks, each bank returning to the other the checks drawn against it which for any reason it refuses to pay; the bank receiving the check crediting the same to the bank returning it, just as though the same were paid in cash, and charging the amount of such check to the person depositing it.

Loans on Collateral.—The cashier of the bank is the man to whom the sufficiency of collateral is usually referred when a loan is sought, and oftentimes loans of hundreds of thousands of dollars to well known houses are negotiated over the telephone wires, the houses sending the collateral over by messenger. Of course, these loans being usually call loans, if the collateral is not satisfactory, are immediately called in or other collateral demanded. Such loans are only made to houses with whom the bank has long had dealings, and whose commercial rating is very high. The writer has known of half a million dollars being negotiated by telephone message. It is understood that the borrower will furnish satisfactory collateral, and the loan is generally simply placed to the credit of the borrower on the books of the bank.

The Management of a Bank; the Officers by whom its Business is Conducted, and their Respective Duties.—Necessarily the management of a bank is largely dependent upon its location and the character and amount of its business, but speaking broadly it is safe to say that the management of all large banks of deposit, and the method and manner in which their business is conducted, is essentially the same and differs only in detail.

The highest power of the bank is lodged in the Board of Directors, whom we will consider first.

Board of Directors.—In banks of deposit, both State and National, the Board of Directors shall consist of not less than five nor more than thirteen members. A person to be qualified as a Director must be the absolute owner of ten unpledged shares of the capital stock of said bank, and three fourths of the members of the Board must be residents of the State in which such bank is located. The State law provides that in banks whose capital does not exceed $50,000, each director must be possessed in his own right of at least five unpledged shares of the capital stock of such bank; in banks whose capital is in excess of $50,000, each director must be the owner of ten unpledged shares; and three fourths of the members of such Board shall be residents of the State, city, and county where such bank is located.

The selection of the directors of a bank is largely governed by the business which such directors it is thought can bring to the bank, the position they occupy in the different trades or professions, their knowledge of the financial and business standing of persons likely to do business with such bank, and the general reputation they enjoy in the community.

Banks in the larger cities are often located in a neighborhood the business of which is almost exclusively confined to one trade. In New York, for instance, there are banks whose business is derived almost solely from the dry-goods trade, which banks are necessarily located in a convenient locality to such trade. Other banks derive their business from other trades. In the case of banks whose business is confined largely to one trade, the directors are selected naturally with special reference to their influence in that trade, and their knowledge of the standing of firms engaged therein.

While the law only prescribes that a director should be the holder of five or ten shares of stock, the judgment of an intelligent community dictates that a director should have a more substantial interest than this; and, as a matter of fact, most of the directors of banks are chosen, not only on account of the qualifications before mentioned, but on account of their large holdings of stock in the institutions which they serve.

In the first instance, of course, relying to some extent on the advice of the officers of the bank, who are supposed to be particularly well informed as to the character of persons desiring loans, they settle upon the amount of accommodation to be extended to each depositor. In many banks loans are only made upon their approval, and in the first instance no large amount of credit is extended to any person, firm, or corporation without their sanction; and while the exigencies of business are such that it will not permit that all paper should be submitted to them before loans are negotiated thereon, still it is true that loans, being made in many instances subject to call, in order to stand must receive the approval of the Board. And as banks make a certain class of loans only on condition that they may call upon the borrowers at any time to reduce the amount of their indebtedness, which, taken in connection with the above stated fact that the amount, character, and time of accommodation are, in the first instance, prescribed by the Board, relieves the executive officer of much responsibility that is generally supposed to devolve upon him personally.

The compensation of the directors is usually in the form of a charge for each Board meeting attended, although in many banks they receive no specific compensation other than the benefit they derive from the additional value and dividends on their stock to which their advice is supposed to contribute.

Next in importance to the Board of Directors is the executive head of the bank, generally known in the United States as the President; in England, in the case of the Bank of England, as the Governor; and in other banks as the Manager, and in Canada as the Manager, General or Resident, as the case may be.

In the United States the President of a bank is always a member of the Board of Directors, but in England the Manager is never a member of the Board of Trustees or Directors.

President.—The President, with the concurrence and sanction of the Board of Directors, has absolute control over the policy and discipline of the bank, and to him all the other officers except directors are answerable for the faithful discharge of their various duties. He is usually selected with especial reference to his knowledge of the character of the business to be transacted by the bank over which he is called upon to preside, his influence with the trade which the bank desires to reach, his knowledge of credits, and his general business reputation in the community, on which so much depends the success of the bank. It is his province, assuming that he is the active head of the bank, which in some cases he is not—being occasionally simply a figure-head, but this is not generally true in large banks,—to keep himself not only thoroughly posted in regard to the standing of the various persons with whom the bank does business, but also with the condition of the trade in which those people are engaged, because while the person or firm negotiating a loan may be perfectly solvent, it must be borne in mind that a large part of the loans of banks are made against values in the shape of merchandise, and not against the bare paper, and it might easily happen, should the president of a bank or the person in charge of the loans be ignorant of the value of the merchandise on which a particular loan was negotiated, that that merchandise might decrease so rapidly in value as to form no safe security for the loan, and occasion legal proceedings against the makers of the note for the deficiency.

The president should have a pecuniary interest as a stockholder in the bank which he serves. This may not necessarily be larger than the interest of other stockholders or directors, because if the interest he has is his greatest interest, it is an interest sufficient to influence, apart from his reputation which is at stake, his utmost efforts for the benefit and success of the institution whose policy and business he is called upon to direct.

In his official capacity the president is called upon to sign all contracts in behalf of the bank, all the circulating notes, certificates of stock and other evidences of indebtedness issued by the bank, save certificates of deposit and cashier's checks, which are signed by the cashier. The president is required to give no bonds. All the lesser officers holding responsible positions and having directly to do with the bank's assets, are:

Vice-President.—What has been said with reference to the President applies with somewhat modified force to the vice-president, unless he should be the real head of the bank. His duties, in the absence or inability to act of the president, are the same as those of the president. In the larger banks, where there are necessarily many departments, and even these are sometimes subdivided, the vice-president, in addition to being called upon to serve in the absence of the president, often has charge of some particular department, generally the credit department; to his duties in which department the remarks made in relation to the qualifications of the president apply.

Cashier.—The mechanism of the bank is directly under the control of the cashier, who is, however, accountable to the Board of Directors, by whom he is appointed and to whom he gives bonds for the faithful and efficient discharge of the duties, not only of himself, but of his subordinates, over whom he is supposed to exercise a direct supervision.

In banks where the president or vice-president is not actively in charge, the cashier assumes largely the duties and responsibilities which the president would be called upon to assume and perform, but in all banks the cashier is necessarily conversant with the general policy and management of the bank, the line of credits to be extended to its various depositors, and in most instances, either independently or acting on the advice of the directors, regulates the same, and must keep himself acquainted with the condition of the various accounts, so as to determine which accounts are profitable or otherwise.

The cashier is called upon to sign all contracts, agreements, circulating notes, or evidences of debt issued by the bank, besides cashier's checks and certificates of deposit. He also signs checks drawn on other banks. In his absence they are signed by the president; also drafts and notes sent to other banks are endorsed by him.

The cashier also generally conducts the correspondence of the bank, acts as secretary of the Board of Directors, and keeps the minutes of all meetings of the board, as well as of the stockholders.

Assistant Cashier.—The assistant cashier usually exercises special supervision over the discount books, and attends to the notes and bills payable, besides his principal duty which is to relieve the cashier of matters of detail, and to keep himself so thoroughly informed in regard to the working of the bank, the accounts of depositors, etc., that he can readily supply the cashier, vice-president, or president with information in regard to them. In many banks the correspondence is conducted very largely over the signature of the assistant cashier, and he is specially empowered to endorse checks, drafts, etc., for collection.

Paying Teller.—The paying teller is often called the "first teller." His duties are perhaps more exacting than those of any other officer of the bank. He is generally the custodian of its cash, and is personally responsible for the same. In the safe or vault of the bank certain compartments are set aside for his exclusive use, to which compartments in many banks there is an outer and inner door, the combination of one of which is known only to him and the combination of the other is known only to some other officer, usually the cashier. In these compartments are kept the greater part of the cash belonging to the bank, and in which each day, after the close of business, and the balancing and proof of the cash, are placed all the cash, coin, etc., which have been received during the day by the receiving teller, the note teller, and the collection clerks, all of whom turn over to him, on his receipt, the amounts received by them, as also does the paying teller, the cash contents of his till, a drawer arranged into numerous spaces for the convenient holding of bills of various denominations.

Each morning at the opening of business for the day, the paying teller takes from such compartments the amount of money he thinks will be required to pay the checks presented at his window, and later the amount necessary to settle the Clearing-House balance, should his bank be debtor. This balance in normal times is sent in cash to the Clearing House by trusted employés; although, as has been before stated, in times of great financial stringency the Clearing House issues, on the deposit of satisfactory collateral, "Clearing House Certificates," which are receivable by it in payment of debtor balances, and must, of course, to be of any real use, be also accepted by creditor banks in payment of debits to them, as the Clearing House has no other money than that paid in by the debtor banks. With this amount the paying teller is credited.

The paying teller's desk is usually a model in the way of neatness and convenience of arrangement. On top of it to the left are the trays containing coin, piles of gold and silver of various denominations; further to the left and a little in front of these trays are stacks of bills of different denominations done up in packages, each of which has been previously counted and marked. In the till proper, which is a drawer underneath the desk, the bills of unusual denominations are assorted, and those needed to make change where checks are drawn for odd or broken amounts. The bills in the stacks are usually done up fifty in a package, hence a package of ones would contain $50, of twos $100, of fives $250, of tens $500, and of twenties $1000; the larger bills are not generally put up in packages, and when called for, the teller upon taking them out usually puts a slip in the compartment from which they are taken, or the same amount in packages of a smaller denomination, which being in packages while the other bills are not, are readily separable, and answer the purpose intended, which is always to keep the same amount in each section of the till, except those used for making change, and to use the money in the stacks, which facilitates counting after the day's work is over.

In New York City, promptly at ten o'clock, the tellers' windows are opened for the transaction of business, and remain open until three, except on Saturday, when they are closed at twelve.

The day's business now begins. Mr. Smith presents his check to his own order for $500. The teller examines the same, and if it is properly endorsed, Mr. Smith being a well known depositor, keeping a good balance, the check is paid, the teller handing Mr. Smith a package previously counted and known to contain that sum. Mr. Smith must either count the money handed him before he leaves the window, or accept the teller's count. Next comes a person who presents Mr. Brown's check for say $5000 and wants it certified. Mr. Brown has dealt with the bank a number of years, and his account is known to the teller to be generally somewhere in the neighborhood of $6000, but of late his balances have not been so heavy; in fact, there is a vague suspicion capable of instant verification that Mr. Brown's account would only show about $4000 to this credit, and the National Banking Act under which this bank is organized prescribes severe penalties, not only on the bank, but also on the official, for the over-certification of checks. To certify or not to certify! He well knows that a refusal to certify will probably be a serious injury to Mr. Brown's credit, and Mr. Brown's dealings have always been honorable. He does not attempt to verify his suspicion—uncertainty in his case is preferable; he certifies the check, and in the rush of business forgets all about it, and probably never thinks of it again unless Mr. Brown should fail to make good his account; or the teller will say, "I will pay you the money." The teller is allowed a large discretion in the matter of certification. The moment a check is certified, it is charged against the maker. The memory of signatures and faces is even more necessary than a memory of the depositors' credit balances, as the ledger keepers can always furnish the latter, while no one, in the rush of business, but the teller himself, can furnish the former, although it is true he may refer to the signature book for comparison.

In the payment of checks, four considerations should be ever present. *First*, is the person presenting the same entitled to receive the money for which it calls, and unless he is known to the teller he cannot determine, and if not known he must be identified by some one who is known. Many tellers require the person identifying another to write his name under the endorsement of the person identified, so as to recall the name of the person by whom such identification was made. The *Second* consideration is whether the signature is genuine; the *Third* whether the drawer's account is good for the amount called for, and the *Fourth* whether the first and all intermediate endorsements on the check are correct.

The paying teller must also, as much as is within his power, examine the checks returned from the Clearing House for the same reasons that he examines those presented for payment at his window.

When the day's business is over, the paying teller makes up a balance sheet, on one side of which is the total amount paid out, and the amount on hand, which should, of course, equal the amount of cash with which he started business that day. He then receives from the other tellers the amounts paid in to them during the day, for which he receipts. His final proof is then made up and handed to the cashier or assistant cashier, and the money is locked up in the safes or vaults as before described.

Receiving Teller.—The receiving teller (often called the second teller), as his title implies, receives moneys for deposit, but as he pays out none, it is not necessary that he should have the same knowledge of accounts as the paying teller. It is necessary, however, that he should have a thorough familiarity with counterfeit money, as it is to his window the same generally comes. There are several magazines published which give lists and descriptions of all counterfeits, with which lists the receiving teller is supposed to be familiar.

Each morning he starts with an empty till, and each afternoon when the day's business is done turns over the cash and checks deposited with him to the paying teller and receives his receipt therefor. He retains the deposit slips accompanying each deposit, and marks and files the same for future reference. He should require depositors to endorse every check deposited, whether to order or bearer, so that should any check be returned for want of funds or any other reason, he may by looking at the endorsement know who deposited it.

Discount Department.—As discounts constitute the principal business and source of income of all banks of deposit, this department is the most important in the bank, and is usually under the charge of its principal officer or officers. It is conducted in much the same way as the credit department of any large mercantile house, except that a well managed bank, on account of its discounts being generally larger in amount, should make more careful inquiry as to the financial condition of the borrower than is necessary for a business house to do in regard to the persons to whom it extends credit.

The reports of the principal commercial agencies are always on hand and almost hourly referred to; but these printed reports are seldom taken as conclusive. In a case where there is any doubt, later reports are asked for from the office of the agency and generally promptly supplied, beside which the banks make personal inquiry of the intending borrower and of each other as to the amount of paper which the borrower has in the market, etc., and often require a statement of his exact financial condition, and any misrepresentation on his part renders him liable to criminal prosecution.

Naturally, the persons or firms who take up their paper

promptly become favorably known, and can get their paper discounted at the lowest market rates.

Nearly all the large firms and persons actually engaged in business have at times a large amount of paper out, and some business men assert that in order to secure loans either at all or at the lowest rate of discount, it is necessary to keep their paper on the market, as offering it to banks is termed. Some even go so far as to assert the necessity of issuing such paper for this purpose, even if they do not need the money and keep it lying idle in bank.

Discount Clerk.—In all the larger banks the clerk who has charge of the discounts, *i. e.*, the paper purchased by the bank, is called the Discount Clerk. Perhaps it would be well here to explain why these are called discounts. The reason is the paper is sold to the bank, which becomes the owner thereof, paying to the seller the amount of the face of the paper less the interest on the amount actually paid, which is deducted therefrom and termed a discount. On the acceptance of a discount the amount of interest to be deducted is at once taken therefrom and the balance paid to the seller of the paper.

In the discounting of paper, interest is first charged on the face amount of the paper and then credited at the same rate on the amount of the discount, as the discount not being paid over to the seller of the paper, and he in the first instance being charged interest on the whole amount should be credited with interest on that amount which he does not receive. To illustrate, A presents his paper for $10,000, having one year to run. B agrees to discount it at six per cent. The discount on $10,000 at six per cent. for one year would be $600, so that A would be actually receiving but $9400 while paying interest on $10,000. A therefore should be credited with the interest on the sum of $600 which he does not receive. The computation would then stand as follows:

Loan $10,000, less 6 per cent. discount................	$9400
Plus 6 per cent. interest on amount not paid, $600..........	36
	$9436

which would be the sum payable to A.

All paper offered to a bank for discount is first handed to the discount clerk, by whom it is entered in a book called the "Offering Book," which, in addition to setting forth the particulars of the paper offered, often also states the amount of paper already purchased from the person offering the same.

After the paper has been accepted it is entered in the "Dealers' Discount Book," which is so ruled as to provide columns in which to enter the names of the maker, the endorser, place of payment, due date, days to run, discount, amount of exchange, and net proceeds. Postings to the ledger are made direct from this book. The discount clerk also enters paper discounted in books called "Ticklers." Some banks have domestic ticklers, in which are entered domestic discounts, and foreign ticklers, foreign discounts. The tickler is a book used to tickle or refresh the memory, from which it probably derives its name. The total footings of the ticklers should agree with the total of bills discounted.

As both the names of the drawer and the endorser of each piece of paper offered for discount is set forth not only in the Offering Book, but also in the Ticklers, by reference to these books, should it be suspected that two persons or firms are exchanging paper or endorsing for each other, that fact could be ascertained.

In some banks, paper offered for discount and accepted is numbered in red ink and filed in packages. Other banks, however, will permit no writing of any description or even the puncturing of the paper by a pin.

It is considered unwise to make paper payable to the order of the bank, but rather, and the general practice among business men is, to make it payable to their own order, and then endorse it.

The discount clerk is the custodian of and has in his possession the major part of bills receivable, and each night he deposits the same in the compartment of the vault or safe set apart for that purpose. Each morning they are taken out by himself. Should an officer desire to inspect a note, the discount clerk is called upon to produce it, and the same is inspected in his presence, he being responsible for the safe-keeping of such paper.

As paper for discount is handed him in the first instance, and after being entered in the Offering Book is presented to the officer or officers to decide whether it will be accepted or not, and when a decision has been reached, is returned to him, if accepted marked " A," to be entered in the proper books, and if rejected marked " R," to be returned to the persons offering the same for discount, naturally persons come into frequent contact with the discount clerk, in order to receive information as to what disposition has been made of their offerings.

It is also the duty of the discount clerk to send paper falling due outside of the city in which his bank is located, to the bank's correspondent in the city where the same is payable. This paper is usually sent for collection, as few New York banks keep accounts in foreign banks (by foreign banks are meant any banks outside the city of New York); although it does occasionally happen that New York banks at times re-discount their paper with other banks, but more frequently the foreign banks re-discount in the New York banks, or deposit their paper as collateral for loans. Discounted paper sent to correspondents for collection is usually transmitted through the mail, and when information of its payment is received, the collecting bank, if it does not remit therefor, is debited with the same and " Bills Discounted " credited. If it does remit " Cash " is debited and " Bills Discounted " credited. It is desirable that such paper should be sent to the correspondent from a fortnight to ten days before maturity.

Note Teller.— In the larger banks where there is a special teller who attends to the collection and payment of notes, he is known as the note teller, sometimes called the third teller. He receives checks certified or uncertified or cash in payment of notes, of which there are two kinds: first, the notes which have been discounted by the bank and the payments for which become a part of the funds of the bank, the bank having already purchased the same; and, second, notes deposited for collection, the payments for which are credited to the depositors of the same. Should any notes either for collection or discount not be paid when presented, the teller hands the same over to the notary of the bank for presentation to and demand on the maker, when, if not paid, they are protested. Such presentation and protest are necessary in order to hold the endorsers. It is of the utmost importance that the note teller should make no mistake in the date of presentation of a note to the drawer, at the place where the note is made payable, because, should a note be presented a day after its maturity and the drawer decline or be unable to pay the same, the endorsers cannot be compelled to pay it.

Book-keeper. "The book-keeper" is used in contradistinction to the ledger keepers, who are also book-keepers. He is the person directly responsible for the general books of the bank, and the other book-keepers and ledger keepers are immediately under his control.

In no business is it so necessary as in banking that the books should be kept written up to date, especially the depositors' accounts, else errors may and probably will occur which would do great damage to the bank. All accounts should be posted to date so that the exact condition of each account can be ascertained at the beginning of each day's business. It is the rule in most banks to have checks entered up in the Customers' Ledger immediately after payment or certification, and before the clerks leave the bank for the day to enter up to their respective accounts all deposits. Should any check forming part of a deposit be returned unpaid the person depositing the same is debited therewith. Most banks make it a rule that their depositors shall not draw against that portion of their deposit consisting of checks the day of deposit.

The teller and collection and discount clerks have books which are kept exclusively by them and are only referred to by the book-keeper to post or prove his books, which are not books of original entry.

The pass-books are written up by the ledger keepers.

The books should be so kept that a complete statement of the bank's condition could be furnished within a day, and all accounts which would influence the Board of Directors or other officers in the making or rejecting of discounts or loans should be written up to date.

While the ruling of some books in the various banks may differ in a minor degree, practically the same system prevails in all large banks. In the smaller banks and the country banks fewer books are required and used than in the larger, one book in many instances answering in the place of two and sometimes three.

In order to keep the books properly written up it is necessary that the book-keeper should have a sufficient number of assistants, and that each man should do the work assigned him systematically and accurately.

Runners.—Runners, usually young men, are employed to present notes, drafts, and other promises to pay ; notes are presented to the makers ; if they are not in, a notice is left, a printed slip with which the runner is provided, stating that the bank holds such and such a note payable to the order of ——— for the amount for which it was drawn, and giving the last day when payment for the same will be received. Drafts, of course, are presented to the person on whom drawn, if on sight for payment, and if time drafts for acceptance. In case of the absence of the person on whom they are drawn a like notice is left.

In regard to notes presented on the last day of payment it is important that the runner should report promptly to the note teller a failure to collect, so that the paper may be placed in the hands of the notary to make the necessary presentation, and, in the event of non-payment, protest and notice to the endorsers. Generally notice is given the maker several days before maturity, after which notice the maker is expected to call at the bank and pay the same by the morning of maturity; if he does not do so the bank again presents the note. (For presentation, protest, and notice to endorsers see "Notary.")

The bank is in charge of the porter from the time the watchman who has care of the bank at night leaves in the morning till the clerks arrive and the books are put in their proper places, and again from the time the clerks leave till the watchman comes on duty.

How to Open a Bank Account.—The first thing is to have the necessary amount of money with which to open it. Many of the New York banks of deposit refuse to receive accounts averaging less than a thousand dollars, and there is one well-known bank in New York which will not receive an account which averages less than twenty-five thousand dollars.

The next thing to do is to secure an introduction to the cashier, preferably by a depositor of the bank. You are then questioned as to the amount of balance you intend to keep on hand, and what accommodation you expect from the bank.

As the various banks have different rules in regard to the amount of deposit which, as they term it, "entitles a depositor to accommodation," none can be here stated. The larger and more prosperous a bank, the less anxious it is generally to secure new accounts, and the more independent in the matter of accommodation, so that it is not always best to keep your account in a large bank, if that account is a comparatively small one, and it is probable that accommodation will be needed.

The preliminaries being satisfactorily arranged, you are introduced to the receiving teller, who receives your deposit and gives you credit for the same in a book, which is handed you, termed the "pass book," on one side of which are credited the amounts deposited, and on the other, when your book is sent in to be written up, *i. e.*, balanced with the bank's books, is debited with the checks drawn by you against those credits.

You are next introduced to the paying teller, and requested to write your signature in a book kept for that purpose in the bank and called the "Signature Book," and you are given a check book. The cashier, if you are of sufficient importance, accompanies you to the door and you are politely bowed out, and you have opened your bank account, and your hard-earned wealth is in the possession of a soulless corporation which knows no favor, or should know none.

Bank pass books should be handed in, at least once a month, to the proper ledger keeper, to be written up, and, on the return of your checks and book, the checks and entries in the pass book ought to be carefully compared with the stubs in the check book, and, if the account is found correct, the checks should be done up in a package and marked checks on the bank on which they are drawn, from........to........and put away in a safe place, as generally an endorsed check is the best obtainable evidence of a payment.

If any discrepancy is found to exist between the bank's balance and the balance the depositor thinks is due him, the bank should be immediately notified and the pass book taken back for comparison.

Course of a Deposit.—As deposits are divided into two kinds, checks and currency, we will have to consider the same separately, as they do not follow the same course.

First: In regard to currency, the amount of which must be stated on the deposit slip of the depositor, who is provided therewith by the bank. This currency is paid in at the window of the receiving teller and by him credited, together with the rest of the deposit, to the person making the same, first on the pass book, then on the teller's book, and finally by the ledger keeper on the ledger, and is placed in the receiving teller's till, mixed with the funds of the bank, of which it becomes a part, and its identity is lost.

As to checks. First we will consider those which are drawn upon the bank in which the depositor has his account. These checks, as in the case of currency, are set out on the deposit slips and are handed to the receiving teller, who credits the depositor with the amount thereof as before described. The total amount of the deposit of which such checks form a part is placed in the depositor's account to his credit. The checks are passed to the ledger keeper in charge of the ledger in which the drawers' accounts are kept and are there debited to said accounts. At the end of a given period, as above stated, they are returned to the drawers when their pass books are balanced.

In regard to checks drawn on other banks, the credit is made to the depositor depositing the same, in the manner above described, but the checks, instead of going through the books of the bank, are assorted by the assistant teller and placed in numbered boxes, the numbers of which correspond to the numbers assigned said banks at the Clearing House.

After the close of business hours the checks on each bank are done up in a separate package and the total amount, together with the bank's name, is written thereon. The total amount of checks on all the Clearing-House banks, or those clearing through them, are then stated on the Clearing-House sheet, which can, of course, only show their debits, as their holdings against this bank are not yet known. The next morning at ten o'clock the clearing clerks of the various banks meet at the Clearing House, and after presenting their bank's Clearing-House sheet to the Clearing House, exchange the checks of their respective banks, as is described in the article on the Clearing House.

The clerk of the Clearing House then gives to the clerk of each bank a statement, showing the net total either due to or owing by his bank from all the other banks. In case the bank is a debtor this amount has to be paid in by one o'clock; and in case it is a creditor the amount due is paid over to it by two oclock.

The clerks after this exchange of checks return to their respective banks and the different checks are charged up to the various drawers thereof, and finally returned to them as before explained.

CHAPTER V.

New York Clearing House.

LOCATED at present in the modest four-story brownstone building, at the corner of Pine and Nassau Streets, is the "New York Clearing House Association," formed by the principal banks of this city, for the purpose of effecting clearances or exchanges of checks, drafts, etc., between each other. The association is now erecting a new home on Cedar Street.

This association was formed in 1853 with a membership of fifty-five banks, whose capital aggregated $47,000,000. Its present membership consists of sixty-six banks with an aggregate capital of $62,622,700 and a surplus of $71,046,800. While this increase has not been as rapid as might have been supposed and perhaps as has taken place in some other directions, it should be borne in mind that the strength of a bank or a banking institution does not entirely rest upon the amount of its capital nor even of its surplus, and when it is considered that this association was organized by the fifty-five strongest banks in the city, and it is remembered that these banks, with but few exceptions, still retain that leading position, and that only institutions of the very highest character are admitted to membership, the wisdom and conservatism displayed in thus restricting the membership will be appreciated. It may be said that in addition to the Federal supervision in the case of national banks, and the State supervision in the case of State banks and trust companies, all members of this association are subject to the almost daily supervision of committees appointed by, or officers of, the Clearing House.

The conditions of membership are the payment of an initiation fee ranging from $5000 for banks of a capital of half a million to $7500 for banks with a capital of five millions. Further, each member irrespective of capital pays yearly $200, besides which there is a charge varying from 35 to 40 cents on each million dollars cleared.

In addition to the examination spoken of, each member must file weekly a statement of loans, specie, legal-tender circulation, deposits, etc.

The officers and committees of the Clearing House Association are chosen from the banks by which it is formed. The Assistant Treasurer of the United States, owing to the importance of the clearings of the Sub-Treasury, is a member by courtesy, as is said by way of being polite, but largely for the convenience of the banks and to avoid individual presentation of claims against the Sub-Treasury.

This association is designed to provide a place and method by which the risk, expense, and loss of time necessary in the presentation of the demands of one bank against each of the other banks, members of this association, and of the claims of each of those other banks in turn against it and against each other, may be avoided. The method by which this is accomplished in brief is by the presentation by a bank of its entire demands on all other banks to the Clearing House, with which the bank is credited. The Clearing House receives from all other banks, members, the claims against said bank, and if the claims of said bank are in excess of the claims against it, then the Clearing House pays to it such excess; in case the demands against such bank are in excess of its claims against other banks, then the bank must pay the excess to the Clearing House, the Clearing House distributing such excess among the banks to which it may be due.

In England, as early as the latter part of the eighteenth century, the necessity of such institutions was recognized, and in fact in several of the cities of England clearing house associations were then established.

The great utility of such an institution need only be mentioned to commend itself immediately to any one acquainted with finance, but perhaps an illustration would not be amiss. Not long since one of the larger members of this association presented to it demands against the other members of the association amounting to about $4,000,000, and these other members presented to the association demands against it only fifty cents short of the amount of its claims against them. Only the balance between these two amounts was paid over, the two principal amounts being set off against each other; a transaction of $8,000,000 was thus accomplished by the set off of credit against debit and the payment of the balance of fifty cents.

The machinery by which these exchanges or clearances are accomplished is as follows: The manager and his staff are in their respective positions on the platform at 10 A.M. This platform is situated at the western end of the large room on the third floor, in which room are assembled at the respective desks allotted to them the "delivery and "settling clerks" of the various members of the association. Each delivery clerk brings the demands held by his bank against the other members, done up in separate parcels, this work having been accomplished the day before by the assistant tellers in his bank. The settling clerks now present to the manager of the association a memorandum giving the amount of the total demands against the other members, with which amounts the bank represented by said settling clerk is credited on a proof sheet kept by the "Proof Clerk."

The clerks now go to the respective desks allotted to their banks on one of the three rows of desks located in this room, and the actual clearances begin as follows: The delivery clerk at desk No. 1 delivers to the settling clerk of No. 2 all demands of No. 1 against No. 2, obtaining a receipt therefor. At the same time No. 2's delivery clerk has delivered to No. 3's settling clerk the demands of No. 2 against No. 3, upon his receipt. This mode of settling prevails throughout the room until each member has presented his demands against every other bank and every other member's demands have been presented against it, which usually consumes about twenty minutes. After these settlements have been effected the settling clerks send the result of the demands against their respective banks on slips to the proof clerk by whom they are entered to the debit of such bank. The proof clerk now adds up the total debits and credits, which should, of course, agree, because what is a credit of one member is a debit of another, and vice versa. In half an hour more the differences between member and member are announced. Those members whose credits are in excess of their debits are termed creditor banks and those whose debits are in excess of the credits are termed debtor banks. The creditor banks collect, as soon as practicable, after the settlement of the debtor banks, the amounts due them, which amounts, of course, have to be paid in by the debtor banks, and which amounts these debtor banks are required to pay in cash, not later than half-past one.

To give an accurate idea of the importance of this Clearing-House Association, it may be interesting to note that while the clearings of the New York Clearing House for the year ending December 31, 1894, amounted to $24,387,807,019.92, although for the last ten years the average annual clearances have been $35,000,000,000, those of all the other clearing houses outside of New York amounted to less than $21,000,000,000. It is estimated that the clearings of the London Clearing House, the next most important to the New York Clearing House, amount annually to about $20,000,000,000.

But not only has the Clearing House been useful in the discharge of its ordinary business of effecting clearances, but on account of the respect and confidence in its methods and management, inspired by its conservatism, it has been able at least three times within the last twenty years to come to the aid of the banks, and incidentally to that of the public, and to either avert or greatly ameliorate the severity of a money panic by the issuance of certificates against collateral acceptable to a committee appointed by it. These certificates were issued to the extent of 75 per cent. of the usual market values of the securities held by such committee as collateral to their issue, and were used in the settlement of the daily balances between its members, and, of course, released just that amount of money into circulation and to that extent relieved the stringency of the money market. Such certificates were issued in 1890 to the extent of $15,000,000, about the time of the embarrassment of the Barings, when the money markets of the whole world were more or less convulsed. The denominations of these certificates were five, ten, and twenty thousand dollars. They were all taken up within five months after their issue. Another issue of certificates to the amount of $41,000,000 was made on June 15, 1893, which was all retired by November 1st of the same year. The following is a copy of one of these certificates:

<table>
<tr><td>[On the back of the certificate is the printed inscription:] Paid to the Clearing House By..........</td><td>FIVE THOUSAND DOLLARS.</td><td colspan="2">No...... $5000.

LOAN COMMITTEE OF THE NEW YORK CLEARING-HOUSE ASSOCIATION.

New York,..........1893.

This certifies that the............has deposited with this committee securities in accordance with the proceedings of a meeting of the Association, held November 11th, 1890, upon which this certificate is issued. This certificate will be received in payment of balances at the Clearing House for the sum of Five Thousand Dollars, from any member of the Clearing-House Association.</td></tr>
<tr><td></td><td></td><td>On the surrender of this certificate by the depositing bank above named, the committee will endorse the amount as a payment on the obligation of said bank held by them, and will surrender a proportionate share of the collateral securities held therefor.

$5000.</td><td>..................
....
....
....
....   COMMITTEE.</td></tr>
</table>

The government of this institution is entrusted to its principal committee, the Clearing-House Committee, which is composed of members elected by the various banks of the association. This committee has the executive management of all matters pertaining to the association. The next most important committees are the Arbitration, the Conference, and the Admission Committees. The executive management of the Clearing House is in charge of Mr. William Sherer, the present able manager, and a staff of assistants.

CHAPTER VI.

Savings Banks.

SAVINGS banks, so named from the fact that they are designed to be the depository of savings, rather than of general accounts subject to immediate check.

These banks, with the exception of those in the District of Columbia (which are necessarily organized under the Federal Laws), are organized and exist under the laws of the States in which they are located.

As these banks are the custodians of the surplus earnings above the immediate necessities of their depositors and often represent their entire available assets, the laws of this State, in particular, have thrown around them numerous safeguards, not only for the protection of the depositors, but of the institutions themselves.

The law is so exhaustive in its treatment of the class and kind of security on which savings banks may make loans or invest their moneys, that it is impossible to give more than a brief résumé.

In the matter of the regulations under which moneys are received, interest paid or credited to the depositors' accounts, loans effected, etc., the constitution and by-laws of the institution often govern in the practicable workings, but the constitution and by-laws are always subject to the rules laid down in the statute law.

Article III. of the Banking Laws of the State of New York pertains to savings banks and prescribes (Section 100) that thirteen or more persons, two thirds of whom shall be residents of the county where the proposed bank shall be located, may become a savings bank by executing a certificate in duplicate, one copy of which shall be filed in the office of the Clerk of such County, and the other in the office of the Superintendent of Banks within sixty days after its acknowledgment, setting forth:

1. The name by which the corporation shall be known.
2. The place where its business is to be transacted, designating the particular city, village, or town, and if in a city, the ward therein.
3. The name, residence, and, if in a city, the street and number, occupation and post-office address of each member of the corporation.
4. A declaration that each member of the corporation will accept the responsibilities and faithfully discharge the duties of a trustee in such corporation when authorized according to the provisions of law.

It is necessary that a notice of intention to organize shall be published at least once a week for four weeks previous to filing such certificate in at least one newspaper of the largest circulation published in the city, village, or town in which such bank is proposed to be located, or if no newspaper is published therein, then some newspaper published in the county, or if none is published in the county, then in a newspaper published in the adjoining county.

This notice shall specify the names of the proposed incorporators, also the name of the bank and the location of the same. A copy of such notice shall be sent to every savings bank doing business in such county at least fifteen days before the filing thereof.

If the above regulations have not been complied with to the satisfaction of the Superintendent, he shall refuse to file such certificate until it shall be amended in conformity with the provisions of the law and the regulations thereof complied with, but if such regulations have been complied with and the certificate is accompanied with satisfactory evidence of the proper publication and service in good faith of such notice, he shall forthwith endorse the same over his official signature "Filed for Examination" with the date of such endorsement.

The Superintendent shall thereupon ascertain from the best sources of information at his command whether greater convenience of access will be afforded depositors by opening a savings bank in the place designated, whether the population in the neighborhood designated affords a reasonable promise of adequate support to the enterprise, and whether the responsibility of the persons named in the certificate is such as to command the confidence of the community in which such savings bank is proposed to be located.

If the Superintendent shall be satisfied that the organization of the savings bank will be a public benefit, he shall, within sixty days after the same has been filed by him for examination, issue a certificate to the persons named in such certificate authorizing them to open an office for the deposit of savings as designated in the certificate.

Such certificate shall be filed in the office of the County Clerk of the County in which the savings bank is to be located; and the Superintendent of Banking shall also file a duplicate of such certificate in his own office.

If the Superintendent shall not be satisfied that the establishment of a savings bank is expedient and desirable, he shall, within sixty days after the filing thereof, give notice to said County Clerk that he refuses to issue a certificate, which notice shall forthwith be filed by the County Clerk with the certificate of incorporation of such savings bank.

Upon the filing of any certificate of authorization the persons named therein and their successors shall thereupon become and be a corporation vested with all the powers and charged with all the liabilities conferred and imposed by law upon savings banks, and shall have power to receive on deposit money and invest the same and declare credit and pay dividends thereon and transact the business of a savings bank. They possess, however, only such powers, rights, and privileges as are conferred by the banking law, notwithstanding anything to the contrary in their respective charters. The same thing may be said as to their duties and liabilities.

After the receipt of such certificate of authorization the bank must begin business within a year, but the Superintendent may, for reasons satisfactory to himself, extend the time not exceeding one year.

The Board of Trustees consists of not less than thirteen, and to it the entire management and control is entrusted; they may elect a President and two Vice-Presidents, and such other officers as they deem fit. The persons named in the certificate of authorization are the first trustees. A vacancy in the Board is filled by the Board as soon as practicable at a regular meeting after the vacancy occurs. Only residents of the State are eligible to election as trustees, and removal from the State by a trustee acts as a vacation of office.

The Board of Trustees may, from time to time, make such by-laws, rules, and regulations, not inconsistent with law, as they may think proper for the election of officers, for prescribing their respective powers and duties, the manner of discharging the same, for the appointment and duties of committees, and generally for transacting, managing, and directing the affairs of the corporation, a copy of which should be transmitted to the Superintendent of Banks, who should also be notified of any amendment or change therein.

Regular meetings of trustees, seven being necessary to constitute a quorum, shall be held as often as once a month for the purpose of receiving the reports of their officers and committees and for the transaction of other business.

The statute provides that the office of trustee becomes vacant whenever its incumbent becomes a trustee, officer, clerk, or employee of any other savings bank, or when he shall borrow directly or indirectly, any of the funds of the savings bank in which he is a trustee, or become a surety or guarantor for any money borrowed of or a loan made by such savings bank, or when he shall fail to attend the regular meetings of the Board, or perform any of the duties devolved upon him as such trustee, for six successive months, without having been previously excused by the Board for such failure ; but the trustee vacating his office by failure to attend meetings, or to discharge his duties, may, in the discretion of the Board, be eligible to re-election.

The trustees shall have power to require the officers, clerks, and agents of such bank to furnish security for the faithful performance of their duties.

No trustee of any such corporation can have any interest in the gains or profits thereof, nor as such receive any payment for his services, except that such of the trustees as are officers of the corporation or who act as the committee to examine vouchers and assets may receive such compensation as a majority of the Board deem reasonable. No trustee or officer of any such corporation shall for himself or as an agent or partner of others borrow any of its funds on deposits, or in any manner use the same except to make such current and necessary payments as are authorized by the Board of Trustees; nor shall any trustee or officer of any such corporation become an endorser or surety, or become in any manner an obligor for moneys loaned by or borrowed of such corporation.

The sums deposited with any savings bank, and any dividends or interest credited thereto, shall be repaid to the depositors respectively, or to their legal representatives, after demand and under such regulations as the Board of Trustees may prescribe. Such regulations shall be posted in the room where the business of the corporation is transacted, and printed in the pass-books furnished by it, and constitute evidence, between the corporation and the depositors holding the same, of the terms upon which the deposits therein acknowledged are made.

Every such corporation may limit the aggregate amount which any one person or society may deposit to such sum as it may deem expedient to receive, and may, in its discretion, refuse to receive a deposit, and may also at any time return all or any part of any deposit. The aggregate amount of deposits to the credit of any individual at any time may not exceed three thousand dollars, exclusive of deposits arising from judicial sales or trust funds or interest ; and to the credit of any society or corporation at any time, shall not exceed five thousand dollars, exclusive of accrued interest, unless such deposit was made prior to May 17, 1875, or pursuant to an order of a court of record.

Any deposit made by or in the name of any minor, shall be held for the exclusive right and benefit of such depositor, and free from the control or lien of all other persons, except creditors, and shall be paid to the person in whose name the deposit shall have been made, and the receipt or acquittance of such minor shall be a valid and sufficient release and discharge for such deposit or any part thereof to the corporation.

A deposit made by a person in trust for another shall, in the event of the death of the trustee, be paid to the person for whom the deposit was made.

"The trustees of any savings bank may invest the money deposited therein and the income derived therefrom only as follows :

"1. In the stocks or bonds, or interest-bearing notes or obligations of the United States, or those for which the faith of the United States is pledged to provide for the payment of the interest and principal, including the bonds of the District of Columbia.

"2. In the stocks or bonds or interest-bearing obligations of this State, issued pursuant to the authority of any law of the State.

"3. In the stocks or bonds or interest-bearing obligations of any State of the United States which has not within ten years previous to making such investments by such corporations defaulted in the payment of any part of either principal or interest of any debt authorized by the Legislature of any such State to be contracted.

"4. In the stocks or bonds of any city, county, town, or village, school district bonds, and union free school district bonds, issued for school purposes, or in the interest-bearing obligations of any city or county of this State, issued pursuant to the authority of any law of the State for the payment of which the faith and credit of the municipality issuing them are pledged.

"5. In bonds and mortgages on unencumbered real property situated in this State, worth at least twice the amount loaned thereon. Not more than sixty-five per cent. of the whole amount on deposit shall be so loaned or invested. If the loan is on unimproved real property, the amount loaned thereon shall not be more than forty per cent. of its actual value. No investment in any bond and mortgage shall be made by any savings bank, except upon a report of a committee of its trustees charged with the duty of investigating the same, who shall certify to the value of the premises mortgaged or to be mortgaged according to their best judgment, and such report shall be filed and preserved among the records of the corporation.

"6. In real property subject to the provisions of the next section."

"Every such corporation may purchase, hold, or convey real property only as follows :

"1. A plot whereon is erected or may be erected a building or buildings requisite for the convenient transaction of its business, and from portions of which, not required for its own use, a revenue may be derived. The cost of such building or buildings and lot shall in no case exceed fifty percentum of the net surplus of the corporation, except by written permission of the Superintendent of Banks.

"2. Such as shall have been purchased by it at sales upon the foreclosure of mortgages owned by it, or on judgments or decrees obtained or rendered for debts due on it, or in settlements effected to secure such debts. All such real property shall be sold by such corporation within five years after the same shall be vested in it, unless, upon application by the Board of Trustees, the Superintendent shall extend the time within which such sale shall be made.

"Every such corporation may, with the approval in writing and under the seal of the Superintendent of Banks, change its location within the limits of any city or town wherein it may be established. In effecting such change of location such corporation owning a banking house and lot, may purchase such additional plot under the provisions of subdivision one, of this section, as the corporation may require ; and such banking house and lot previously owned and occupied shall be sold as provided in this subdivision concerning real property acquired in satisfaction of debts.

" For the purpose of meeting current payments and expenses in excess of the receipts, there may be kept an available fund not exceeding ten percentum of the whole amount of deposits with such corporation. Such available fund may be loaned upon pledge of securities, but not in excess of ninety percentum of the cash market value of such securities so pledged.

"Should any of such securities depreciate in value, after making any loan thereon, the trustees shall require the immediate payment of such loan or additional security therefor, so that the amount loaned shall at no time exceed ninety percentum of the market value of the securities pledged for the same."

Such savings bank may also deposit temporarily in the banks or trust companies authorized by statute, the excess of current daily receipts over the payments, until the same can be judiciously invested in the securities required by law. Should it appear to the Superintendent of Banks that the trustees of any savings bank are violating the spirit and intent of the statute in this respect by keeping permanently uninvested all, or an undue proportion of the moneys received by them, he may report the facts to the Attorney-General, who shall proceed against such corporation in the same manner as against Banks of Deposit.

The trustees of any savings bank must not loan the moneys deposited with them upon any other personal securities whatever, and in all cases of loans upon real property, a sufficient bond secured by a mortgage thereon must be required of the owner.

Whenever money is loaned upon improved property, such property must be insured by the borrower, and the policy of insurance thereof assigned to the savings bank, and in case the borrower neglects to insure or keep insured such improved property, the Superintendent of Banks may insure the same at the cost and expense of the borrower.

No savings bank should directly or indirectly deal or trade in real property in any other case or for any other purpose than is authorized by this article, or deal or trade in any goods, wares, merchandise or commodities whatever, except such personal property as may be necessary in the transaction of its business; nor shall any savings bank or any officer thereof in his regular attendance upon the business of the bank, in any manner buy or sell exchange gold or silver, or collect or protest promissory notes or time bills of exchange.

Savings banks may, however, sell gold or silver received in payment of interest or principal of obligations owned by them or from depositors in the regular course of business, and may pay regular depositors, when requested by them, by draft upon deposits to the credit of the bank in the city of New York, and charge current rates of exchange for such drafts.

No savings bank may issue any certificate of deposit payable either on demand or at a fixed day, or pay any interest except regular dividends upon any deposits or balances, or pay any interest, deposit, or any check drawn upon itself by a depositor, unless the pass-book of the depositor be produced, and the proper entry be made therein at the time of the transaction.

The Board of Trustees may, by their by-laws, provide for making payments in case of loss of pass-book, or other exceptional cases where the pass-book cannot be produced without loss or serious inconvenience to depositors; but the right to make such payments ceases when so directed by the Superintendent of Banks, upon his being satisfied that such right is being improperly exercised by any savings bank; payments, however, may be made upon the judgment or order of a court or the power of attorney of a depositor.

The trustees of every such corporation may regulate the rate of interest or dividends not to exceed five per centum per annum upon the deposits therewith, in such a manner that depositors shall receive, as nearly as may be, all the profits of such corporation, after deducting necessary expenses and reserving such amounts as the trustees may deem expedient as a surplus fund for the security of the depositors, which, to the amount of fifteen per centum of its deposits, the trustees of any such corporation may gradually accumulate and hold, to meet any contingency or loss in its business from the depreciation of its securities or otherwise. The trustees usually classify their depositors according to the character, amount, and duration of their dealings with the corporation, and regulate the interest or dividends allowed in such manner that each depositor shall receive the same ratable portion of interest or dividends as all others of his class.

The trustees of any such corporation should not declare or allow interest on any deposit for a longer period than the same has been deposited, except that deposits made not later than the tenth day of the month commencing any semi-annual interest period, or the third day of any month, or withdrawn upon one of the last three days of the month ending any quarterly or semi-annual interest period, may have interest declared upon them for the whole of the period or month when so deposited or withdrawn..

No dividends or interest should be declared, credited, or

paid, except by the authority of a vote of the Board of Trustees, duly entered upon their minutes, whereon should be recorded the ayes and nays upon each vote; but accounts closed between dividend periods may be credited with interest at the rate of the last dividend, computing from the last dividend period to the date when closed, if the by-laws so provide. Whenever any interest or dividend shall be declared and credited in excess of the interest or profits earned and appearing to the credit of the corporation, the trustees voting for such dividend are jointly and severally liable to the corporation for the amount of such excess so declared and credited.

The trustees of any such corporation whose surplus amounts to fifteen per centum of its deposits, at least once in three years, shall divide equitably the accumulation beyond such authorized surplus as an extra dividend to depositors, in excess of the regular dividends authorized.

A notice posted conspicuously in a bank of a change in the rate of interest shall be equivalent to a personal notice.

In determining the per cent. of surplus held by any savings bank, its interest-paying stocks and bonds should not be estimated above their par value or above their market value if below par. Its bonds and mortgages on which there are no arrears of interest for a longer period than six months are to be estimated at their face, and its real property at not above cost. The Superintendent of Banks determines the valuation of such stocks or bonds, or bonds and mortgages, as are in arrears of interest for six months or more, and of all other investments, from the best information he can obtain, and he may change the valuation thereof from time to time as he may obtain other and further information.

The trustees of every savings bank, by a committee of not less than three of their number, on or before the first days of January and July in each year, must thoroughly examine the books, vouchers, and assets of such savings bank and its affairs generally. The statement or schedule of assets and liabilities reported to the Superintendent of Banks for the first of January and July in each year should be based upon such examination, and shall be verified by the oath of a majority of the trustees making it; and the trustees of any savings bank may require such examination at such other times as they shall prescribe. The trustees must, as often as once in each six months during each year, cause to be taken an accurate balance of their depositors' ledgers, and in their semi-annual report to the Superintendent they must state the fact that such balance has been taken.

All the property of any bank or trust company which becomes insolvent, shall, after providing for the payment of its circulating notes, be applied to the payment in full of any sum or sums of money deposited therewith by any savings bank.

The Superintendent shall receive the moneys so deposited with him by the trustees of any solvent savings bank voluntarily closing its business, and all moneys which may be deposited with him by the receivers of insolvent savings banks pursuant to the provisions of any law or the order of any court, and shall receive a receipt therefor, and forthwith deposit the same in some solvent savings bank or savings banks to the credit of the Superintendent of Banks in his name of office, in trust for the depositors and creditors of the closed savings bank from which they were received. The Superintendent shall report to the Legislature annually in his report the names of such closed savings banks and the sums of unclaimed and unpaid deposits to the credit of each of them respectively.

The Superintendent may pay over to the persons respectively entitled thereto the moneys so held by him upon being furnished with satisfactory evidence of their right to the same. In cases of doubt or of conflicting claims, he may require an order of the Supreme Court authorizing and directing the payment thereof. He may apply the interest earned by the moneys so held by him towards defraying the expenses in the payment and distribution of such unclaimed dividends to the depositors and creditors entitled to receive the same, and he shall include, in his annual report to the Legislature, a statement of the amount of interest earned by such unclaimed dividends.

CHAPTER VII.

Trust Companies.

THE important field covered by Trust Companies, together with the fact of their comparatively recent growth, warrants and, in fact, necessitates a rather lengthy treatment of the subject.

By many it is erroneously supposed that these companies are organized to compete for business with banks, both state and national. A careful review, however, of the powers and privileges granted banks, both national and state, including savings banks, must convince the thoughtful reader that such is not the case, and while it may appear at first glance that many small accounts which are now kept in trust companies would otherwise be deposited in savings banks, it must be borne in mind that the restrictions and regulations of savings banks in regard to the drawing out of money, it being necessary for the depositor not only to make out a check but to present his pass-book in person, or hand the pass-book to the person presenting the check, are so irksome, that many of these accounts cannot be conveniently and would not be kept therein. In fact, about the only thing in common between a trust company and a savings bank is that both are required by law to pay a certain per cent. of interest upon deposits. The trust company, as hereafter stated, being compelled to pay two per cent., while savings banks are prohibited from allowing a higher rate than five.

In order to point out more clearly the difference between the business conducted by a trust company and that conducted by an ordinary bank of deposit, it will necessitate a brief statement of the business conducted by such banks, which is given more fully in other portions of this work, particularly those chapters referring to banks of deposit. Succinctly stated, the business of a bank of deposit (omitting now all reference to the issuing of circulating notes) is to receive money on deposit from its depositors, to whom it pays no interest whatever, but in lieu thereof and as compensation for the use of such moneys (only 25 per cent. of which national banks in the reserve cities are required to keep on hand to meet the checks of its depositors, and state banks are only required to keep 15 per cent.; the balance of which deposits are loaned to various borrowers), it agrees to discount acceptable commercial paper offered by such depositors in a recognized proportion to the amount of such deposits. In order to be in a position to do this it follows that its loans must be of comparatively small amounts on rapidly maturing obligations; this, of course, bars out loans on real estate or on settled securities. National banks are prohibited by law from making loans on real estate, and are only permitted to receive real estate as additional security for loans previously made, and while State banks of deposit are not prohibited by the State law from so doing, nevertheless, as a matter of good banking, they also carefully avoid loans of this character. In other words, the policy of a bank is first to secure large deposits on which they have to pay no interest, and to make a great number of small loans on short-time paper; while that of a trust company is to make loans large in amount running for a considerable time, and to receive only deposits which will not be immediately drawn out or seriously diminished, but which they must be able to loan at a higher rate than two per cent., which the law requires them to pay the depositor.

In the complex life of highly civilized and wealthy communities, this leaves a field open, which field, among others, trust companies are designed to cover.

The class of persons who constitute their depositors are salaried and professional men, who deposit moneys for which they have no immediate or shortly anticipated need; business men accumulating a fund for some specific purpose or their individual profits; married women with separate estates, who deposit the principal, drawing, as a rule, only the interest thereon; administrators, executors, trustees, and committees, whose deposits are generally permanent, and not likely to fluctuate greatly in amount; assignees and receivers, whose deposits, though for a shorter time, are of practically a uniform amount while they last.

From the comparatively stationary and uniform character of its deposits, not to speak of the amount in its hands as executor, administrator, assignee, receiver, or committee, and over which it has absolute control, trust companies are in a position, and find it advantageous, to make loans of larger amount and longer duration than do banks; and as real estate is the one thing of greatest and most staple value in a community, it naturally forms the most desirable thing on which to make such loans.

But before money can be loaned or invested to advantage, either in real estate or in stocks and bonds, it is necessary that a sufficient amount should be accumulated. It is in the collection and accumulation of these amounts which, until they have arrived at a sufficiently large sum, are deposited daily by the trust companies in banks, and on which daily balances the banks allow them interest for the use of such money, that the trust company becomes, not a competitor, but a powerful auxiliary to banks of deposit; gathering in and bringing together, as they do, accounts which would be of no value to the banks, but which, when consolidated into one account and deposited by a trust company, become of great value.

Thus far we have spoken of trust companies almost exclusively in their relation to banks. It must be borne in mind that this is not the chief object, but merely an incident growing out of their organization. We will now consider the real object of their formation, which is:

To act in a fiduciary capacity as fiscal agent, trustee, executor, administrator, assignee, receiver, or committee either for individuals or corporations. Heretofore these various offices and the duties pertaining to them have been discharged by individuals.

The advantages of entrusting the performance of such important duties to a corporation whose life is perpetual during its corporate existence, which in this State is fifty years, and whose charter can be renewed, which is never sick or incapacitated for the discharge of its duties, whose management is confided to some of the most successful, wealthy, and reputable business and professional men in the community, whose combined experience and knowledge of affairs must be greater than that of even the most astute and well-informed business man, besides which they devote an amount of time and labor to the study and investigation of property and business affairs, the value of real and personal property, which it would be obviously impossible for one person to do, and their capital surplus and assets, which are invested not alone in one industry, but in many, and which are liable for the faithful performance of their duties, furnish greater security than those of an individual trustee. That the appointment of such a company in any of the above capacities is more desirable than that of an individual, whose time is necessarily largely employed in his own affairs, and whose tenure of life and capacity is uncertain, is too manifest to require argument.

To enumerate the different trusts which are best reposed in these companies is to repeat Section 156 of the Banking Laws of this State, which is quoted farther on, and to which the reader is referred.

While the law does not specifically state that trust companies shall receive deeds, agreements, securities, or papers or things in escrow, still, on account of the confidence which they inspire, they are often used for such purpose.

Probably the greatest and most common field of usefulness occupied by trust companies is acting in the capacity of trustee of stock and bondholders in the formation or reorganization of corporations. A corporation is organized, but before its securities can be advantageously brought to the attention of the investing public, it becomes necessary that some one in whom the public have implicit confidence, and who will not be swayed by personal considerations or friendships, should investigate the property which has been incorporated, inquire into the title to its plant, the legality of its franchises, see that the mortgage is properly drawn and covers the property which it purports to mortgage, and that all the legal requirements in regard to the incorporation of the company, the filing of its certificate of incorporation, the payment in of the capital required, the payment to the State of the corporation tax, and all other legal requirements have been duly complied with, and certify to the regularity thereof, and to investigate, supervise, and certify to the issue of bonds, and to the issue and registration of stock, and that there has been no over-issue in either case. Who can do this better than a trust company, they frequently being the authorized registrar of the stock of the corporation?

Not only have companies to be organized, but almost as frequently reorganized, when it becomes necessary for the stockholders to secure unity of action upon their part, to respectively appoint some one to act in their stead, to receive and register the outstanding securities, and, upon the deposit with it of a fixed amount, to reorganize the company and to issue new securities for the old, and to register and transmit to the depositors new securities in the proportion agreed upon in place of the securities deposited.

Very often the formulating of the plan by which this re-organization is accomplished and the fixing of the basis of exchange of the old securities for the new is undertaken and carried through by a trust company.

The procuring of a well known company to undertake such re-organization in most instances tends greatly to the success of the re-organization, and the fact that a company of good repute is the trustee or registrar of the bonds and stock of a corporation adds very appreciably to the value of such securities.

Trust companies also act as agents for the payment of obligations maturing at future dates, such as the premiums on policies of insurance, assessments on stocks, interest on mortgages, etc., and for the collection of coupons, of interest, of premiums, and so on.

As agents for the stock and bond holders of various kinds of corporations, who desire to act as a unit.

Also as registrar, where such certificates may be registered so as to indemnify the holder against loss in case such certificate should be lost or destroyed.

In the case of individuals, they act as the trustees of special funds for the benefit of married women, or minors, for insane persons, habitual drunkards, lunatics, or for devisees whom the giver may regard as incompetent to take care of the funds so placed in trust. For a corporation for the accumulation of a sinking fund, etc.

Trust Companies are organized exclusively under the laws of the State in which they are located, and are subject to the supervision of the State Banking Department, the same as State Banks.

The powers and privileges granted them are much greater than those granted banks, except that they are not permitted to issue circulating notes, but may in all other ways perform the functions of a bank in addition to those specially conferred on them. These powers and privileges are best enumerated in the language of the law under which they are organized.

"Section 156 : Upon the filing of any such certificate of authorization of a trust company, the persons named therein and their successors shall thereupon and thereby become a corporation, and in addition to the powers conferred by the general and stock corporation laws, shall have power :

"1. To act as the fiscal or transfer agent of any State, municipality, body politic, or corporation ; and in such capacity to receive and disburse money, and transfer, register, and countersign certificates of stock, bonds, or other evidences of indebtedness.

"2. To receive deposits of trust money, securities, and other personal property from any person or corporation, and to loan money on real or personal securities.

"3. To lease, hold, purchase, and convey any and all real property necessary in the transaction of its business, or which the purposes of the corporation may require, or which it shall acquire in satisfaction or partial satisfaction of debts due the corporation under sales, judgments, or mortgages, or in settlement or partial settlement of debts due the corporation by any of its debtors.

"4. To act as trustee under any mortgage or bond issued by any municipality, body politic, or corporation, and accept and execute any other municipal or corporate trust not inconsistent with the laws of this State.

"5. To accept trusts from and execute trusts for married women, in respect to their separate property, and to be their agent in the management of such property, or to transact any business in relation thereto.

"6. To act under the order of appointment of any court of record as guardian, receiver, or trustee of the estate of any minor, the annual income of which shall not be less than one hundred dollars, and as depositary of any moneys paid into court, whether for the benefit of any such minor, or other person, corporation, or party.

"7. To take, accept, and execute any and all such legal trusts, duties, and powers in regard to the holding, management, and disposition of any estate, real or personal, and the rents and profits thereof, or the sale thereof, as may be granted or confided to it by any court of record, or by any person, corporation, municipality, or other authority; and it shall be accountable to all parties in interest for the faithful discharge of every such trust, duty, or power which it may so accept.

"8. To take, accept, and execute any and all such trusts and powers of whatever nature or description as may be conferred upon or intrusted or committed to it by any person or persons, or any body politic, corporation, or other authority, by grant, assignment, transfer, devise, bequest, or otherwise, or which may be intrusted or committed or transferred to it, or vested in it by order of any court of record, or any surrogate, and to receive and take and hold any property or estate, real or personal, which may be the subject of any such trust.

"9. To purchase, invest in, and sell stocks, bills of exchange, bonds and mortgages, and other securities; and when moneys, or securities for moneys, are borrowed or received on deposit, or for investment, the bonds or obligations of the company may be given therefor, but it shall have no right to issue bills to circulate as money.

"10. To be appointed and to accept the appointment of executor of or trustee under the last will and testament, or administrator with or without the will annexed, of the estate of any deceased person, and to be appointed and to act as the committee of the estates of lunatics, idiots, persons of unsound mind, and habitual drunkards.

"No such corporation shall have any right or power to make any contract, or to accept or execute any trust whatever, which it would not be lawful for any individual to make, accept, or execute.

"No loan shall be made by any such corporation, directly, or indirectly, to any director or officer thereof.

"No such corporation shall transact its ordinary business by branch office in any city not named in its Certificate of Incorporation or Charter as the place where its business is to be transacted."

Thirteen or more persons may form a trust company, upon filing a certificate stating the name of such company, its place of business, the amount of its capital, and the number of shares into which it is divided, the name, residence, and post-office address of each member of the corporation, and the term of the existence of such company, which shall not exceed fifty years, and a declaration that each member of such corporation will, if elected a director, faithfully discharge the obligations and responsibilities of such office. This certificate must be filed with the Superintendent of Banking of the State within sixty days after its execution, and a duplicate must be filed in the office of the county clerk of the county where such company is to carry on business.

The minimum capital of such companies shall be as follows: In cities containing

25,000 inhabitants or less	$100,000
25,000 inhabitants or more	150,000
100,000 to 250,000	200,000
More than 250,000	500,000

Before filing such certificate notice must be published at least once a week for four successive weeks in a newspaper to be designated by the Superintendent of Banks in the city where such trust company is to be located, and shall set forth the facts so stated in the certificate of organization. This notice must be sent to every trust company doing business in such city at least fifteen days before the filing of the organization certificate.

The Superintendent upon the receipt of such certificate conforming to the provisions of this act, as to execution, notice, etc., shall file the same, and he shall then proceed to ascertain the fitness of the persons named for the discharge of the trust which they ask permission to assume, and if such investigation prove satisfactory, he shall within sixty days after the filing of such certificate, and after knowledge that the entire capital stock has been paid in, in cash, issue under his seal a "Certificate of Authorization" to the incorporators to commence business, which shall be transmitted to the County Clerk, who shall file the same and attach it to the organization certificate and record both certificates in the records of incorporation. A duplicate of such certificate of authorization shall be filed by the Superintendent in his office.

The Superintendent, may, however, if he deem such organization inexpedient refuse to issue a certificate of authorization, and shall file a notice of such refusal with said County Clerk.

Section 157 provides that letters testamentary, of guardianship, of administration with the will annexed, and the like, may, in a proper case, be granted to trust Companies, the only exception being that of simple letters of administration to which, in a like case, the Public Administrator is entitled.

Upon the appointment of a trust company as executor, the Court does not require the filing of a bond for the faithful performance of its duties as in the case of an individual, but the capital stock, property, and effects of such trust company shall be held liable therefor, and the debts due by said corporation as executor, administrator, guardian, trustee, committee, or depositary shall have the preference. Power, however, is given the courts to require trust companies to give security, and upon their failure so to do the court is empowered to remove such trust company from the exercise of such trust.

They may be required to furnish statements and accounts as executor, administrator, guardian, trustee, etc., in the same manner as a natural person.

" The capital of every such corporation shall be invested in bonds and mortgages on unincumbered real property in this State worth at least double the amount loaned thereon, or in the stocks or bonds of this State, or of the United States, or of any county, or incorporated city of this State duly authorized by law to be issued.

"The moneys received by any such corporation in trust may be invested in its discretion in the securities of the same kind in which its capital is required to be invested, or in the stocks or bonds of any State of the United States, or in such real or personal securities as it may deem proper. No such corporation shall hold stock in any private corporation to an amount in excess of ten per cent. of the capital of the corporation holding such stock."

Interest must be paid on all sums of money over one hundred dollars collected and received by such corporation acting as executor, administrator, guardian, trustee, receiver, etc., of any court, or in any fiduciary capacity under such appointment, or as a depositary of moneys paid into court at a rate of not less than two per cent. per annum, until the money so received shall be expended or distributed. All of such interest moneys which are not collected annually shall be added to the principal, and interest thereon shall be paid.

"The affairs of every such corporation shall be managed and its corporate powers exercised by a Board of Directors of such number, not less than thirteen or more than twenty-four, as shall, from time to time, be prescribed in its by-Laws. No person can be a director who is not the holder of at least ten shares of the capital stock of the corporation. The persons named in the organization certificate, or such of them respectively as shall become holders of at least ten shares of such stock, shall constitute the first Board of Directors, and may add to their number *not exceeding* the limit of *twenty-four*, and shall severally continue in office until others are elected to fill their respective places. Within six months from the time when such corporation shall commence business, the first Board of Directors shall classify themselves by lot into three classes, as nearly equal as may be. The term of office of the first class shall expire on the third Wednesday of January next following such classification; the term of office of the second class shall expire one year thereafter; and the term of office of the third class shall expire two years thereafter. At or before the expiration of the term of the first class, and annually thereafter, a number of directors shall be elected equal to the number of directors whose term will then expire, who shall hold their offices for three years or until their successors are elected.

"Such election shall be held at the office of the corporation and at such time and upon such public notice, not less than ten days, by advertisement in at least one newspaper, approved by the Superintendent of Banks, published in the city where such corporation is located, as shall be prescribed in the by-laws."

In case of failure to elect any director on the day named, the directors whose terms of office do not that year expire, may proceed to elect a number of directors equal to the number in the class whose term that year expires, or such number as may have failed of re-election. The persons so elected, together with the directors whose terms of office shall not that year expire, shall constitute the Board of Directors until another election shall be held according to law. Vacancies occurring in the intervals of elections shall be filled by the Board.

"If default shall be made in the payment of any debt or liability contracted by any such corporation, the stockholders thereof shall be individually responsible, equally and ratably, for the then existing debts of the corporation, but no stockholder shall be liable for the debts of the corporation to an amount exceeding the par value of the respective shares of stock by him held in such corporation at the time of such default.

"For all losses of money which the capital stock shall not be sufficient to satisfy, the directors shall be responsible in the same manner and to the same extent that directors are now responsible in law or equity.

"Every trust company incorporated by a special law shall possess the powers of trust companies incorporated under the general law, and shall be subject to such provisions thereof as are not inconsistent with the special laws relating to such specially chartered company."

The consolidation or merger of trust companies is provided for by an act which went into effect April 23, 1895. See page 102 State Banks.

It is true that while trust companies are compelled by law, as stated in Section 160, to pay interest on all sums in their hands held in certain capacities, yet the rate of interest is lower than that paid by savings banks, although the money on deposit in the trust company is subject to immediate withdrawal, whereas a savings bank may require, according to its constitution and by-laws and the regulations printed in its pass-books, a notice of sixty days.

The sources of income are much more diversified than in the case of banks. Drawing a large part of their revenue from acting in the different fiduciary capacities for which they are created, and for which services they charge a commission, and being less restricted as to the character, nature, and time of their loans, they can make many which the banks cannot. A very large portion of its loans are upon, or secured by, real estate. In fact, loans upon real estate in the cities are effected, almost exclusively, through savings banks, trust and life insurance companies.

Probably the largest source of income of trust companies of New York is acting as the financial agent of corporations.

CHAPTER VIII.

Safe Deposit Companies—Building and Mutual Loan Associations—Co-operative Loan Associations—Mortgage and Debenture Companies.

Safe Deposit Companies.

THESE companies may be aptly called the "warehouses of finance," occupying the same relation to it that storage warehouses do to commerce.

Article VII. of the State banking laws, which provides for the organization of these companies, states that they may be incorporated by five or more persons for the purpose of taking and receiving upon deposit as bailee for safe keeping and storage jewelry, plate, money, specie, bullion, stocks, bonds, securities, and valuable papers of any kind, and other valuable personal property, and guaranteeing their safety upon such terms and for such compensation as may be agreed upon by it and the respective bailors (depositors) thereof; and to let out vaults, safes, and other receptacles for the uses and purposes of such corporations, by making and filing with the County Clerk of the County, where the same may be located, and the Superintendent of Banking, a certificate similar to that required of other corporations organized under the banking law.

The law provides that its capital shall not be more than $1,000,000 nor less than $100,000, except in cities or villages of less than 100,000 inhabitants, where the same shall not be less than $10,000; the term of its corporate existence shall not exceed fifty years; it shall not commence or transact business, not make any loans or advances on any property left with it for storage or safe keeping, until the whole amount of its capital stock has been paid in; and until its certificate has been approved by the Superintendent of Banks and duly filed, as in the case of other banking corporations.

Its affairs shall be managed by not less than five or more than thirteen directors, who shall be stockholders, and a majority of whom shall be citizens of this State, which directors shall, after the first year, be annually elected at the time and place prescribed by its laws, notice of which shall be published ten days before the election in a newspaper in the place where its business is conducted.

The directors may make such by-laws as they shall deem proper for the management, disposition of the stocks, property, and business affairs of the corporation; prescribing the duties of officers and employees, the manner of the appointment and election of all officers, and for carrying on all kinds of business within the objects and purposes of the corporation.

There shall be a President, to be selected from among the directors, and such subordinate officers as the by-laws may designate, who may be appointed or elected. The Board may require of the officers and employees of the company such security or bonds for the faithful performance of their duties as it may deem necessary.

The stockholders shall be jointly and severally liable for all debts due and owing by the corporation to an amount equal to the par value of their stock therein over and above such stock, to be recovered of the stockholders who are such when the debt is contracted or the loss or damage sustained, or of any subsequent stockholder. Any stockholder who may have paid any demand against such corporation either voluntarily or by compulsion shall have a right to resort to the rest of the stockholders who are liable to contribution; and the dissolution of the corporation shall not release or affect the liability of any stockholder which may have been incurred before dissolution.

If the rent due for any safe or box shall remain unpaid for three years, the company may cause to be sent to the person in whose name the safe or box stands, a written notice in a registered letter, directed to him at the address recorded on its books, notifying him that if the rent due is not paid within sixty days, then it will cause the said safe or box to be opened in the presence of its president, secretary, or treasurer, and a notary public not in its employ, and the contents thereof to be taken therefrom, to be sealed by the notary in a package upon which he shall distinctly mark the name and address of the person in whose name the same may stand upon the books of the company, and the estimated value thereof, and the package so sealed and addressed, when marked for identification by the notary, will be placed by him in one of the general safes or boxes of the corporation. Upon the expiration of sixty days from the date of mailing such notice, if such rent is not then paid, the company may itself proceed and direct the notary to act as above, after doing which his proceedings shall be fully set out by him in his own handwriting and under his official seal in a book to be kept by the corporation for that purpose.

The capital of these companies, when merely used as a place for the storage of valuables, is not so much a matter of importance as the character of the precautions taken to avoid allowing any one not entitled having access to the boxes or safes, the kind of identification required, the fact that its walls are fire- and burglar-proof, as none of these companies have sufficient capital to make good the loss of valuables which the loss of the contents of one safe might entail.

Each box or safe holder is furnished by the company

with a box or safe, and the key or combination to it, and is made known to the outer and inner doorkeepers. He is always given a password, by the use of which he can secure admittance, if not otherwise recognized by the doorkeepers. The safes and boxes are arranged in rows one above another on the walls and in the middle of a large fire-proof vault, the entrance to which is guarded by heavy iron bar doors; the windows, where there are any, are guarded in the same way. In this vault, at convenient places, are cages made of iron, in which subscribers may go and lock themselves in, no one from the outside except an attendant being able to enter, and there cut their coupons, examine their securities, etc., in absolute safety. After a subscriber leaves one of these cages, a trusted employee enters the same and makes a careful search to see if the subscriber has left any paper or thing of value, and if he has, the same is taken and put in charge of the proper officer, who returns the same to the subscriber.

It is not only much safer and more secure to keep valuables in the safe and boxes of these companies than in safes at an office or residence, but oftentimes more convenient.

The location of the company is a controlling element in the charges made by it. There is no uniform charge by all companies for the same size safe or box. In each company the rent is regulated by the size of the safe or box rented.

Nearly all men of means have their safes and boxes in one or more of these companies, and when their families go away from home send their jewels and silver to be stored; and even when they are home the family jewels, when not in actual use, are so deposited for safe keeping.

In regard to consolidation see page 102, State Banks.

Building and Mutual Loan Associations.

(Commonly called Building and Loan Associations.)

The very large amount of money invested in these associations, which in 1893 in the United States was about $900,000,000, $37,285,173 of which was in the State of New York, and $25,000,000 in the State of New Jersey, together with their rapid growth and wide spread, require a somewhat lengthy statement of their objects and aims, which, while they differ slightly in individual cases, are, taken broadly, the same.

In New York these associations are organized, under Article V. of the Banking Laws of the State of New York, 1892, which defines the purpose for which they are created to be:

"The accumulation of a fund for the purchase of real property, the erection of buildings, the making of improvements on lands, the payment of encumbrances thereon, and to aid its members in the accomplishment of all or any of the above objects, and the accumulation of a fund to be returned to its members who do not obtain such advances when it shall amount to a certain sum per share, to be specified in the certificate of incorporation."

The method by which these aims are sought to be accomplished perhaps demand some explanation.

The basis of these associations is that of a co-operative savings institution, in which each member has like privileges and obligations with each other member, according to the series and number of shares held by him. There is, however, one marked difference between the plan of saving followed by these associations and the general method pursued, and that is, while all savings are voluntary in the beginning, after a subscriber begins saving by the plan adopted by these associations, the continuance of such savings becomes compulsory to a certain extent, that is, to as great an extent as the infliction of penalties in the shape of fines, and either entire or partial forfeiture of the amounts previously paid in can make them so, but while the law gives the association the right in its by-laws to provide for absolute forfeiture, this right is rarely ever exercised. Some of the associations provide after notice of thirty days payments may cease, and the amounts already paid in, with such interest as the Board of Managers may allow, will be paid to the withdrawing subscriber, after which all penalties and forfeitures cease. By the ordinary methods of saving one can continue or discontinue his savings as he pleases. Of course, if it becomes desirable to discontinue the payment of the monthly installments known as dues, it is generally possible for the subscriber to sell his right in past savings, which are represented by the shares standing in his name.

The method of accumulation of the fund is this: The association is composed of subscribers, to each subscriber is issued such number of shares as he is willing to pledge himself to pay for until they obtain a given value, generally $200, by the payment of a monthly installment of $1 on each share. Obviously it would take, in the absence of interest on the money so paid in, 200 months to bring these shares up to that value, but the earning capacity of money, properly invested, is such that it has been found that, instead of taking 200 months, it will probably not take more than 120 months, or ten years, for these shares to reach their face value of $200. In this time, ten years, instead of paying in $200 per share, the subscriber has only paid in $120, and the $120 so paid in has earned the additional $80 to bring his shares up to their face value.

In order to become a subscriber of such association it is necessary to enter into a contract with the association to pay subscriptions on a stated day each month, or suffer certain penalties and forfeitures.

The profit of the subscriber, either in case he becomes

a borrower from the association or otherwise, is solely in the fact that at the end of a given time he receives back the money he paid into the association, plus such interest as it may have earned and his proportion of the forfeitures and penalties inflicted upon defaulting subscribers.

The holder of each share is entitled to borrow from the association out of the moneys which it may have on hand to loan, on acceptable real property, either improved or to be improved under the direction of the association, a sum equal to the face value of the shares held by him, but on the further condition that he must pay a premium, generally not less than 50 cents a share, for securing such loan, beyond the legal rate of interest, which he is to pay for the use of the money advanced. Some of the companies also permit a member who has not already borrowed to build or acquire property, to borrow for other purposes than acquiring property at the legal rate of interest, on the deposit of his shares as collateral, to the extent of 90 per cent. of the amount then paid in on such shares. In a prominent company, with which the writer is acquainted, the members availed themselves of this privilege to the extent of $50,000 during the depression of 1893.

The by-laws of many associations prescribe that the funds in hand to be loaned shall at stated times be put up and bid for, and the same loaned to the person bidding the highest rate of interest, and at the same time offering satisfactory security, but this plan is now being quite generally abandoned in favor of what is known as the "gross premium serial plan," by which a certain premium per share is charged.

The theory and principle upon which loans are made to the subscribers are that all the subscribers will not wish to borrow at the same time, and therefore that the money of those who do not desire to borrow may be loaned to those who do.

Article V. of the Banking Laws of the State of New York prescribes that building and mutual loan corporations may be organized by not less than nine persons for the purposes before stated, by making, acknowledging, and filing a certificate of incorporation setting forth:

1. The name of the corporation.
2. The location of its principal business office.
3. When its regular meetings shall be held, and how special meetings may be called.
4. What shall be a quorum to transact business at its meetings.
5. How members shall be admitted, and their qualifications.
6. What officers, directors, or attorneys of the corporation there shall be, and how and when chosen.
7. The duties of such officers, directors, or attorneys, and how removed or suspended from office.
8. The names of the persons who shall be such officers and directors for its first year, and until others are chosen or appointed in their places.
9. The entrance fee of new members and new shares.
10. The amount of each share.
11. The monthly or weekly dues per share.
12. The redemption fee on shares on which advances shall be made.
13. The fees to be paid on the transfer of shares.
14. The penalties for non-payment of dues or fees, or other violation of the provisions of the certificate.
15. The manner of redemption of shares by advances made thereon.
16. The mortgage security to be taken on such advances, and how the same may be changed.
17. The manner of the transfer or withdrawal of shares.
18. The manner of investing funds not required for advances on shares.

19. The qualification of voters at its meetings and the mode of voting.

20. The ultimate amount to be paid to the owners of unredeemed shares.

21. The manner of altering or amending the certificate of incorporation.

22. Such other provisions not inconsistent with law as shall be necessary for the convenient and effective transaction of its business.

This certificate must be approved by the Superintendent of Banks, and filed in the office of the Clerk of the County in which the principal office of the corporation is located. A certified copy must also be filed with the Superintendent of Banks, after which the subscribers thereto and their successors shall become a corporation by the name specified in said certificate.

The directors may demand from the members and stockholders the sums of money subscribed for at such times and in such installments as the certificate of incorporation shall prescribe, under penalty of forfeiting the shares of stock subscribed for and all previous payments made, if payment is not made within sixty days after personal demand or notice published for six successive weeks in the newspaper published nearest to the principal place of business of the corporation.

The association may borrow money for temporary purposes not inconsistent with the objects of this organization, but no such loans shall be of longer duration than two years, nor shall its indebtedness for money so borrowed at any one time exceed one fourth of the aggregate amount of its shares and parts of shares and the income actually paid in and received. No loan shall be made to any member or stockholder exceeding in amount the par value of the capital stock subscribed for by said member.

Parents and guardians may hold stock for their minor children or wards, provided the cost of such shares be defrayed from the personal earnings of such children or wards, or gifts from persons other than their parents.

Dividends from the earnings shall be payable as prescribed in the articles of incorporation.

"No holder of redeemed shares shall claim to be exempt from making the monthly or other stated payments provided in the certificate of incorporation on the ground that by reason of losses or otherwise the corporation has continued longer than was originally anticipated, whereby the payments made on such shares may amount to more than the amount originally advanced, with legal interest thereon ; nor shall the imposition of fines for non-payment of dues or fees or other violation of the certificate of incorporation, nor the making of any monthly payment required by the certificate of incorporation, or of any premium for loans made to members, be deemed a violation of the provisions of any statute against usury.

"All the shareholders of any such corporation shall be individually liable to the creditors to an amount equal to the amount of stock held by them respectively for all debts contracted by it. The directors or other officers of every such corporation shall be personally liable for any fraudulent use, disposition, or investment of any moneys or property belonging to it, or for any loss which shall be incurred by any investment made by any such directors or officers, other than such as are mentioned in, and authorized by, this article ; but no director or other officer shall be so liable unless he authorized, sanctioned, approved of or made such fraudulent use, disposition, or investment."

The shares held by the members and stockholders of every such corporation shall be exempt from sale on execution for debt to an extent not exceeding $600 in such shares at their par value.

"Any existing corporation formed solely for the purposes mentioned in this article, or any of them, may, by a vote of the persons holding a majority of the voting shares of stock of such corporation at any regular meeting after this article shall take effect, become entitled to the benefit of this article on complying with Section 170 of this chaper, or such portions thereof as have not been previously complied with."

The consolidation or merger of Building and Mutual Loan Associations and Co-operative Loan Associations is provided for by "An Act to Amend the Banking Law," which became a law April 23, 1895. See State Banks, page 102. In the case of these associations the act provides that dissenting shareholders may demand cancellation of their stock or liquidation of their indebtedness, the value of which stock, or the amount of which indebtedness is to be determined by three appraisers, to be appointed by the Supreme Court of the district in which the county of domicile of the corporation is located, upon application made by such stockholders upon eight days' notice to the corporation, within sixty days after merger.

Co-operative Loan Associations.

These associations may be organized by not less than fifteen persons.

The objects sought are practically the same as those of Building and Mutual Loan Associations.

A certificate of organization must be filed with the Superintendent of Banks at Albany, and a copy with the County Clerk of the County where the principal office of such Company is located, which certificate must be approved by the Superintendent of Banks before the subscribers and their successors shall become a corporation by the name specified.

The officers of such association shall be a President, Vice-President, Treasurer, and Secretary, all of whom shall be *ex-officio* members of the Board of Directors, which Board shall consist of not less than nine members, exclusive of *ex-officio* members.

By-laws shall be adopted prescribing the terms of office, the duties and compensation of officers, the time of their election, and of periodical meetings of the officers and shareholders, how special meetings may be called regulating the due conduct of the business of the corporation, defining the duties of its officers and committees, the mode of determining and declaring the withdrawing value of shares, and making such other regulations in regard to the transaction of the business of the corporation as are not inconsistent with law.

The Board of Directors shall each year determine the compensation of the Treasurer and Secretary, and they may appoint and remove at pleasure an attorney for the corporation.

The capital stock, not to exceed one million dollars, divided into shares of the matured value of two hundred dollars each, shall consist of the accumulated savings of its members which it holds. The total number of outstanding shares at any one time shall not exceed ten thousand. The shares shall be issued in yearly or half yearly series, and at such times as shall be prescribed by the by-laws. No shares of a prior series shall be issued after the issuing of shares of a new series. No person shall hold more than ten unpledged or more than twenty pledged shares in any one series.

Savings paid to the corporation upon shares shall be called dues. At or before each stated monthly or semi-monthly meeting of the Board of Directors, each shareholder shall pay to the board or a committee thereof, one dollar dues upon each share of stock held by him until the share reaches the value of two hundred dollars, or is withdrawn, cancelled, or forfeited. Payment of dues on shares of each series shall commence from its issue. Fines may be imposed and collected, not exceeding 10 per cent. for each month in arrears, for every dollar of dues or interest which a shareholder shall refuse or neglect to pay at the time it is due. An entrance fee may also be charged, not exceeding twenty-five cents on every share of stock issued by the corporation.

Unlike in the case of a building and loan association, the law prescribes that a member may withdraw the accumulations upon his share after one month's written notice to the Secretary, which withdrawing shareholder shall be paid the withdrawal value of his share as prescribed by the by-laws at the last distribution of profits before the notice of withdrawal, together with all it has paid since such distribution, and such interest on the value of the shares at the time of the last distribution, and on the dues thereafter paid, as the by-laws shall determine, less any fines unpaid and a proportionate share of any unadjusted loss; but not more than one half of the receipts of the corporation, and when the corporation is indebted on matured shares, not more than one third of such receipts shall be applicable to the payment of withdrawing shareholders. Withdrawing shareholders shall be paid in the order in which their notices of withdrawal were filed with the Secretary. The board of directors may in their discretion, under rules made by them, retire the unpledged shares of any series at any time after four years from the date of their issue by enforcing withdrawals of the same; but the shareholders whose shares are to be retired shall be determined by lot, and they shall be paid the full value of their shares, less all fines and their proportionate part of any adjusted loss.

Upon an unpledged share of a given series reaching the value of two hundred dollars, all payment of dues thereon shall cease, and the holder be paid out of the funds of the corporation $200 therefor, with such rate of interest as shall be determined by the by-laws from the time the board of directors shall have declared such shares to be matured until paid; but at no time shall more than one third of the receipts of the corporation be applicable to the payment of matured shares without the consent of the board of directors, who shall also determine the order of the payment of matured shares.

At each monthly stated meeting, immediately following the receipt of dues and interest, the board of directors shall offer to members of the corporation desiring to borrow, all accumulations applicable to that purpose, in sums of two hundred dollars, the value of a matured share, or a multiple thereof, or the fractional parts of one third of one half thereof. If more than one member desires to borrow, the right to the loan shall be determined by an open bidding of a premium per share, and the member bidding the highest premium shall be entitled to the loan upon giving proper security; and the amount of the premium paid shall be deducted from the sum loaned at the time of loaning, and the receipt thereof shall not be deemed a violation of the usury laws. No member can borrow a larger sum than shall be equal to the matured value of the shares held by him. A borrowing member, for each share or fractional part thereof borrowed upon, shall, in addition to the dues on his shares, pay monthly interest on his loan at the rate of six per cent. per annum, or such lower rate as the by-laws shall name, until the shares borrowed upon reach the matured value of two hundred dollars each, or the loan is repaid; and when such matured value is reached, the loan upon it shall be paid out of the share, and the proper surrender and acquittances be made. See last paragraph Building and Mutual Loan Associations.

Mortgage and Debenture Companies.

These companies are of comparatively recent growth and are a necessity of the unnaturally rapid development of our Western agricultural sections by persons who, without the aid afforded by these companies, would be unable to retain their holdings, which often in the first instance were simply pre-empted Government lands, the holders owning little more than the land itself, and not having the means with which to erect suitable buildings thereon and to purchase the implements required for its cultivation. Settlers of this class usually, in order to procure capital, mortgage their lands as soon as they have any commercial value, which, of course, is as soon as they can produce anything which can be marketed.

Holders of the mortgages on such lands, as a rule, reside in the money centres of our country, which are mainly on the Atlantic seaboard, and can make no personal examination of the land on which they loan. This work falls within the province of the mortgage companies, who, through their agents, make examinations of the lands, extend the loans, and then through their representatives, principally in the East, sell the mortgages to investors.

The farming lands of several Western States are mortgaged to more than half of their appraised value, which mortgages have been in no small degree negotiated through mortgage and debenture companies.

When properly conducted, their loans carefully chosen, and the company economically managed, the mortgages of such companies certainly offer a fair investment, and companies of this description are of great use in bringing together the borrower and the lender in a way quite impossible without their aid.

Each company, as a rule, confines itself principally to a given area, frequently taking the name of the State or section where its loans are located.

CHAPTER IX.

Private Bankers—Brokers—Stock Brokers—Note Brokers—Puts and Calls.

Private Bankers.—In an estimate of the financial strength of a great city, or a country, few of us, our minds filled with the enormous aggregation of capital of banks, take into consideration what an important element is the private banker, who, practically unrestricted as to his dealings, investments, and ventures, save by the consideration of receiving good security for his advances and avoiding placing his own or his clients' funds where they may be insecure, or regained only at expense and loss of interest, undertakes and promotes enterprises which National and State banks, by law, are prohibited from doing. Still less do we consider that while the aggregate capital and surplus of the National and State banks of New York City, clearing through the New York Clearing House, for instance, does not exceed perhaps $134,000,000, that of the private bankers more numerous 't is true, more than trebles this amount, and while $5,000,000 is the largest capital of any of our banks, there are certainly half a dozen or more private banking firms in the city of New York whose individual capital is not less than $10,000,000.

Private bankers, like banks, receive money from one person and loan it to another, sometimes paying interest on the money which they receive, and always charging interest on that which they loan; the difference between the two being their profit.

By far the larger portion of their business is in the furtherance of new enterprises, and the reorganization of old, the forming of companies, the consolidation of already existing corporations or businesses, the selling and buying of exchange, and the sale and issuance of letters of credit, certificates of deposit, etc.

Private bankers in the United States have all the privileges granted to State banks generally, but are not subject to the same restrictions excepting when they issue circulating notes, which they can do under the laws of most States, then they become subject to the same restrictions and limitations in that respect as State banks; but while they possess that right it is rendered of no practical value to them by the National tax of ten per cent. on the circulating notes of other than National banks.

In England at present, and in this country up to the imposition of the National tax above alluded to, the issuance of circulating notes was a source of considerable revenue.

The business of banking and promoting, now being generally carried on by the same firms, is usually so intimately connected as to be almost inseparable; most of the larger banking houses deriving the greater part of their incomes from the promotion of various enterprises, by which is meant the furnishing to those enterprises in exchange for its securities a sufficient amount of money to enable them to begin and continue their operations.

The reorganization of various properties also furnishes a large field of usefulness, and offers very handsome profits and commissions.

They enter into contracts with companies, by which they agree to advance them money to a given amount, receiving for such advances the bonds and stock of such companies at a given price. These they dispose of to their clients and customers. On such transactions they make two profits, one being the interest on the money loaned, and the other the advance in price on the securities, or a commission on the sale.

To enumerate all the sources of income of private bankers is to name the various businesses of the country, in all of which they are more or less directly interested, and which they assist and are assisting daily.

Perhaps no great industry owes more to their generous assistance than do the railroads, whose securities are largely owned and almost exclusively placed by them; and when it is borne in mind that the railroad interests of the United States represent some nine billion of dollars, or nearly one fifth of the whole wealth of the country, and but for their existence vast tracts which now have great value would be comparatively valueness, it may be seen to what an extent the development of the West in particular is due to the foresight and enterprise of the private banker.

But vast interests and values are perhaps quite as much affected by the maintenance of existing enterprises as by the creation or extension of new ones, and oftentimes the reorganization of a railroad is as important to the interests of the section which it traverses as the building of a new road would be to another section.

The consolidation of properties either friendly or antagonistic, for the purpose of eliminating competition, reducing expenses, or increasing earnings, is a source of almost constant employment for the larger houses.

In the organization of a company the method of procedure is something like this: We will take a railroad company, for instance. Certain persons desiring to build a road from one point to another, after making inquiries as to the probable business which can be secured, make estimates as to the cost of the right of way—in many instances a large portion of which can be secured without cost, the land being given to the company either by the persons whose lands will be traversed, in the hope of making the remainder more valuable, or grants are made by the State, county, and in many instances by the National government, which has given millions of acres to the transcontinental lines ; plans are then submitted to some railroad contractor, who makes an estimate as to the cost of construction of such a road as is desired, a rough survey having first been made. These plans together with the contractor's estimates are all submitted to the banking house, which if it agrees to take up the matter perfects the organization of the company, by procuring the passage of an act to that effect by the State or States in which it is located, and after the filing of its certificate of organization, the payment of such fees and taxes as are necessary to complete such organization, proceeds through the directors and stockholders to issue its mortgage bonds and stock, of which it retains or subsequently receives a certain portion as security for advances which they agree to and do make. These securities they then place among their customers. The agreement frequently is that they will only supply the company with such sums as they can realize from a sale of its securities, for which sale they charge a commission. The securities issued by the company in excess of the amount necessary to procure these advances are retained by it in its treasury.

In the reorganization of companies the usual method is for the security holders to deposit with some trust company, usually named by the bankers effecting the reorganization, their securities. After a sufficient proportion have been deposited to insure the success of the reorganization, and after the completion of the necessary preliminaries, the depositors receive securities of the new company at the rate agreed upon in the reorganization agreement.

When a property is put in the hands of a receiver, a reorganization is about the only thing to be done, as the company is bound to be reorganized either by the purchaser or the creditors, generally the bondholders. These reorganizations are usually very profitable to the bankers consummating them.

Brokers.—There are so many kinds of brokers, in fact, as many kinds as there are commodities or paper representing values to be sold and purchased, that it is impossible to speak of them all. Our remarks will therefore be confined to Stock Brokers and Brokers of Commercial Paper, commonly known as Note Brokers.

Stock Brokers.—The principal places of business of the stock broker in New York is the Stock Exchange, and the Consolidated Exchange, where most active stocks are dealt in, but in addition to these stock brokers, members of one or both exchanges, there are a large number who belong to no exchange, and who deal largely in street railway and gas stocks, and State, municipal, and county bonds and warrants, called " Investment Securities." The number of brokers in New York engaged in the sale of securities is certainly several thousand.

While most of the banking houses in New York do what is known as a "banking and brokerage business," there are a great many brokers whose business is solely confined to the buying and selling of stocks and bonds; and some trade almost wholly in the securities of certain properties.

A membership in one or more of the principal exchanges of the country is now considered a pre-requisite to success, and there are comparatively few of the chief houses who do not have memberships in several. In New York a membership in the "New York Stock Exchange" is indispensable to the carrying on of a large stock-brokerage business, although some of the brokers on the "Consolidated Stock and Petroleum Exchange" do considerable business.

Stock brokers rise in various gradations from the "curbstone" broker who buys and sells stock on the curb-stone, the broker who holds forth in some of the rooms known by various names, but better known to the public as "bucket" shops, until you finally come to the opulent Stock Exchange man who drives to his office in his carriage, and buys and sells stocks by the thousand or ten thousand shares.

That New York is not suffering from a dearth of stock brokers may be inferred from the fact that the Stock Exchange furnishes 1100, the Consolidated as many more, —and they seem, during a busy market, literally to spring out of the curb of New Street.

There can scarcely be less than six or seven thousand men engaged daily in New York in various ways in the increasing or decreasing of the prices of various stocks and bonds, especially if we include the brokers who, belonging to no exchange, make a specialty of State, city, and county bonds, which are rarely, if ever, dealt in on the exchanges.

Many of the commission houses, brokers who, for a commission, buy and sell for others, make it a part of their articles of partnership that the members of their firm shall not speculate on either their individual or firm account. There are many good reasons for this. The first is that the firm may not be injured by the speculation of its members, and find itself suddenly embarrassed by losses of which it had no knowledge; and the second is that members of said firm shall be in a position to advise their customers disinterestedly, which, of course, they might not and probably would not be if they were themselves large buyers or sellers of stocks, the price of which they desired to see increased or decreased; and, thirdly, this rule being known, the customers would have greater faith in and reliance upon the advice given them. For the same reasons, and the additional one that speculation at times offers great temptation to dishonesty and the betrayal of trusts, the clerks of many houses are prohibited from speculating.

A brief description of the way in which business is done in a well conducted office perhaps would not be out of place. We will confine it to the office of a member of the Stock Exchange. The first thing in the morning, is the opening of the mail to see what orders have been sent in. Such of these as are not to be attended to by the members of the firm are assigned to other brokers. The cashier reports the condition of the firm's finances—balances in banks, and what loans, if any, are needed. Negotiations often are had simply by telephone message, and the loan arranged, it being understood, of course, that proper security will be deposited to cover it. The opening of the Exchange at ten o'clock finds all brokers with any business to transact on the floor, and with the exception of a short interval for lunch, although many brokers do not allow themselves even this respite, they usually remain there till three o'clock, when business on the floor is over for the day. From ten to three, however, the broker has been in frequent communication, by messenger and telephone, with his offiee. His duties on the floor of the exchange, while described at greater length in the article on the New York Stock Exchange, are, briefly, to execute the orders of his customers.

The charge made for the buying or selling of a stock is one eighth of one per cent. of the face value of such stock. All the shares on the Stock Exchange, with two exceptions, being of the face value of one hundred dollars a share, and these two are fifty dollars a share, one hundred shares of one hundred dollars per share is the smallest quantity of stock bought or sold on the Stock Exchange, and in the case of the exceptions just mentioned two shares of fifty dollars each are counted as one, so that not less than two hundred shares of these stocks are dealt in. This represents a par value of ten thousand dollars, one eighth of one per cent. of which would be $12.50. This is the price charged persons not members of the Exchange, but one member may do business for another member at as low a rate as $2 per hundred shares. The penalty for the violation of these rules is fine, suspension, or expulsion from the Exchange, as the Governing Committee may elect.

In most of the larger offices there are great blackboards with the names of all the principal stocks, cotton, wheat, lard, etc., near which are one or more tickers from which the quotations are taken and written on the board with great rapidity, this of itself occupying the time of one and sometimes more clerks. Standing and seated around the room, intently watching the blackboard, are the customers of the firm. Many of them have pads in their hands, on which to write their orders, which are handed to clerks, and by them checked and handed to the telephone clerk, telegraph operators, or messengers, as the case may be, by whom they are immediately sent or delivered.

After the Exchange business is over the brokers return to their offices, and the business of the day is written up, the correspondence attended to, etc.

Some of the principal houses while having as many as three or four Stock Exchange members, do a large share of their buying and selling through other brokers, to conceal their identity from their fellow-brokers, a knowledge of which might tend to injure their interests.

Quite a number of brokers are known as "Specialists." They devote their time to one particular stock, and can always be found at the part of the floor where that stock is traded in. These men, however, do most of their business for other brokers, and are called "$2 Brokers."

A very large proportion of the buying and selling of stock is done on *margin*, and a comparatively small percentage of outright purchases are made. Some brokers require a larger margin than others, and all brokers require heavier margins on some stocks than on others, while there are stocks which no broker will buy on margin.

The amount of margin required is dependent not alone on the character of the stock, but also on the condition of the money market, and all brokers reserve to themselves the right to call for more margin.

As a rule, any of the active stocks which are fairly steady can be bought on a ten per cent. margin. That is, by depositing one thousand dollars with your broker you can buy one hundred shares of stock. In speculating on margin it should be remembered that while the smaller the percentage of margin the greater the number of shares which can be purchased for a given sum, yet, in case of the market going against the speculator, the sooner the margin becomes exhausted, before which event he has either to put up more margin or lose what he has already deposited, whereas the same amount of money representing a larger margin on a smaller purchase would have more than covered the fall, and a later recovery of the price of the stock may leave him a profit.

Another matter for a speculator to consider is the interest charge made by the broker, in purchases on margins, the usual charge being five per cent., and, of course, if your money is earning less it is evidently to your advantage not to borrow at a higher rate than your own money is earning. The broker charges the customer interest on the difference between the margin deposited and the amount it takes to buy the stock outright. Thus, if on a purchase of $10,000 of stock selling at par $1000 is deposited as margin, $9000 more is necessary to complete the purchase; this the broker either furnishes or becomes liable for, holding the stock as security, and charging his customer interest on the $9000 until the stock is either all paid for or again sold; and while this amounts to only a little over $1.30 per day, we must not forget that if the stock is held for any length of time it takes quite a substantial slice out of the profits, if it does not entirely absorb them.

But a small proportion of the purchases on the Exchange are made for investment, most being made for a quick sale, or "turn" as it is called, the purchaser or seller intending to buy or sell as soon as he can make a profit by doing so; the broker in the event of a profit paying him the difference between the price at which he buys and that at which he sells, less his commissions and interest charges; or in case of a loss, applying the customer's margin to the payment of such loss, the broker's commissions and interest charges. Should the commissions and interest exceed the margin deposited, then the client has to make good the deficiency.

Where stocks are bought outright and paid for, they are delivered to the purchaser, or held by the broker for him, subject to the owner's order.

Brokers' offices generally have telegraph and telephone facilities, tickers, and every means of obtaining immediate information in regard to the state of the crops, the finances of the country, and of the world, and everything else that may have an influence on the stock market, and there is scarcely a better informed man as to the material condition of the different parts of the country than the broker, whose success in business is largely due to the correctness of the advice he gives his clients.

Conditions and circumstances which influence the price of stocks are so numerous as to defy exhaustive statement, but a few of the most important will be given.

First, the condition of the property; next, the condition of the country from which the company draws its business, whether it is such as to warrant a continuation of the present condition of affairs, and in that connection, of course, must be considered the yield of the section, whether it be an agricultural, mining, or lumber section. Next, the management of the company, the ratio of its earnings to expenses, the presence of competitors, and, in fact, everything that might tend to make it a more profitable or a less profitable investment. The general condition of the money market must be considered carefully, and especially in the case of new companies, or those requiring assistance, to be procured by the borrowing of money upon their securities; for when the money market is easy they can place their securities at a better price than if it is tight, but they must in any event, in the case of railroads, have the money to build their tracks or extend their operations. On a tight market they have to sell more stock to secure the same amount of money than in an easy market, or incur a greater obligation, as each share, no matter what price it sells at, is an obligation of the company for the amount written on its face. Another consideration is the class of persons by whom the larger part of the stock is held, whether they are persons who would on a slight "scare" have to relinquish their "holdings," as the stock would necessarily decline in price under heavy offerings.

In the case of companies requiring no such assistance, where the stock is bought for investment, and the property is well known to be a "dividend payer," the condition of the money market is of less consequence, as the tightness of money will not to the same degree affect the earning capacity of the company.

Consolidation of properties nearly always tends to increase the price of their securities, unless there is a disproportionate issue of securities, because it is assumed that competition is thereby largely eliminated, expenses reduced, rates raised, and net earnings increased.

Traffic agreements, which are contracts entered into by two or more railroads drawing their business from the same section or sections, by which they agree upon a uniform rate for given services, and a certain apportionment of the business, is in effect a consolidation to a certain extent, and always tends to increase the price of the stock of the companies parties to it. These agreements have become an absolute necessity in many cases, to avoid bankruptcy of the roads entering into them, competition having become so fierce that in many instances they were doing business at absolutely ruinous rates, and a continuation of such competition must result in the ruin of many of the parties concerned.

Rumors that certain companies will show increased earnings or decreased earnings, that they will fail to declare dividends on certain issues of stock, or that they will declare larger dividends, that they will fail to pay coupons falling due on certain dates, and, in fact, anything that will have a tendency to increase or decrease the price of its securities, are diligently circulated for the purpose of affecting the market; also stories as to the solvency of known large holders of its stocks; and while the law has done its utmost to punish the circulating false reports, it cannot keep foolish people from becoming frightened or over-sanguine, as the case may be; and many have been the failures caused by the circulation and the heeding of such rumors or "tips," as they are called, many people for the time apparently forgetting that the tips which they are happy in possessing have been purposely given to them with the object of inducing them to do something to the advantage of others. For instance, nothing could be more obviously to the advantage of a person "short" of a particular stock, and who naturally wishes to buy it at the lowest price, than the circulation of a report among the holders of that stock, that the receipts of the company showed a falling off, or that a competitor's business had greatly increased, or that it had received concessions prejudicial to the company whose stock he was short of; and it is a very easy matter to intimate or insinuate this to some friend of the holders, who in repeating the same simply furthers the plans of his friend's enemy.

The price of stocks is further influenced by the formation of "pools," in which a number of persons "pool" their interests, join together, for the purpose of buying or selling, and increasing or decreasing, the price of one or more stocks. When the object is to increase the price of a stock, they are called "bull pools," and when the object is to decrease the price "bear pools." Naturally, only persons having large holdings will join in a bull pool, and those short of, or having no, or comparatively insignificant, holdings, in a bear pool.

The method of operation depends largely upon the stock and whether the pool is a bull or a bear pool. If a bull pool, as much stock as can be is purchased for future delivery. The sellers of this stock generally do not have the amount sold, but expect to be able to purchase the same before the date of delivery at a lower price than the one at which they sold it; a still hunt is then made by the bulls and as much stock as possible bought, still for future delivery, if possible. The pool now begins to buy up the stock as rapidly as it is offered on the market, the stock becomes scarce and the price advances, bids are made in excess of the amount offered, and the sellers who sold stock which they did not and do not possess, "the shorts," now come in to buy, or "to cover," as it is technically termed, but discover that there is very little or no stock to be had, in which case they have either to buy what little there is to be had, sending the market still higher, or pay the purchasers, "the bulls," the difference between the price at which they agreed to deliver and the price of the stock in the market. The success of a bull pool is dependent upon the ability of the pool to take all or a very large portion of the stock offered, upon the condition of the property during the operation of the pool, and to put the sellers, or shorts, in a position where they are compelled to purchase from the pool at practically the price it chooses to dictate, or at any rate at a price which will leave the bulls a profit after all their holdings have been disposed of. These pools are seldom formed for other than speculative purposes, and seldom have the money to buy all the stock for which they contract outright. They generally operate with a stock of medium issue, rather than one of either very large or very small issue, as in one case the stock would probably be too scattered and it would require too much money, while in the other their design, on account of the limited issue, would become apparent at an early stage, and their object defeated.

A pool is generally managed by one of its members, who has absolute power over the holdings of the others, which are pooled and under his control. As a complete record is kept of all bonds and stocks of every corporation on its books, and while, of course, the entries of transfer do not always show the real owners, still a thoroughly posted operator can approximately determine what portion of its securities are held for investment and what are being actively dealt in on the exchange, and for ordinary purposes only the latter portion need be considered.

Both the bulls and the shorts will do whatever they can to influence the market in their respective favors.

A bear pool is formed and controlled in the same manner, usually by persons short of a particular stock, who sell stocks, not in their possession, for future delivery and by their constant offerings to sell, seek to reduce the price so that they may be enabled to buy at a lower price than the price at which the stock has been sold. Inasmuch as they have to keep selling to depress the market while they are buying to fill their maturing contracts, as it would never do to have all the contracts mature at the same time, it requires most adroit management, as they must, in order to be successful, sell on the market which they have themselves lowered, and are compelled to keep on hand a much larger amount than they buy in order to make the pool a success.

Note Brokers.

This is the name usually given to men whose business is procuring the discount of commercial paper, notes. For various reasons there are comparatively few men engaged in this department of finance as compared with the other departments; and their dealings are largely restricted to what are known as outside borrowers, borrowers residing outside of the place where the loan is sought, or who desire accommodation from other than their usual banks or lenders, because most business men whose credit is good can nearly always secure all the money they need from the different banks in which they keep their accounts, and it is only when a man wants to go beyond this that he puts his paper in the hands of brokers, who usually simply procure its discount by some one else, but sometimes they buy the paper themselves, and either hold it or re-discount it at a lower rate.

As a rule, however, they are simply middlemen between the borrowers and the lenders, and receive a certain commission from the borrower for procuring the discount.

People who have no regular line of accommodation at one or more banks, or who have exhausted that line and wish to place their notes somewhere else, should consult the note broker.

Puts and Calls.

These words are so technical in their meaning as to require special explanation, which is best given by a statement of the method by which this business is transacted. Thus: A sells his agreement to B for a certain sum to "put" to him at a given day at the price named in such agreement a stated number of shares of a particular stock, giving B the privilege of calling for the delivery at the time and price agreed upon.

If the stock in the meantime goes down so that A can purchase the same for a less price than the price at which he agreed to deliver it, B either pays A the difference between the price at which the stock shall be delivered and the price at which the same can be purchased in the market or receives the stock and pays therefor the price agreed upon. In the event of the stock going up, A either delivers to B the stock at the agreed time or price or pays to B the difference between the price at which he agreed to deliver the stock and its market price.

CHAPTER X.

Exchanges—New York Stock Exchange.

Exchanges.—Exchanges are meeting-places for persons engaged in the buying and selling or exchanging of commodities or values, or the titles to such commodities or values.

The exchanges of the present day may differ in degree but not in kind from the guilds of the Saxons, and the meeting-places of the early merchants. Their growth has been so gradual and imperceptible, keeping pace with commerce, but never outstripping it, as to have occasioned but little comment historically; and while we are informed that they were a well established part of the commercial life of the Florentine period, and gradually crept northward as the centre of commerce changed from Southern to Western Europe, still in all the essentials they existed, so soon as a large number of persons met with any regularity at a specified place to exchange their goods.

To the merchant or broker the exchange occupies in one sense the same relation as the merchant or distributing agent does to the producer and consumer. It is the medium through which he is brought in contact with those who desire to sell, and those who wish to buy, and he can consequently either sell or buy as he wishes. The exchange saves him the trouble and loss of time necessary to ascertain the person with whom he may exchange, just as the country merchant saves the farmer the trouble of finding a purchaser for his wheat or cotton; and as the country storekeeper brings the manufacturer and the farmer together, so the exchange brings the different merchants together.

To realize the enormous saving of time and money and the economizing of energy effected by these institutions, let us for a minute suppose the business of a great community conducted without them, and each seller groping around for a buyer, and the buyer searching for a seller. Such a condition would be wholly incompatible with the life of our century.

All of our cities, even the smaller ones, have their Boards of Trade, and exchanges for the principal commodity dealt in, and even our villages have what to them answers the same purpose, some common meeting-place for buyers and sellers.

The relative importance of the different exchanges is usually determined by the sales, and naturally in different sections and cities different exchanges become more or less important than in others. Thus, in New York, the Stock Exchange is the most important exchange, owing to the enormous transactions annually effected, while in Western cities exchanges for the sale of produce, and in the larger Southern cities those for the sale of cotton, are the most important.

In most of the larger cities all the chief trades and businesses have their particular exchanges, where the people interested in those trades meet.

Outside of a mere mention of the principles of exchanges in general, it is not within the purview of this work, to deal with any exchanges but those relating particularly to finance; and as an illustration of the workings of such exchanges, and because it is perhaps the most interesting and generally discussed institution of this kind in our country, we have decided to discuss somewhat in detail—

The New York Stock Exchange.—A voluntary unincorporated association founded in the year 1792, which, after various migrations downtown, settled in 1867 in its present magnificent home at 16 Broad Street.

There are entrances to the building on three streets, the main one on Broad Street, access to which is had by a flight of marble steps leading into a corridor, on either side of which are elevators running to the upper floors, where the bond room, library, executive offices, and the offices of the clerks of the exchange are situated. These elevators also lead to the Visitors' Gallery, which runs partly round the main hall. On Wall Street, there is an entrance used by brokers, but to a larger extent by sightseers, who go usually by this ingress to the gallery just mentioned. On New Street there are two entrances, one at the northern and the other at the southern end of the building, which are used exclusively by members, their clerks, and the employees of the exchange.

All entrances lead to the "floor" of the Exchange, which is on the level of Wall and New Street, but above that of Broad. This "floor" is a large room almost square, with a sort of a bay-window effect on the Broad Street side, produced by the irregular extension of the hall in that direction. Opposite this is a large board, divided into different colored blocks, which blocks are further subdivided into smaller blocks, each of which, in a short time it will be discovered, discloses a number in the same fashion as an hotel annunciator. The number so disclosed is the number assigned to some broker or firm, and indicates to him that some one wishes to communicate with him. The board is in reality an annunciator, and without some such contrivance it would be quite impossible, owing to the noise and confusion, to secure the attention of a broker on the floor.

Looking down on the crowd of brokers beneath, the scene from the gallery is one which never fails to create a strong impression on the mind, and especially so when the market is active, and there are hundreds of brokers buying and selling. There is audible but one continuous roar of voices, no one distinguishable from the rest, although every now and then you may distinguish "five hundred $\frac{7}{8}$ths, two hundred $\frac{1}{4}$th," etc.; the five hundred and the two hundred meaning the number of shares, and the $\frac{7}{8}$ths or $\frac{1}{4}$th representing the fraction of a cent at which the stock is offered, no one deeming it necessary, except in case of an unusual rise or fall in stocks, to state the whole number of cents, as that is presumed to be known by everybody on the floor. Nor is the name of the stock called, the seller or purchaser simply goes to that portion of the room where that stock is dealt in, which place is marked by an iron stand supporting a placard on which is printed its name. This, of course, applies merely to the principal active stocks. There are many stocks which are not active stocks, and which are not dealt in to such an amount as to have any separate place assigned to them, but are grouped with a number of other stocks, in which case the broker announces the name of the stock and the price at which he offers the same.

On busy days, from six to seven hundred brokers are often on the floor at the same moment, some offering and others bidding, waving their arms, gesticulating, and generally trying to attract the attention of some particular person, or rushing about from crowd to crowd, and from stand to stand, endeavoring to fill their orders.

The fee fixed by the Stock Exchange, which brokers are to charge to persons not members of the Exchange, is one-eighth of one per cent. of the face value of the stock for buying, and the same for selling, so that to buy and sell a stock it costs one-fourth of one per cent. The rate below which no broker is allowed to deal with his fellow-brokers is two dollars a hundred shares for selling, and two dollars a hundred shares for buying.

The 15th of September and Christmas Eve are days which are not religiously observed in the Exchange, but they are observed with equal regularity if less decorum. White hats are considered especially unorthodox on the 15th of September, by which time every well-informed broker is supposed to have accumulated sufficient worldly goods to purchase a Fall hat, but if he has not, he certainly will have to buy one on margin.

Only citizens of the United States over twenty-one years of age are eligible to membership, and are admitted only after application to, and a thorough investigation by, the Admissions Committee, and the payment for a certificate of membership which may have been purchased from some other member of the Exchange, but no certificate is of any value so far as its use is concerned by the individual purchasing it, until his application has been approved of by the Admissions Committee, and such membership must be held free and clear of all debt and liability. The seat to which it entitles its holder is subject to sale by the Exchange in discharge of the obligations of its holder to other members; any surplus remaining over being paid to such holder or his legal representatives.

The owner of a seat may sell the same by nominating a successor acceptable to the above-named committee, This committee may, upon the death of a member, transfer his membership, and after the Exchange has paid all demands properly chargeable against the proceeds of such transfer, it turns the remainder over to his heirs. On the decease of a member, his family receives from the Gratuity Fund ten thousand dollars, this being regarded purely as a gift by the Exchange, and subject to no claims whatever.

All stock purchased or sold must be delivered between 1.15 and 2.15 P.M. If not delivered by the last-named hour, the Exchange is notified, and demand is made for the stock. All stock purchased must be paid for on presentation, most houses requiring certified checks. It is here that over-certification is greatest, many banks finding it necessary to so accommodate their broker customers, who almost invariably make good such over-drafts before the close of the day, but certainly within a reasonable time. The banks generally regarding such a check as an implied notice of a deposit sufficient to more than meet it, the stock itself, for which such check is given often with more stock is deposited as collateral to make good such check, and as this stock is generally by commission houses bought for some one else, the check of which purchaser will be doubtlessly received and deposited the same day, the banks really do not take as much risk as is generally supposed when dealing with reputable houses.

There are about eleven hundred members, and as the seats are worth about $18,000 apiece at the present time, the cost of these memberships alone represents something over twenty million dollars. All the larger houses have on the Exchange one or more members, or clerks.

Most of the principal operators and firms doing the greatest volume of business are members more for the sake of getting the benefit of the rates which brokers are allowed to charge each other than for the purpose of actually dealing themselves on the floor, as their presence would often defeat the object they have in view. Nearly all of their larger purchases and sellings are done through other brokers: and it is a common thing for an operator desiring to keep his identity a secret, or to mislead others, to send some member, or some broker known to represent him to sell a small amount of stock, while some other broker, supposed to represent opposed interests buys a large amount of the same stock for his account. But if we should attempt to describe the various methods resorted to to deceive and frighten the unwary, we would have no room in this work for other equally important matters. It is sufficient to say that the Wall Street man is ingenious to a degree seldom paralleled in other businesses.

CHAPTER XI.

Corporations, Officers, Etc.

Corporations.—Many enterprises, businesses, and industries require such a large amount of capital in their organization and operation, as well as the certainty that these operations will not suddenly be suspended by the death of one individual, nor interfered with by the settlement and division of assets rendered necessary by the retirement of a general or special partner, and the public interest in them is often so great, as to render their conduct by individuals not only inadvisable, but often impossible.

To meet these objections, corporations, or companies, associations of men for the prosecution of one or more objects, are formed under the laws of different countries. They are granted various privileges which neither are nor can be given individuals, the chief of which is legal perpetuity, or at any rate existence for a given time, if they fulfil the requirements imposed upon them by the power granting them their charter.

The object of their formation is not only to secure the perpetuity of an enterprise, but to secure and maintain sufficient capital to continue it when formed; and this can only be accomplished by making the shares of the various persons interested easily transferable; and definitely settling the proportion of their interests. Again, many persons who would be glad to buy a stated interest, the liability on which was specified, in an enterprise, which interest they could readily transfer, would be unwilling to become partners, either general or special, in the same thing.

Corporations are formed to carry on all kinds of businesses and enterprises which men either individually or as firms engage in, save generally those requiring the personal rendering of technical or professional services, although even this field is now encroached upon by the title companies, which employ large numbers of lawyers whose sole occupation is the examining of titles to real estate, and also by dental companies employing a number of dentists, and other novel corporate enterprises.

Companies are most commonly organized to conduct industries of considerable magnitude requiring a large capital, employing numerous hands, and possessing valuable franchises, usually derived from the Federal or State governments.

The principal companies, generally speaking, are those engaged in transportation, mining, and manufacturing, and the transmission of intelligence, *i. e.*, telegraph companies, press associations, etc., although a great many large mercantile houses have of late reorganized as corporations.

We will take, by way of illustration, the case of a person owning valuable mining lands, but without the capital necessary to make them available and valuable. Assistance from others must be had, and the most common way of obtaining such assistance is by the formation of a company by the owner of the lands, and the persons willing to furnish the capital, or so much of it as is necessary to begin operations; on the formation of such company the land owner transferring them to the company for so much stock or money, and the people furnishing the money receiving stock for the money furnished.

To a limited extent the same result may be attained

by a partnership, but if the amount needed is large, and has to be subscribed by a number of people, it is found that the partnership becomes unwieldy, and the interests of the several partners difficult of adjustment.

Having brought together the persons desiring to form such corporation, the next step is to proceed with the organization, which is accomplished in substantially the same way in all States, but the regulations, requirements, and restrictions of many of the States differ, some being more and others less severe. The laws of the same State also differ with respect to the various kinds of companies.

Before organizing, it is very important for the incorporators to decide upon the State under whose laws they will organize, and a judicious decision on this point can generally best be arrived at by following the advice of some well known corporation lawyer.

Except in the case of companies which derive privileges from the States where they operate, a company may, as a rule, become incorporated under the laws of whatever State it pleases, and the incorporation of a company under the laws of another State does not exempt it from the restrictions on, or duties to be performed by, like companies organized under the laws of the State in which it transacts its business.

In all States the first thing to be done is to file with the proper State officer, usually the Secretary of State, a certificate of incorporation, stating the Act under which the company is organized, if the character of the company is such that it can organize under a given Act (some companies, being permitted only by special Act of the Legislature to organize).

In the case of railroads and other corporations, organized by special Act of the Legislature, it is necessary to secure the passage of such an Act before any further step is taken, and then, if the company intends to operate in or through certain cities, a resolution or ordinance of the Board of Aldermen, or the Common Council, or whoever may have control of such privileges, and generally to further obtain the consent of the property holders owning two-thirds in value of the real estate in the streets of such city through which the road will run.

While in the State of New York there must be remitted with the certificate of incorporation a tax of one-eighth of one per cent. on the capital stock of the company sought to be organized, together with the fees charged for the receiving and issuance of the necessary papers, in many States no such tax is imposed, and only a charge by the Secretary of State is made.

The importance of having the organization properly incorporated and all the legal requirements attended to cannot be too strenuously dwelt upon ; and good business men have come to realize that the certificate of a well known legal firm as to the clearness of the title, the compliance with statutory legislation, and other legal requirements add a value to the securities of the company far in excess of the cost of the services rendered.

A Certificate of incorporation must be filed with the Secretary of State containing the name and object of the company, the names of the directors for the first year (usually chosen by the subscribers to the stock), the number of directors who shall thereafter govern, the amount of capital stock, and the location of the company's principal office, to which is usually added a provision for the increase or decrease of capital stock. The payment of the tax, which is levied upon the proposed capital of most companies, should usually accompany the certificate.

Under the laws of none of our States of which the writer is aware is a company required to begin operations with the full amount of its capital stock paid in, except in the case of trust companies of the State of New York.

In most cases this would be an obvious impossibility, owing to the inability of any man or number of men placing the stock and bonds of a company immediately upon its organization. In fact, most companies reserve a portion of their bonds and stocks in their treasury in anticipation of future needs.

Attached to the certificate of incorporation should be a copy of the constitution and by-laws.

Companies operating in one State, but organized under the laws of another, are required to name a resident attorney in fact, possessed of the usual powers given such attorneys.

According to the laws of some of the States, the principal office of such company must be in the State under the laws of which it is organized, where its books—especially its stock and transfer books—must be kept, but this is not always so, especially in the case of West Virginia. Companies organized under the laws of the State of New York are required to have a certain per cent. of their directors, according to the character of the corporation, residents of the State.

Privileges or concessions are usually granted upon certain conditions, varying according to the character of the company, the nature of its business, and the source from which they are received.

As to the distinction between and the rights of stockholders, and bondholders, and stock and bonds, see Chapter XIV.

Officers.—A few suggestions as to the duties of the President, Vice-President, Secretary, and Treasurer of a Corporation.

In order to conduct business with dispatch and certainty, and to enter into contracts which will be binding upon both parties, it is necessary not only that a person having dealings with corporations should have some knowledge of the powers of the officers of such corporations, but also that the officers themselves should know the extent and limitations of their powers and duties, so that they may exercise these duties and powers within their legitimate range. It has, therefore, been thought wise to make a few general comments on this subject.

The President, as the head of a corporation and its chief officer, would naturally be spoken of first, though in some cases instead of a President, a Corporation or Company is managed by Commissioners or a Committee who may or may not have a Chairman, but, as a general thing, each Corporation has its President.

Before proceeding specifically to enumerate the duties of these officers, it is well to state that their powers are usually prescribed by the Constitution and By-Laws of the Company which they serve ; in some companies the powers of the officers being very great and in others more limited. And while in some cases the duties of one officer are assigned to some other officer, notably in the case of the Secretary and Treasurer, yet as a rule the officers subsequently named have substantially the following duties assigned them.

President.—The President is always a member of the Board of Directors or Trustees, and usually its Chairman. He is vested with power to enter into and sign contracts, deeds, agreements, and various other legal documents by direction of the Board of Directors or Trustees.

He is expected to be present and preside at all meetings of the Board of Directors and Stockholders. To him is entrusted the general management of the Company and the employment of its subordinates. Other officers who employ clerks or laborers derive their power from him.

All important documents with the Company should bear the signature of the President.

Vice-President.—The Vice-President, in the absence of the President, performs the duties assigned him ; but when the President is present, the Vice-President's duties are principally those of an assistant to the President, although, in large corporations Vice-Presidents usually have charge of some particular department.

Secretary.—The Secretary's duties are confined principally to the keeping of the records of the Company, consisting of the meetings of the Board of Directors and the meetings of the stockholders, the issuance of calls to such meetings, and the submission of the Annual Reports placed in his hands to the Board of Directors and the stockholders; to the conduct of the correspondence; and he is generally called upon to attest all documents signed by the President, to sign the bonds and coupons attached thereto, certificates of stock, and to see to the transfer of stock certificates, and to attach the seal of the Corporation to all contracts requiring such seal.

Under the By-Laws of many institutions the Secretary is made Assistant-Treasurer, so that in the absence of the Treasurer he may perform the duties pertaining to that office.

The office of Secretary and Treasurer are also frequently combined, in which case, in addition to the duties above enumerated, he discharges those duties which the Treasurer is usually called upon to perform.

Treasurer.—The Treasurer is more particularly the financial man of a company, and under his direction are kept the books, showing the assets and liabilities of the Company, and its general business transactions. It is his duty, with the direction of the Board of Directors, to designate a bank in which the funds of the Corporation shall be deposited, and therein to deposit them.

He is also required (by most companies) to countersign all contracts, checks, notes, and other evidences of debt or promises to pay, which have to be signed by the President.

General Manager.—The General Manager, while not

necessarily a member of the Board of Directors, and supposed to be subordinate to the President, is perhaps the one officer with whom the public deals most directly, and whose power it is most important that they should understand.

His power, as stated, is derived principally from the President as under the constitution of most companies the General Manager is appointed by the President, but when appointed by the Board of Directors is answerable to them. In such case his duties and powers are prescribed in the By-Laws.

It is ordinarily safe to assume that the General Manager has power to enter into contracts for supplies and such material as is legitimately needed in the operation of the particular business under his control, and to make agreements for the employment of clerks and laborers and others necessary to the operation of the company.

In the case of a contract involving a large sum of money, or one which it is not commonly known that the General Manager has power to bind the company upon, it is wise to have the same ratified and confirmed by the President. There are, however, certain contracts and deeds which even the President has not the power to enter into, these, as a general rule, are contracts disposing of some portion of the assets or franchises of the company, the power to dispose of which rests with the stockholders only.

The issuance of new stocks or bonds can only be legally done by the direction of the stockholders.

In many companies, while the President and Treasurer finally sign a contract, still their power is limited, and they are only empowered so to do after the passage of a resolution to that effect by the Board of Directors.

Of course, it is obviously impossible to give more than the briefest outline of the duties of the various officers of a corporation, and when a person is in doubt as to the ability of a particular officer or of particular officers to bind a company, it is always best to consult some reputable attorney in respect thereto, because there is no greater source of litigation than the repudiation of contracts by corporations, the defence almost invariably set up being that the officer exceeded his power.

CHAPTER XII.

Stocks, Bonds, Warrants, and Receivers' Certificates.

No work on Finance would be complete without some treatment of this subject, and while it is a rather recent development of finance, it constitutes to-day one of its most important divisions. The size of this book, however, permits only of a very brief discussion of the subject.

As certificates of stock or shares are written evidence of the rights of their holders, transferable on sale or registration, and bonds are subsequently issued by authorization and direction of these holders, we will follow in our treatment of the subject, this order.

Before proceeding to a particular consideration of stocks and bonds, it seems necessary to say a word as to the necessity of their issuance.

One of the objects of incorporation is to afford the public an opportunity to subscribe the requisite capital for the organization and operation of an enterprise, and after the purchase of its plant and franchises partly if not wholly by the money paid in by the shareholders, it issues its bonds, secured by a mortgage on its assets, or some part thereof, with which to secure whatever money may be needed for its further completion and operation.

Stocks.

Shares, in the United States generally called "Stock," are certificates issued by a corporation, certifying that the person in whose name they are written and stand registered on the books of the company, is entitled to a portion of the corporation's profits, to the right, by vote, to participate in its management, and, according to the character of the shares, liable to assessment for its debts. It must be borne in mind, however, that all stock is not registered, nor is all assessable. The shareholder is, for the time being, a limited partner in the enterprise by which his shares are issued, but this interest is more readily transferable, and his rights having been previously determined, are more easily disposed of, than in the case of an ordinary special partnership interest.

While all shares entitle their holders to a certain proportion of the net earnings of the corporation, it must be remembered that these earnings can only be computed and distributed among the shareholders after the payment of all obligations of the company, such as operating expenses, fixed charges, etc., inasmuch as the shareholder is regarded in law as a partner in the enterprise, and therefore the last person entitled to share in the distribution of its assets. Bondholders, on the contrary, are creditors of the corporation, having loaned or advanced it money, receiving as evidence of such loan, a bond secured by a mortgage on the property and earning capacity of the company. Because of this liability of the shareholders (in the case of assessable shares) and their position as special partners, they are given the control of the company, whereas the bondholders being in the position of lenders or creditors of such corporations are not generally accorded any voice in the management of a solvent company, although there are being issued by some few corporations, bonds giving their owners certain rights of participation in the corporate management in the event of certain contingencies arising. This, however, is in direct contravention of the principles upon which shares and bonds are issued and held, and is not, therefore, very popular or resorted to often.

The rights and liabilities of shareholders are determined not alone by the language of the share, but also by the statute law of the State or country from which the corporation issuing such shares derives its powers.

Having broadly defined shares we must now proceed to a more specific consideration of their different kinds, the six principal kinds being: 1st, Assessable; 2d, Non-Assessable; 3d, Preferred; and 4th, Common; and all shares belong to one or more of these kinds. A 5th kind of share, known as Cumulative, is issued, and a 6th, Non-Cumulative.

Assessable.—The stock of many corporations under the laws of the United States and the States, under one of which they must organize, is made assessable; thus the shareholders of national banks are made liable to the amount of the value of their stock to the creditors of the bank. In other words, a holder of $100,000 of the shares of a national bank would be liable to assessment to that amount in addition to the application of the money paid in for the purchase of the stock. Many transportation and industrial companies issue assessable stock, and a purchase of this stock in any but a sound and well-managed corporation is attended with considerable responsibility. The limit of assessment, however, in all cases is 100 per cent. upon the face of the shares. Assessable stock may, instead of being an asset of its holder, become an actual liability, on account of the responsibility assumed in the payment of assessments, and it often becomes impossible to give it away.

In case of the insolvency of a corporation issuing assessable stock, bondholders and other creditors may institute civil actions to recover their pro rata contributions from each holder of assessable stock.

Non-Assessable Stock.—No explanation is needed as to the character of this stock. It carries with it all the rights and privileges, but none of the liabilities and responsibilities inherent in an assessable stock, and the utmost obligatory loss that can be sustained by its holder is that of the amount paid for the stock. The holder of non-assessable stock, however, may, in common with other holders, voluntarily consent to the payment of an assessment for the purpose of putting the corporation issuing the stock in a better financial condition.

Preferred Stock.—Preferred here means that the stock so called has a preference over other stock in the payment of dividends. It does not affect the general character of the stock, which may be assessable or non-assessable, cumulative or non-cumulative. The effect of the word is simply to entitle the holder of such stock to be the first to participate in the net earnings of the corporation. This stock is also further divided into first, second, and sometimes even third preferred, all of which come before common stock. All stock, however, generally has the same voting rights, although occasionally where a special guarantee is made the preferred stockholders, putting them in the peculiar position of being partly owners and partly creditors of the corporation, they are deprived of the right to vote, and the controlling power is exercised solely by the common shareholders. But the dividend to which the preferred stockholders may become entitled is generally specifically stated, and any surplus remaining after such payment goes to the common shareholder. In a few isolated cases of extraordinarily successful companies, it has been found that, after the payment of the specified dividends to the preferred shareholders, the amount remaining as a dividend to the common shareholders was so largely in excess of the dividend payable to the preferred that provision was made that after payment of a certain dividend to both preferred and common shareholders the balance should be divided equally between them. The value of the preferred, as well as all other stocks, may be seriously impaired, not only by the incurring of floating debt, but by the making and issuing of bonds secured by mortgages; but inasmuch as these bonds and other debts can be incurred and the obligations can be ratified only by the action of the shareholders, through their representatives, the directors or trustees of a corporation, attempts on the part of shareholders to repudiate such obligations have almost invariably been rendered futile by the decrees of our courts, because even though the issue of such obligations should be proven to be fraudulent, the innocent holder should not be made to suffer for such wrong, but the agents of the shareholders who exceeded or abused their powers might be held accountable.

Common Stock.—After pointing out the distinction between preferred and common stock, which necessarily involved an explanation of the right of the common stockholders, little need be said in this regard.

While the common shares are the last to participate in the distribution of the net earnings of a company after the payment of accrued indebtedness, in exceptional cases where these net earnings are very large and a limit is placed on the dividends payable on anterior stocks, the common becomes more valuable than the preferred.

Cumulative.—A cumulative stock is one on which the corporation agrees to pay dividends past due and unpaid before declaring a dividend on stocks coming after it in the distribution of net earnings, and is necessarily a preferred stock, to that extent at least.

The cumulative feature of a stock at best can only be effective as against subsequent shareholders, as all accrued debts of the company must be provided for before either present or past dividends can be declared. The cumulative feature, while it adds an additional value to preferred stock, to the same extent lessens the chances of participation in earnings by the common stock, and hence decreases its value.

Non-Cumulative Stock is stock without this provision for the payment of past due dividends.

Unless specifically stated, the dividends on a stock are non-cumulative, and in the case of the issue of only common or capital stock this cumulative provision would be of no effect in any event, because the shareholders could at best do no more than participate in the final net earnings, and even without a cumulative clause, if those final net earnings were sufficient to pay past due dividends, could declare the same; unless restricted by law, as some of our corporations possessing valuable franchises from States and cities have been, from declaring dividends in excess of a certain percentage per year, although this restriction has been generally avoided by the issue of an amount of stock sufficient to bring the dividends within the maximum rate which the law permits to be declared. Thus, if after paying all fixed charges a corporation with a capital stock of $10,000,000 should have final net earnings of $1,200,000, and the law prohibited the declaring of a dividend in excess of 6 per cent. on the stock of the company, by doubling the amount of its capital stock it would then be enabled to pay just 6 per cent. and thus come within the restriction of the law. Various laws have been enacted looking to the prevention of what is known as the watering of stock, even going to the extent of compelling the corporation to reduce the charge for its commodities or services; yet so long as such corporation is able to declare a fair dividend on its issue of stock, so long will there be a market for that stock.

In the absence of governmental restriction as to the amount of dividend paid, it sometimes happens, in the case of very successful corporations, that their stock becomes more valuable than their bonds, the bonds being a fixed charge the interest upon which is specified, while the dividends upon the stock may amount to a larger percentage of interest than that paid on the bonds, besides carrying with it the control of the company.

Common stock is sometimes given to purchasers of bonds as a bonus, and of course carries with it the right to participate as shareholders in the management of the corporation.

Promoters' Shares.—Promoters' shares are issued by corporations in payment of the services of the promoters in the organization of such companies. The issue of this stock, while quite common in England, is very infrequent in this country, payment being usually demanded by our bankers or promoters either in money, mortgage bonds, perferred, or common stock. A promoter's share is entitled to participation in the final net earnings of a company only after payment of all accrued obligations, including the establishment of any sinking fund or surplus which either the articles of incorporation or the constitution and by-laws or the bonds or mortgages provide for; but, as it is entitled to absorb the final amount remaining, in the absence of provision in the other stocks to the contrary, after the above payments they sometimes become very valuable.

Dividends.—Dividends, it must be remembered, stand to the stockholder in the same relation that the division of the profits of a private business do to the partners therein, consequently they should only be declared, and can legally only be paid, after the payment of all accrued indebtedness, including the setting aside and creation of any fund or funds which the corporation binds itself to its creditors to create and set aside.

Stocks are sold "dividend" or "ex-dividend." When a dividend is declared a day is fixed for the closing of the transfer books of the company, after which date no transfers can be made until the books have been reopened. On the morning of the day that the books are closed the stock is sold on the New York Stock Exchange "ex-dividend"—an amount equal to that of the dividend declared being deducted from the price at which the stock would ordinarily be sold. It is needless to say that this applies only to sales on the exchange, as a private purchaser can stipulate that the dividend be included, or not, as he chooses—the result, however, being practically the same.

Guaranteed Stock.—Stocks of subsidiary, auxiliary, leased, or rented properties are often—in fact generally—guaranteed by the principal company. Usually in case of lease or rental, however, only the interest is guaranteed by the lessee company, unless it be a lease for a period which means practical ownership or control, when both principal and interest are guaranteed.

In the case of a leased company such a guarantee constitutes a claim which must be paid even before the fixed charges of the lessee company. The default of payment abrogates the contract, with the institution of such penalty against the guarantor as may be stipulated. Thus often companies which were at one time very prosperous are dragged down by the weight of guarantees on securities of their connections or branches which were hastily and unwisely taken into their systems.

Trust companies and bankers are frequently appointed as the fiscal agents of corporations for the purpose of registering and certifying to the regularity of the issue of stocks.

A brief explanation of such terms as "Assented" stock, "First Assessment paid," etc., is desirable. Stocks thus designated usually remain in the hands of holders, and their character is only so far changed as indicated by the words which are stamped or written upon them. This is done by the trustee. In cases where an assessment is found necessary, the holders of the security assessed are requested to bring such security to the firm, bank, or trust company having the matter in charge, and have them certify by stamping or writing upon the security that the assessment has been paid. The same applies to the assent of security holders to any plan for merging them into, or exchanging for, other or new issues. They are thus stamped in order that they may be distinguished from others which have not paid the "assessment" or "assented" to the plan, as it will readily be seen that the compliance with the terms proposed in either case may affect the market values of the securities to a considerable extent.

The exchange quotations distinguish such securities by prefixing the abbreviations "1st (or 2d) Asst. pd." or "Assented," as the case may be. There are many other conditions under which bonds and stocks are stamped, in order to signify their acceptance of various propositions. The above instances are merely cited as illustrations.

Bonds.

The following observations on the above subject will be confined entirely to government and corporate bonds.

A bond is an instrument by which the maker binds himself under certain conditions to the performance of some particular thing. Government, State, or municipal bonds, properly so called, are seldom secured by a mortgage on anything beyond a certain portion of the taxing power of the maker, which may be pledged to the holder for the payment of the interest and principal of such bond. Village, town, district, county, and State warrants partake of the nature of bonds, and, in common with bonds issued by municipalities and States, are known as Investment Securities, and will be treated of under that head, to which the reader is referred.

Corporate Bonds.—The bonds of corporations are commonly known as mortgage bonds, and are secured by a mortgage upon its entire plant, franchises, and assets, or a portion thereof, the exact portion of which is or should be always stated in the mortgage to which the bond refers.

Attached to these bonds are coupons payable at given periods, generally semi-annually, stating that the holder is entitled to the interest then falling due. This is very convenient, as the coupon containing the number of the bond and signed by the proper officer or officers, without the presentation of the bond itself, shows the holder of such coupon to be entitled to the interest in it named, and of course is transferable on delivery.

A corporate bond, in common with all other bonds, is a written evidence of the obligation of the corporation to perform certain acts therein named in consideration of the payment to the company of a specified value (it is not intended to convey the impression that bonds are always sold for the amount stated on their face, they sometimes being sold at a premium and other times at a discount), for which the bond is a receipt, and a bondholder, consequently, is in the position of a creditor of the company, which, until the payment and cancellation of such bond, is indebted to him for the payment for which the bond is a receipt.

The rights of bondholders are determined by the language of the bond, as well as by the language of the mortgage securing the same, and the laws governing the issue of such bonds.

At the present time a mortgage securing the payment of corporate bonds is usually placed in the hands of a trustee, generally some trust company, which is supposed to act in behalf of the bondholders as a unit, and which is empowered by the language of the bond, in the event of the failure of the corporation to perform the obligations it assumes in said bond, to foreclose the mortgage and divide the proceeds of sale among the bondholders.

The practical question, and the one which really regulates the amount of the issue of bonds, is the ability of the company to finance or place them on the market. Where the bonded indebtedness is in excess of the value of the mortgaged property and the earning capacity of the corporation, it is much more difficult to secure purchasers than where the mortgaged property and the earning capacity forms an ample security for such bonds.

The laws in most States are designed especially for the benefit and protection of the public from the usurpation of power by corporations, and as in many companies—especially railroad and telegraph companies—valuable franchises are afforded them by the government, it in turn restricts the exercise of those franchises and limits a corporation in various ways, too numerous even to suggest here, and it is very essential to a determination of the value of either a share or a bond to know, first, the power given such corporation, and next, the legal limitations and restrictions upon the exercise of its corporate powers.

It must be borne in mind that bonds can only be issued by the consent and direction of the shareholders, because of the fact that their property becomes mortgaged in payment of such bonds, making them necessary parties.

Bonds of corporations constitute a variety of obligations, and are widely different in character and value. In the case of railroads, bonds are issued against the main line and branches, against the securities in their possession, against its rolling stock and equipment, and against its present or future earnings. In some cases bonds are secured by little, if anything, besides the promise and ability of the issuing corporation to pay.

The bonds of gas, telegraph, and electric companies are somewhat less complex and fewer in kind than those issued by railroad companies.

The denomination and nature of a bond, name of company issuing same, rate of interest, kind of coin in which it is to be redeemed, and the date of payment of principal are generally stated in its title, thus:

"$1000. ——— Railroad Co. First Mortgage, 5 % Gold Bond, Due 1903."

Also the name of the guaranteeing company, when the bond is guaranteed by another company.

Among the kinds of bonds dealt in on the New York Stock Exchange are the following: First Mortgage Bonds, Second Mortgage Bonds, Third Mortgage Bonds, First, Second, and Third Consolidated Mortgage Bonds, Income, First, Second, and Third Preference Bonds, Collateral Trust Bonds, Debenture Bonds, General Mortgage Bonds, Convertible Bonds, Sinking Fund Bonds, Improvement and Extension Bonds, Car Trust Bonds.

First Mortgage Bonds.—As the term implies, these bonds constitute a first lien upon the property of the company which issues them, that is, upon all property actually owned by the company at the time when the issue is made. In case, however, of the future absorption of other properties, a question naturally arises as to the right of the bondholders under the clauses generally contained in first mortgage bonds, constituting the bond a first lien "upon all property now owned or hereafter acquired," etc. When this provision is made there can be no doubt as to the rights of the holders of the first mortgage bonds, provided that in future acquirements of other companies the property of such companies has not been placed under a mortgage issued prior to its absorption. In the latter case the previous mortgage existing on the property acquired cannot be superseded by that of the company which absorbs it. Thus, in the case of many of the larger railway systems, we see mortgages which one not familiar with the properties would assume to be a first lien upon the entire plant, but which are really a first mortgage on only a portion of the system.

Second and Third Mortgage Bonds, in view of the above, need no description here. The claims of holders under these mortgages naturally coming in proper sequence. It is scarcely necessary to add that when such mortgages exist the interest thereon is paid after that of the first mortgage has been satisfied.

Consolidated Mortgage Bonds are generally issued to take up and fund the prior bonds existing on one or more parts of a system, but unless they possess a greater marketable value than is possessed by the bonds they are designed to replace, the holders of the other bonds will not part with them. A consolidated mortgage bond can only become a first lien on the assets and earnings of a property by the retirement of prior mortgages. Many companies, in issuing these bonds, retain in their treasuries a certain portion for the purpose of retiring previous bond issues, but as these prior bondholders are under no legal obligation to make such exchange, so long as they refuse so to do consolidated mortgage bonds constitute only a subsequent lien on the property and earnings.

Second Consolidated Bonds are issued by some corporations, and their bondholders are subsequent lienors to the first consolidated bondholders, in the same manner that the second mortgage bondholder comes after the first mortgage bondholder.

Income Bonds.—As indicated by their name, are usually secured by a mortgage on the earnings or income of a corporation after the payment of prior claims thereon. When secured by collateral they are known as "Collateral Income Bonds." Being frequently issued without a mortgage or some actual present security for their ultimate redemption, a sinking fund oftentimes is created for that purpose. These bonds are frequently nothing more than a promissory note of the issuer, with coupons attached, bearing a certain rate of interest payable at a specified date, in which case they are wholly dependent for their marketable value upon the earning capacity of the company.

Income bonds, in common with all other bonds, being a prior lien on the earnings of a corporation to that of any stock, often seriously decrease the value of such stock by diminishing the amount of earnings applicable for dividends thereon. In the case of St. John *vs.* Erie Railroad, it was sought by the preferred stockholders through the courts to compel the road to continue the payment of dividends on their stock, but the Court took the ground that the preferred stockholders, having voted for the incurring of this obligation, having ratified the action of the Board of Directors, and having used the money for betterments, *i. e.*, for their own benefit, were estopped from disclaiming the obligation, and that dividends on their stock could only be paid after the payment of interest on these bonds.

Collateral Trust Bonds.—As their name implies, these bonds are issued against collateral deposited with a trustee (most commonly some trust company), giving the trustee power to sell the collateral and redeem the bonds upon failure of the issuer to fulfil the conditions undertaken.

Collateral trust bonds consist of two sorts; first, the "Collateral Trust," where specific collateral is placed in the hands of a trustee to insure the performance by the corporation issuing these bonds of the payment of interest and principal when due. This collateral cannot be changed or converted. And secondly, "Convertible Collateral Trust Bonds," in which collateral is placed in the hands of the trustee for the same purpose as in the case of collateral trust bonds, but which collateral may be exchanged or converted at the option of the issuer with the consent of the trustee or bondholders. The collateral deposited to secure both bonds usually consists of the securities of other companies possessed by the issuers of such bonds.

Often, in addition to the collateral deposited with the trustee, a mortgage is made of a certain part of the property and assets of the corporation and given as further security.

For several reasons a convertible collateral trust bond would seem to be a more desirable bond than an inconvertible one, first, because the inconvertible bond is secured by an unchangeable security which may depreciate in value, when the holders of such bonds could not call upon the issuers to deposit further security, nor by the terms of the bond and mortgage could the issuers take advantage of any increase in the market value of the collateral, to dispose of it to their own or the bondholders' benefit. Of course it is true that in the case of convertible collateral the security is subject to the same depreciation, but here advantage may be taken of any appreciation in the collaterals, and other collaterals greater in value may be purchased, or should the collateral be sold, the proceeds of such sale can be deposited with the trustee to take up a certain portion of such bonds. Convertible collateral bonds frequently contain a provision giving the company the right to redeem them at a given price after a certain number of years.

The value of a collateral trust bond, either convertible or inconvertible, like that of any other bond, depends upon the collateral by which it is secured and the earning capacity of the issuer. These bonds are frequently issued upon the absorption by one corporation of one or more smaller companies.

Debenture Bonds.—A debenture bond is difficult to define exactly. It is generally considered to be little more or less than a note given by a company—a promise to pay. In the case of the debentures issued by the Chicago & Northwestern, due 1909 and 1933, respectively, and paying 5 per cent. interest, it is provided that " any future mortgage of the company, excepting any mortgages for the enlargement, betterment, or extension of the company's property, shall include these debentures."

A debenture bond may be a general lien on the property of a company, and like an income bond it generally contains specific provisions for liens on certain property and assets of a company, subject to the rights of prior mortgages.

In some States, where the laws in regard to mortgages are onerous, a debenture is issued by a company in preference to a second or third mortgage. As will be seen in the case above cited, they are also, in some instances, protected from being superseded by future mortgages, and must be included therein. Debenture bonds frequently contain a sinking-fund clause.

Like all other obligations, their value depends upon the character and standing of the corporations issuing them, and while in some cases they may represent little or nothing, when issued by companies of high standing they are desirable investments.

These bonds are also largely issued by mortgage and debenture companies, and are generally secured by the placing of mortgages given to the issuing company to secure loans on real estate, in the hands of a trustee, and constitute the collateral on which these bonds are issued.

General Mortgage Bonds.—As the name implies, they are a *general* mortgage on the property of a company. Like a consolidated bond, they may be a first lien on one portion of a system, a second on another, and so on. The value of a bond of this character can be ascertained only by knowing to what extent prior mortgage liens exist, and the value and earning power of the property by which it is issued and secured.

Sinking Fund.—Provision may be made in any bond for the creation and accumulation of a sinking fund with which to redeem such bond at maturity. This fund is generally accumulated by the setting aside each half year or year of an amount equal to a certain per cent. of the issue of bonds which it is created to pay. It constitutes a contract on the part of the issuer with the lender, is an obligation as binding upon the issuer as provision for the payment of coupons, and must be provided for out of the earnings of the company.

Redemption before Maturity.—A clause reserving to the company the right to redeem after the expiration of a certain time and before maturity may be incorporated in any bond.

Many bonds, on account of the incorporation of these various features, can hardly be designated as belonging to a particular class, but partake in some respects of the nature of several different classes of bonds.

Improvement and Extension Bonds.—These bonds are issued against improvements, betterments, additions, extensions, etc. In the case of extensions they may be a first lien upon the extension itself. They are guaranteed by the company under whose name they are issued. Some of these bonds, when they represent the outlay of money for permanent improvements and betterments, are considered an excellent investment. On the other hand, as is too often the case, unfortunately, bonds of this class are issued to cover expenditures which, properly, should have been chargeable to "operating expenses," and were not so charged by reason of reckless or incompetent management.

Car Trust Bonds.—These bonds are secured by a mortgage on the cars of the company named therein, and in case of the failure of the maker to meet the payments or perform the obligations therein incurred, the holders may seize the cars thereby mortgaged. They are generally issued by Car Trust or Rolling Stock companies.

Remarks.—In the foregoing pages we have endeavored to give a brief description of the bonds principally dealt in on the New York Stock Exchange and among financial institutions and investors. It is not our province to define the exact legal status of the different kinds of bonds; that can only be determined by experienced lawyers. The exact rights of the holder of a general or consolidated, an income or debenture bond, depend upon many circumstances and conditions, the laws of the State or

States under which the mortgagor is organized, the amount covered by prior mortgages, and the provisions of the bond itself.

Many bonds partake of the nature of several classes—thus a First Consolidated Sinking Fund, a General Consolidated. A General or an Income Bond where no second mortgage exists on a property may be practically on the same footing as a second mortgage on another property. In many cases a first mortgage is little better than worthless—in other instances a Debenture Bond may sell at a premium.

Some of our large corporations have so great a mania for issuing new obligations that it becomes difficult to invent a proper title for all of their bonds. It may be stated as a general rule, however, that very few corporations, and none of high standing, issue bonds which in their nature conflict with one another; thus we seldom see a consolidated mortgage bond and a general mortgage issued on the same property, or second and third mortgages where a consolidated, a collateral, or a general mortgage exists. In the first place the laws of many States seek to prevent confusion of rights; in the second, and what is more important to the companies, the investing public will not purchase at a good price securities on whose title a cloud rests.

Certificates of Indebtedness (Floating Debts).—Certificates of Indebtedness are frequently issued by corporations as evidence of their floating, accrued, unfunded debts. The holders of these certificates possess a claim on the property and assets of the company for the amount stated in such certificates, and if it is not paid within the time named they may apply for the appointment of a receiver.

Trust Company Receipts, Certificates of Deposit, etc.

Trust Companies' receipts and certificates of deposit, although securities which are of a temporary nature, require a brief description, as they are often listed, bought, and sold on the Stock Exchange the same as securities of a more permanent nature.

The certificates of deposit usually represent the deposit of securities under some plan for the readjustment, consolidation, or reorganization of properties, such securities being held in trust until the same has been effected.

The receipt by the trustee to the depositor for the security deposited with it enable such depositor to avoid the inconvenience and loss which he might suffer from inability to use the security so deposited ; the title to such security being transferable by the holder of the certificate, or it may be used by the holder as collateral in the securing of a loan.

Receivers' Certificates.

Once a property is placed under the management of a receiver, it is in the hands of the Court under whose jurisdiction the receivership has been granted.

The rules which ordinarily apply to the financiering of a corporation as regards its stock and bonds may, at the will of the receiver, if approved by the Court, be set aside. The receiver operates the property, under the direction of the Court, for the benefit of its security holders.

Receivers' Certificates are issued for the purpose of obtaining money for the company, and are seldom resorted to except in cases of absolute necessity or of great emergency. When a company is practically bankrupt and unable to either sell or obtain a loan upon its assets or securities ; when its plant, or road-bed and equipment, as the case may be, is in such condition as to render operation unsafe or impracticable ; or when payments for rentals, loans, cars necessary to conduct traffic, etc., must be made, otherwise involving disintegration of its system, or still further and more disastrous losses in earnings, it then becomes necessary to issue these certificates. They must be approved by the Court, and if objection is made to their issuance by security holders, a hearing is granted their attorney or counsel before such approval is granted.

When receivers' certificates have been duly approved and issued, they take precedence over every other obligation of a company, first mortgage bonds included. They constitute a first lien upon its earnings (excepting only the wages of employees and necessary expenses of operation), and upon its property.

In the face of any determined opposition from holders of first mortgage bonds or other securities of the company, and the submitting of evidence that such issue of certificates is unnecessary, their issue will hardly be allowed. They seldom cover an amount large enough to jeopardize or imperil the rights of bondholders; and, as stated above, are issued only to prevent further and greater losses which would ensue from the lack of funds which they are intended to raise.

These certificates, even when put forth by the receiver of the most hopelessly overburdened and overmortgaged company, are generally considered a perfectly safe investment by the most conservative financiers.

Investment Securities.

The United States, the different States, counties, townships, cities, villages, and school districts issue bonds payable at a specified date, on the principal of which interest is paid at the rate therein specified. These bonds are not secured by a mortgage on any real present value, and their worth consists entirely in the ability of the issuer through its taxing power to meet the obligations incurred.

States and cities issue also refunding bonds, which are bonds to refund either other bonds, or to secure funds to provide for the payment of outstanding obligations. The

Federal Government, State governments, city and county governments have also in many instances issued bonds to assist in corporate enterprises of a semi-public nature, such as the building of bridges, the laying of railroads, the erection of waterworks, etc.

Many cities issue bonds to provide for improvements; and some cities issue special assessment bonds, chargeable against the abutting property. By way of illustration: if they want to pave a street, or make other improvements of a local character in a particular part of the city, the city issues bonds chargeable against the property in the district benefited, but not against the whole city; the city merely acting as agent for the collection and payment of interest and principal.

Many of the States and cities issue Interest Warrants, which are payable within a given time, bearing a specified rate of interest, and are issued to provide needed funds.

These warrants are either paid at maturity or funded in bonds by their makers.

CHAPTER XIII.

Commercial Houses—Commercial Agencies.

Commercial Houses.—In order to form any just estimate of the financial operations of any large city, and in fact of the financial institutions, properly so-called, therein, it is necessary that we should have some adequate idea of the method by which the business of our larger commercial houses is conducted. While it is true that the great variety of business in which these houses are engaged necessitates more or less change in detail, the principles governing the management of the financial part of their business is practically the same in all well conducted houses.

It will be necessary, however, to give some brief outline of the method by which, first, the indebtedness is created by the selling of goods, before we come to the indebtedness itself, which constitutes the primary element in the finances of a house, and leads to their first dealings with financial houses. To proceed regularly, we will first consider the system under which the house obtains possession of the goods which it sells.

All large houses are divided primarily into what, for want of a better word, will have to be termed "departments." One, the Buying Department, through which all the goods sold by said house are purchased from various sources, and the other the Selling Department. Both of these departments, according to the magnitude of the business, are of course further divided into sub-departments.

Buying Department.—This department has charge of the goods purchased by the house, and is usually presided over by some member of the firm, who is supposed to be particularly familiar with the character, quantity, and quality of goods which have the readiest sale, and in which the house most extensively deals. In this department are employed numerous buyers, familiar with the market prices of the particular lines of goods which they have to buy, and whose duty it is to buy such goods as their firm or house may from time to time require, at the best possible prices, and, if occasion offers, to purchase such goods at particularly low prices, in anticipation even of the requirements of their house. These goods are, according to the finances of the house or according to the probabilities of immediate or remote sale, purchased for cash or on time, it being the policy of most houses to purchase for cash only those goods on which they receive a discount for cash, or goods which always have a steady or quick market. As a rule, thirty days is considered cash. These goods, on delivery, are received by the house and assigned to the different departments for which purchased. Each department is charged with the amount of goods so delivered, and credited with the amount sent out by them, the difference between the price paid and the price received for such goods showing the profit or loss of that department.

Selling Department.—The business of most of the larger houses is largely secured through travelling salesmen, to each of whom a certain territory is allotted. It is the business of these salesmen to travel from place to place endeavoring to secure orders for such goods as their houses sell, and not only are they credited with a commission on all goods sold by them personally, but are also generally credited with a commission on goods sold to persons residing within their territory. Some houses employ travelling salesmen only on salary, others on both salary and commission.

Of course all of the large houses have in their stores a number of salesmen on salary, on whose sales no commission is allowed, with which the travelling salesman has nothing to do, and in the amount of which sales he has no interest.

Upon the receipt of orders not paid for in cash, either from travelling salesmen or in the store, the order is submitted first to the Credit Department, which investigates the standing, ability to pay, and general promptness in meeting his obligations of the purchaser. This information is usually obtainable from the mercantile agencies, the chief of which are the R. G. Dun & Co. and the Bradstreets, which publish periodically reports of the standing of all merchants in the country whose assets exceed one thousand dollars. But as these reports are only published quarterly, it often happens that the information given in their publications is several months old, and more recent information is desirable. When such is needed, the credit department asks for a statement up to date of the condition of such purchaser, which information is usually furnished, but sometimes the agencies are necessarily delayed in supplying it. A well-managed credit department will not rely entirely upon the reports of mercantile agencies, knowing that often the reports given to these agencies are highly colored, and while not necessarily dishonest and fraudulent, are liable to be influenced by the expectations of the persons of whom such reports are desired, but will make inquiry among the other houses which they think have probably dealt with the purchaser, and if no satisfactory information is obtained either from the agencies or from their brother merchants, a letter is written the purchaser, asking for letters of reference to persons with whom he has dealt, and usually a letter is likewise written to the travelling salesman, asking for what information he can furnish. If this information is not satisfactory, and the ability of the purchaser to pay is doubted, a careful credit department will immediately recommend that the order be not filled, and this ends the matter. If, however, the purchaser's credit is good, and his obligations are promptly met, the order is next submitted to the order clerk, by whom the prices at which the goods were sold are approved, or not. If not approved, the salesman is usually called to account for selling goods below the prices given him in his weekly price-list, which is compiled by these order clerks under the direction of some member of the firm ; or sometimes on their own responsibility alone, and the order is filled or not, according as the prices are acceptable or otherwise.

Assuming the price to be satisfactory and the credit good, the order is next sent to the various departments and the goods collected together in the Packing Department, where they are packed for shipment. The packages are then sent down to the Shipping Department, where the shipping clerk ships the same to their destination.

From the various departments from which the goods are drawn are sent to the Counting-House Department a list of the goods, and these are entered and invoiced by the entry clerks, who make up bills, which are mailed on the date of the shipment of the goods or at the end of the month, according to the practice prevailing in the particular house or the arrangement between the purchaser and the seller. Next, the entries of the entry clerks in total are entered to the debit of the purchaser by the ledger clerks, in the ledger account of the purchaser.

At the end of the month, or at the time agreed upon, drafts are drawn by the house upon the persons to whom these goods have been shipped. These drafts, according to the necessities of the drawer, are deposited for collection or discount in the bank with which such firm deals, and are there entered for collection or to the credit of the house and sent by the bank to their different agents throughout the country. Such drafts as are not paid upon presentation are returned to the bank, charged against the firm's account, if previously credited, and returned to the firm, and have either to be made good by the firm or are charged against their account, as stated.

Most of the large firms allow a small discount for cash payments.

Commercial Agencies.

No more striking proof can be adduced of the change in our business and financial methods from those prevailing fifty years ago than the very existence of these agencies, now so important a factor in our commercial life. Now all careful business men make a most thorough inquiry in regard to the standing of the persons with whom they have dealings, and as this information is necessarily largely supplied through the quarterly reports of these agencies, and as business men know that any one withholding such information from them simply injures himself, they are themselves willing generally to give the agencies the information sought about their business and finances.

In this country there are two principal agencies, known in almost every village, with branch offices in every city in the States, and also in all the larger towns. These companies furnish, in addition to their quarterly publications supplied each subscriber, information in regard to the present standing of any person engaged in business in any part of the United States or Canada. At stated times they gather information as to the standing of persons in their district, which in a condensed form is contained in the agencies' periodical publications. Where later and immediate information is needed they also obtain that, and forward it to the office or person seeking the same.

Almost every trade also has its special agency, which devotes its energies entirely to that particular trade.

Commercial agencies do not confine their attention solely to the gathering and supplying of information, but are also large collection agencies, besides which their reports of the condition of business, crops, etc., etc., are very generally relied on by both the public and the press.

Bradstreet's and R. G. Dun & Co. are the agencies referred to, each of whom have offices on Broadway, within a couple of blocks of each other. They issue to their subscribers quarterly a large book, conveniently arranged, giving the names of all men in every part of the country, doing a class of business in which they would probably need credit, and giving their ratings, as indicating by letters the amount a man or firm is worth is termed. Should later information than that contained in the last publication be desired, either of these agencies will make every effort to furnish the same to a suscriber.

While it may be said that credits extended nowadays are largely upon the strength of these reports, yet most of the wholesale houses and banks have credit departments of their own in charge of a man whose principal business is to be thoroughly posted on the credits of the people with whom they deal or are likely to deal, and these "credit men" often seek information from each other, when not satisfied with that given by the agencies. Most large extenders of credit are subscribers to both agencies.

The agencies require that books furnished subscribers shall be used only by them or their clerks, and any information furnished a subscriber shall be used only for his benefit; but these requirements are principally honored in their non-observance.

To gather, arrange, condense, print, and disseminate the information collected from every town and village in the United States and Canada, and about almost every merchant or tradesman in each town, requires a vast number of employees scattered all over the country, and this each of the larger agencies has.

Should information furnished by an agency, except where obtained from the injured person, be injurious to the credit of a person, and such information be proven to be false, the courts have held that he has a cause of action against the agency for the damage he has sustained through the injury thereby done to his credit. Or should credit be extended on the strength of information given by a commercial agency, which information was clearly inaccurate, and the agent of such agency could easily have discovered it to be inaccurate, the agency can be held for the damage thereby suffered.

CHAPTER XIV.

Transmission and Remittance of Money—Money Orders—Cheque Banks—Commercial Bills—Cable and Telegraph Transfers.

Transmission and Remittance of Money.

PERHAPS the greatest achievement of modern business and banking is the safety and celerity with which money can be transmitted from person to person and from place to place, although, owing to the high state of development of the financial systems of the world, the actual shipment of money has been minimized to an extent that but few of us realize.

While a great many transactions that once required the shipment of money are now adjusted by bills of exchange, yet there is still, especially in domestic transactions involving small amounts, a necessity for the sending of the money itself; and the certainty with which a dollar or a hundred million dollars may be transported has probably done more than anything else to steady and regulate the finances of the world. In this certainty and quickness of shipment the steam-engine and the telegraph have been the most potent factors, the telegraph putting the whole financial world in instant communication, the steam-engine, with greater certainty than has ever before been attained by human ingenuity, delivering the merchandise of which the telegraph gave notice.

The ability of London, New York, Paris, or Berlin, or, in fact, any other city to call upon other cities and countries of the world for aid, and their power to instantly extend a similar accommodation, has been one of the most important developments of modern progress, making the financial transactions of the most widely separated countries almost as easy and certain of adjustment and settlement as the transactions had between two bankers located in the same city. One result of this rapidity and security of transmission is that the cities or countries which have large amounts of money seeking investment instantly come to the aid of the countries in need of financial assistance, the first desiring to buy and the second to sell or borrow.

The issue of credits, exchange, is so intimately connected with the actual shipment of money as to render a separation of the two here undesirable. Nor is such separation at all necessary, as exchange has already been treated, and only reference will be made to that part of the transmission of money which is accomplished, or rather the actual shipment avoided thereby.

First, as to actual shipment of money, by which is meant the shipment from one point to another of the money itself. This is done by the various steamship, transportation, and express companies in the same way that they carry other commodities, only greater safeguards are used to insure the safety of the money while in transit.

1. By registered letter. This is a letter containing the money to be remitted, and is registered and receipted for at the post-office. The receiver of such letter must receipt for the same upon delivery.

2. By express companies, who carefully count the amount of money to be sent, place the same in an envelope, and securely seal the envelope with sealing-wax in the presence of the person remitting. The envelope is then sent to the person to whom addressed, who, upon delivery, must receipt for the same.

The fact that express companies are known to be the

carriers of large sums of money, and that those sums are always in a particular car, leads to various train robberies, usually at those seasons of the year when great amounts are remitted from the Eastern money centres to the West. It would seem to be safer to send money in ordinary freight cars, where the location of the particular car, and the box or bundle containing it, which need not be even disclosed to the trainmen or conductor, would render its transit much more secure than the present method, although, of course, the objection would be that this would consume too much time, and the money would be earning no interest during its transit.

Payments are most frequently made, not by the shipment of money, but by a transfer of credits. This has been already dwelt upon at considerable length, and the various ways in which credits are transferred will therefore only be enumerated here, and reference made to the pages of this book setting forth the same more in detail.

1. By post-office order, commonly called money orders, which are divided into domestic and international money orders.

"The maximum amount for which a single money order may be issued at an office designated as a 'money order office' is $100, and at an office designated as a 'limited money order office,' $5. When a larger sum is to be sent, additional orders must be obtained. But postmasters are instructed to refuse to issue in one day to the same remitter, and in favor of the same payee, on any one post-office of the fourth class, money orders amounting in the aggregate to more than $300, as such office might not have funds sufficient for immediate payment of any large amount. Fractions of a cent are not to be introduced."

The remitter who desires to relieve the payee or his indorsee or attorney from the inconvenience of proving identity at the office of payment, by the testimony of another person, may do so, at his own risk, which waiver is stamped on the order.

"In the application the given names of the remitter and payee, or the initials thereof, should precede their surnames, respectively. If the payee has only one given name, it should be written in full, if known to the remitter. For example, the name John Jones should be so written, and not as J. Jones. Observance of this rule will tend to prevent mistakes and delay in payment."

"A money order must not be made payable to more than one person or firm."

"Names of firms, places, and streets, as well as amounts, should be written in full and in the plainest manner possible. As in many cases there are several post-offices of the same name in different States, the applicant should be very careful to write legibly the name of the State in which the office he means is located."

The payee named in the order may endorse it to another, but more than one endorsement is prohibited.

These orders should be collected within a year from the date of issue, to collect after which time it is necessary to apply for a duplicate and again pay the amount of the original fee.

FEES CHARGED FOR MONEY ORDERS.

For orders for sums not exceeding $2.50	3 cents.
Over $2.50 and not exceeding 5.00	5 "
" 5.00 " " 10.00	8 "
" 10.00 " " 20.00	10 "
" 20.00 " " 30.00	12 "
" 30.00 " " 40.00	15 "
" 40.00 " " 50.00	18 "
" 50.00 " " 60.00	20 "
" 60.00 " " 75.00	25 "
" 75.00 " " 100.00	30 "

INTERNATIONAL MONEY ORDERS.

What has been said in regard to domestic money orders applies, except as below stated:

"Remitters will please take notice that the maximum amount for which a money order may be drawn, payable in the United Kingdom, Cape Colony, or British Guiana, is $50."

"There is no limitation to the number of international orders that may be issued in one day to a remitter, in favor of the same payee."

"The postmaster must refuse to issue an international order payable to any person, if the surname and the initial letters of that person's given names are not furnished by the applicant, unless the payee be a peer or a bishop, in which case his ordinary title is sufficient. If the payee be a firm, the usual commercial designation of such firm will suffice, such as 'Baring Bros.,' 'Smith & Son,' 'Jones & Co.'"

Rates of commission, in United States currency, charged for issuing all international money orders:

For orders for sums of $10 or less					10 cents.
Over $10 and not exceeding $20					20 "
" 20 " " 30					30 "
" 30 " " 40					40 "
" 40 " " 50					50 "
" 50 " " 60					60 "
" 60 " " 70					70 "
" 70 " " 80					80 "
" 80 " " 90					90 "
" 90 " " 100					$1.00 "

2. By check, either of an individual or bank, certified or uncertified. (See Checks.)

3. By cashier's check. (See Cashier's Checks.)

4. By drafts. (See Drafts.)

5. By bills of exchange, domestic or foreign. (See Domestic Exchange and Foreign Exchange.)

For large amounts this is certainly the method most generally employed for the reasons stated in the chapters devoted to those subjects.

6. By certificates of deposit, receipts from banks or bankers of the deposit of certain sums, made payable to a person designated by the depositor, and payable at the agency of the issuer. (See Certificates of Deposit.)

7. By letters of credit. (See Letter of Credit.)

8. By checks issued by the express companies upon the plan described in the article on Cheque Banks.

9. In Great Britain and Canada by checks of cheque banks. This method does not prevail in this country to any appreciable extent.

Cheque Banks.—Cheque banks operate almost exclusively in England, where they were established more than half a century ago. The object of their existence is to furnish persons desiring to remit money other than by post-office orders a convenient mode for so doing, the bank issuing its check to the individual, payable to the person named by him, upon the payment by the purchaser of the amount of the check plus a small commission. The checks of these banks, whose business is confined to the issuing of such checks, are largely used by persons not having bank accounts and who cannot therefore send their own checks, and who are not willing to take the risk of sending bank notes, which at present in England are not issued in denominations of less than five pounds, and hence are not suitable for the payment of smaller amounts. By way of illustration, a person desiring to remit, say two pounds, will purchase at a cheque bank their check for that amount payable to the order of a person named, and mail the same to the person to whom it is payable, who can cash the same not only at any banker's, but, upon endorsement, at almost any tradesman's.

After endorsement, these checks pass from hand to hand, just the same as any currency. The check is so prepared that it cannot be raised.

This system is very largely used in the British Isles,

and while at first it was unsuccessful, owing to inefficient management, has since grown to enormous proportions.

These banks, however, would be of doubtful utility in this country, and hence have obtained but little foothold.

Commercial Bills.—Next we will consider Commercial Bills, which are drafts drawn by a person or persons in one country on a person or persons in another, in payment of merchandise received, held for account of, or in transit to the persons against whom they are drawn.

These bills are either sent directly abroad for collection or sold by the drawer to some dealer in exchange in his city, most frequently the latter. The price at which they are purchased by the dealers is governed by the condition of the exchange market, and the length of time the bills have to run. Those payable on sight are generally purchased at the market rate for exchange, and those payable on time at the market rate of the exchange, minus the rate of interest prevailing in the country where such bill is payable, from the date of its purchase to the time of its maturity, which interest is deducted when the bill is purchased. It follows that "time bills," as they are called, are nearly always sold at a discount, as it very rarely happens that the discount on exchange is so great as to offset the interest charges.

These bills, when offered for sale, should always be accompanied by warehouse receipt, showing the storage of the goods against which they are drawn to the order of the drawee, or bills of lading showing the shipment of the goods to the person against whom the bill is made out, otherwise the purchaser has no evidence that the draft is drawn against any real value. The bill of lading or warehouse receipt is delivered to the purchaser of the draft, so that he may be in a position to enforce the payment of the draft, or hold the goods, and sell them to reimburse himself.

Cable and Telegraph Transfers.—The system of the transfer of money by telegraphic order originated during the late war, and at first was confined entirely to domestic business. The inception of the system seems to have been this: a person desiring to remit a sum to another at a distant point, deposited the amount to be remitted with a telegraph office and instructed them to send an order by telegraph to their office at the desired point to pay, to the order of the person named, the sum of money deposited, the person named in such order being also sent a telegram, to call at the office and receive the same. This represents the simplest form of a transfer of money, by telegram, and in this form the business is carried on very largely by telegraph companies.

The availability of this method of transfer of money, not only in domestic exchange, but also in foreign exchange, soon became apparent to bankers and commercial men, and if it could be applied successfully by a telegraph company for the transfer of limited amounts, it could certainly be applied to greater advantage by large banking houses or bankers having on hand great sums of money. Probably the next step in the development of this system was the depositing of the actual money with a banker selling telegraphic transfers of money called "cables" and receiving his cable order on his correspondent in another city, for the amount purchased, and also a cable to the person in whose favor the order was drawn apprising him of such order and directing him to call and collect the same. Naturally such transfers are effected at a charge proportionate to the rate of exchange then prevailing to the point on which the transfer was issued, together with the cable and telegraphic charges necessary to consummate such transfer.

Telegraph transfers (by which is meant domestic transfers) are made either by the telegraph companies themselves of small amounts, and of larger amounts principally by banks, whereas cable transfers (by which is meant the transfer of money to foreign countries) are effected through exchange dealers, usually private bankers.

Most papers, in their commercial news, quote ordinary exchange, commercial bills, and cable transfers. The rates of all three differ for the reasons heretofore given in this work.

CHAPTER XV.

Notes—Endorsements—Drafts—Bills of Exchange—Notary Presentation—Protest—Notice of Protest—Checks—Course of Check through a Bank—Cashiers' Checks—Certificates of Deposit—Letters of Credit—Table Showing U. S. Treasurer's Valuation of Foreign Coins—Table Giving Weight of Alloyed and Pure Metal of Units of Value of Principal Countries.

Notes.—A note is a written or a partly printed and written promise made by one or more persons to pay to one or more persons, named or unnamed, a certain sum of money at a given date.

Bouvier's *Law Dictionary* defines a note as "A written promise to pay a certain sum of money, at a future time, unconditionally." This definition, however, does not seem so comprehensive and explicit as that first given.

And as we are dealing with notes as negotiable instruments, we will only consider them when drawn in such form as to hold the maker thereof, for the amount stated in such note, of which the very first element is that the note shall have been given for value, hence all notes should read "Value received."

The following is the form of note generally used:

"$........   NEW YORK............188....
    "....................after date..........promise to
pay to the order of...
....$\frac{}{100}$ Dollars
....
value received.
No........   Due........   ...."

It is a well recognized principle of law that a note given without consideration cannot be enforced by a person having knowledge of that fact, but a note given, though without consideration, may be enforced by an innocent holder, who purchased the same for a consideration.

Notes may be drawn by any number of persons, payable to one or more persons, and are transferable by endorsement.

Notes may be endorsed in some nine different ways, each imposing a different liability upon the endorser or endorsers thereof. The different kinds of endorsements are stated with much brevity and clearness by Mr. Bolles in his work on *Practical Banking*, which we take the liberty of quoting.

"An endorsement may be (1) in full, or (2) in blank; it may be (3) absolute, or (4) unconditional; it may be (5) restrictive; it may be (6) without recourse on the endorser; and there may be (7) joint endorsements of the instrument, (8) successive endorsements, and (9) irregular ones. An endorsement in full mentions the name of the person in whose favor it is made, and to whom, or to whose order the sum described in the note is to be paid. An endorsement in blank consists simply of the name of the endorser written on the back of the instrument. 'The receiver of a negotiable instrument endorsed in blank, or any *bond fide* holder of it, may write over it an endorsement in full to himself, or to another, or any contract consistent with the character of an endorsement, but he could not enlarge the liability of the endorser in blank by writing over it a waiver of any of his rights, such as demand and notice.' By an absolute endorsement the endorser binds himself to pay on no other condition than the failure of the prior parties to do so, and of due notice to him of their failure, while a conditional endorsement contains some other condition to the endorser's liability. An endorsement may be so worded as to restrict the further negotiability of the instrument; it is then called a restrictive endorsement. The words 'for collection,' which are frequently written on notes that are put in a bank to be collected render the endorsement restrictive. The endorser in such a case may prove that he is not the owner of the note, and did not mean to give a title to it or its proceeds when collected. Such an endorsement merely makes the endorsee agent for the endorser in collecting the note. The sixth kind is a qualified endorsement, or endorsement without recourse. This consists in writing the words 'without recourse,' or 'at the endorsee's own risk' on the back of the note. The endorser is then a mere assignor of the title to the note, and is relieved of all responsibility for its payment. A joint endorsement is made when a note is payable to several persons who are not partners. Successive endorsements are those made by several persons on a note, the legal effect of which is to subject them as to each other in the order they endorse. The endorsement imparts a several and successive, and not a joint obligation. Lastly may be mentioned irregular endorsements, which may originate in various ways. But in all cases an endorser guarantees the genuineness of all the preceding endorsements."

It may be well to add that, in the use of irregular endorsements, a person placing his name upon the back of a negotiable note or bill is presumed, in law, to have intended to become liable as second endorser, and that on the face of the paper, without explanation, he is regarded as second endorser and therefore not liable to the payee, who is supposed to be the first endorser. The explanation required is that such endorsement was made for the sole purpose of giving the maker credit with the payee.

Drafts.—A draft is a written order drawn by one or more persons in favor of one or more persons on a third person or persons for a specified amount payable at a named date.

On the next page is given the usual form:

"$1000.
                    "NEW YORK, January 10, 1893.

   "*Ten days after sight* pay to the order of *John Doe*

         one thousand dollars value received

and charge the same to account of

              "*Smith, Brown, & Co.*

"No. *1045*.

"To

   "*James Stimpson & Co.*
         "*Brattleboro, Vt.*"

. The principal distinction between a check and a draft is that a draft is generally drawn on some person or corporation residing or doing business in a different place from that in which the drawer resides, and is dependent for its payment upon the acceptance of the person against whom it is drawn, and who may decline to accept or pay it, and no criminal liability would attach to the drawer, whereas a check is drawn only against a deposit of money or a previously agreed credit, and the drawer of which, should there be no funds to meet it, renders himself liable to criminal prosecution, or the bank or banker refusing to pay such check if there are funds, to a civil action for damages for the injury to the drawer's credit and reputation.

After a draft is accepted it becomes a promise to pay on the part of the acceptor, and he can be held thereon as on a note.

Drafts constitute the most common form of domestic exchange and are purchased by both individuals and banks for that purpose.

They may be transferred to another by the person in

whose favor they are drawn, by indorsement in any of the different forms given in regard to notes.

When these drafts are drawn against a person to whom merchandise has been sold or consigned they are known as commercial bills. They sometimes take the name of the produce which they are drawn against; thus we have "cotton bills" drawn against the sales of cotton, and so on.

The persons selling or consigning the merchandise draws his draft against the buyer or consignee, and with the order for the merchandise, and the warehouse certificate or bill of lading attached to such draft (technically known as "the papers"), offers the same for sale to his bank, which purchases the same at the market rate of exchange on the place at which the draft is payable, less interest on the amount of the draft from the date of its purchase to its maturity, which is deducted from the amount paid over. The draft is then sent to its place of payment for collection, and when collected the amount is either remitted or credited to the bank. The same bank will also sell exchange on the city at which its draft is payable, but at a higher rate than it will purchase at, as no bank can afford to sell exchange as cheap as it will buy it.

The dealings in domestic exchange are confined almost entirely to banks, whereas dealings in foreign exchange are conducted almost entirely through private houses, known as Dealers in Exchange.

Bills of Exchange.—The chapter on exchange is designed to give the principles governing exchange, rather than the machinery by which such exchange is effected. Hence it is necessary to say a few words about the papers commonly used in the purchase and sale of exchange.

First will be considered bills of exchange, which are used almost exclusively in foreign exchange, and of which the following is the general form:

"New York, August 1, 1893.

" Exchange for £100.

" Ten days after sight of this our First of Exchange (second and third of the same tenor and date unpaid) pay to the order of James Brown One Hundred Pounds sterling, and charge the same, without further advice, to

"Drexel & Co.

" To
    "Baring Brothers,
        "London.

" No. 420."

From the above it will be seen that these bills are issued in triplicate, each copy bearing the same number, and upon the payment of one the others are rendered void. The reason for this issuance in triplicate is to provide against loss, two copies being sent, each by a different steamer, or route, and a third retained by the purchaser. These bills are also transferable upon endorsement as in the case of notes and drafts, the person to whom the same is endorsed, or the holder thereof for a consideration, being the legal owner.

"Notary" Presentation,—Protest, Notice of Protest.

In connection with notes, drafts, and bills of exchange, it is very important that some general remarks as to the due presentation, protest, and notice of protest should be made. This necessitates some statement of the duties of the "Notary."

Presentation.—Banks, acting either as principals or collecting agents, as a matter of courtesy and precaution, generally give the makers of notes and the acceptors of drafts and bills of exchange informal notice several days before maturity of the time and place of payment of such paper held by them, by mailing or leaving a notice to that effect at the place where the paper is payable.

During the morning of maturity if such paper is not

paid a formal presentation and demand for payment is made by the bank or holder.

Protest.—At the close of banking hours such matured paper as remains unpaid is handed to the notary for presentation protest and notice to the endorsers or drawers. The notary should, irrespective of any number of previous presentations, again present the paper at its place of payment before protesting the same. In New York and Brooklyn, however, a number of notaries, particularly those who are officers or employés of the banks for which they act, make no personal presentation, and treating the employés of the banks making formal presentations as their clerks, rely upon such presentations for their protests. In these cases the ordinary certificate of protest which affirms a personal presentation by a notary is obviously false, and, to conform to the facts, should be changed to read "has caused the same to be presented," or it was presented, "by my clerk." In which latter instance, while the protest is probably sufficient to hold an endorser or drawer, proof of presentation can only be made by the person who actually presented the paper.

Drafts or bills of exchange may and should be protested immediately upon the refusal of the drawee to accept.

Notice of Protest.—In the case of notes notice of protest should be mailed or presented the day of protest or early the next business day to the last and each preceding endorser on the protested paper. While the notary has discharged his duty by sending notice to the last endorser only, and the preceding endorsers are thereby held, most careful notaries send notice of protest not only to each endorser, but to the last endorser copies which he may himself send to his prior endorsers. In order that a subsequent endorser may maintain an action against his prior endorsers, he should immediately upon or early the day following send a copy of such notice to each preceding endorser.

Where an endorser whose street address is unknown resides in the city in which the paper is payable, notice addressed thus, "John Jones, New York City, N. Y.," and deposited in the General Post Office, is deemed sufficient. Where the address is known or by due diligence can be obtained it should be placed on the envelope.

In the case of drafts or bills of exchange notice of protest should be mailed the drawer and endorsers as above upon failure of the drawee to accept or pay the same.

It has been held in the majority of States, and may be taken to be the law generally, that a notice of protest deposited within the proper time in the General Post Office is sufficient notice to charge the drawer or endorsers. This is certainly the law in New York State. The denial of the receipt of a notice of protest in an action on a promissory note or draft clearly avails nothing. The denial must be of the proper mailing or giving of notice.

Checks.—A check is an order, usually on a banker or bank, to pay either to the person in whose favor it is drawn, or some subsequent endorsee the amount stated on its face. Many checks, however, are drawn to "bearer," in which case the bank may pay the amount called for to the person presenting the same without incurring liability in the event of the wrong person obtaining the money.

The following is the form of check most generally used in New York:

"New York, January 2, 1894.

"No. 513.

".............. NATIONAL BANK.

"Pay to the order of Richard Roe

One Thousand Dollars.

"$1000.00.

"John Doe."

Some banks, however, supply their depositors with what is known as the Chicago check, on which the dollar sign is placed at the end of the line beginning with the words " Pay to the order of."

Richard Roe, in order to receive payment on his check, or to enable another person to do so, must endorse the check, by writing his name across the back of it. The proper way to do this is to place the check face downwards with the beginning of the lines pointed away from the writer, and then write Richard Roe across the back well toward the top, so as to permit of other endorsements. As a rule, it is very unwise to endorse a check merely with the name of the drawee, unless it is the object of such drawer to have some person unknown to the teller collect the same, in which event any person getting possession of the check might collect the money. It is preferable to endorse the check to the person whom it is desired shall be paid, thus:

" Pay to the order of

JOHN BROWN.

RICHARD ROE."

or, if the check is to be deposited, it should be endorsed thus :

" For deposit in................Bank.

" RICHARD ROE."

Then should the check come into the possession of a person not entitled thereto, this prevents him from getting the money therefor.

The signatures on checks have been so often forged or the amounts thereof raised that numerous devices and precautions have been adopted to lead to the immediate detection of either, for neither can be prevented. Perhaps the safest way to ensure the immediate detection of the forgery is to have every blank check in the check-book numbered consecutively by machinery; never draw a check out of its regular order, frequently see that no checks have been abstracted, and in case the stubs and the body of the checks are filled out by clerks, sign the checks before they are torn out of the book. Checkbooks, when not in use, should be locked up in a safe or some other secure place. The check itself should be always of tinted paper, so that if an acid is used to remove any portion of the writing that something else may be substituted, the acid will take out the color along with the ink and render discovery easy.

The method usually adopted in England to prevent the removal of one word or figure and the substitution of another is the employment of chemically prepared check paper, in combination with a chemical ink, when, should the figures or words written on the check be removed by acid, the chemical ingredients of the ink as well as of the paper, combined with the chemicals used to abstract the words or figures, eat a hole in the paper and thus render the insertion of other words or figures impossible.

Lines should be drawn from the end of the name of the person to whom the check is made payable to the end of the line, so as to prevent the insertion of the words "or bearer." The same thing should be done in regard to the line on which the amount is spelled out, otherwise it is easy to insert some word raising the amount. Numerous plans are tried to prevent the raising of checks. The most common at present is to cut, with a machine constructed for that purpose, the figures representing the amount of dollars called for, immediately preceded by a dollar sign and followed by a period. This prevents the insertion of any figure between these signs. The amount of the cents is usually omitted.

Another device is to perforate the figures stating the amount with a stamp prepared for that purpose, which renders it difficult to change the amount of the figures.

Nothing is so difficult to simulate as the natural handwriting, and any teller will say that strained and artificial signatures, even when intricate and embellished with many flourishes, are much easier to forge than those written in the ordinary hand.

In reference to intermediate endorsements of a check, while it is advisable that the receiving or paying teller, as the case may be, should exercise care to such an extent as to see that they have been properly made, and that the check is rightfully in the hands of the person presenting the same for payment or deposit, still it is not possible that a teller should be acquainted with the genuineness of each intermediate endorsement, nor is it necessary, as he is not likely to pay a check to a person unknown to him, and if the check is received for deposit and returned, the depositor's account will simply be charged with the amount of such check which formed a part of his credit.

Checks should be deposited for collection, or cashed, certainly within two days of their receipt, and preferably the same day, where possible, as procrastination in this matter may render the collection impossible.

Persons receiving uncertified checks for large amounts should take them immediately to the bank and have them certified. Such checks are generally certified previous to payment, and if not, as a rule should be.

Course of a Check through a Bank.—The person to whom a check is given presents the same to the paying teller for payment at the bank, who, if the presenter is properly identified, and the drawer's account shows a sufficient net credit, pays the check, which is then charged upon a book kept by him for that purpose, to the account of the drawer, and is then handed over to a clerk who takes the same, along with others, to the bookkeeper keeping the depositors' ledger in which the name of such drawer would appear. The bookkeeper charges the same to the account of the drawer and files the check. At the end of the month or at some stated period when the drawer's passbook is balanced, the amount of the check is entered on a slip, on one side of which are the credits and on the other side the amount of the checks drawn, which, along with the checks marked "Paid" and the pass book in which the balance is recorded, are then returned to the depositor.

Cashiers' Checks.—These are checks issued by banks over the signature of the Cashier for the payment of the sum of money stated therein. They are frequently purchased by persons desiring to remit money, and constitute perhaps one of the commonest forms of exchange. The object of their purchase is that the check of a bank is a more readily transferable instrument than the check of an individual, even when certified. It is usually drawn upon a particular bank, and the charge made therefor is the prevailing rate of exchange upon the city on which it is payable.

Certificates of Deposit.—Certificates of Deposit are often used as a means of transmitting money, and are, of course, necessarily transferable on endorsement.

They are really nothing but receipts from banks that certain amounts of money have been deposited, which they will on demand repay either to the depositors or to some person named in writing by the depositor on the face of such certificate.

A certificate of deposit can also be made payable in whole or in part at some agency of the bank, by the bank directing such payment on its face.

This, however, is not a very frequent method of transmitting money, being much more troublesome and no better than a certified check. It is used mostly by people who either do not have, or do not intend to keep in the bank issuing the same, a regular account.

The following is the common form of such certificate:

<table>
<tr><td rowspan="6">CERTIFICATE OF DEPOSIT.</td><td colspan="2">THE NATIONAL BANK OF _____,</td></tr>
<tr><td>$_____ _____, Mass.,_____ 187__</td></tr>
<tr><td>_____ha__ deposited in this Bank</td></tr>
<tr><td>_____ Dollars</td></tr>
<tr><td>payable to the order of _____
on the return of this Certificate properly endorsed.</td></tr>
<tr><td>No._____   _____
                                              Cashier.</td></tr>
</table>

Letters of Credit.—A Letter of Credit is a letter issued by one or more persons, usually a firm of bankers, addressed to one or any number of persons who may or may not be named therein, authorizing them to pay to the person or persons in whose favor it is drawn, the whole or any part then due of the amount for which it is issued, and guaranteeing the repayment to the persons or firms making such advances.

The usefulness of these letters to travellers consists in the fact that being drawn not against a single house, but practically against every banker in the world, the traveller is not compelled, as in the case of a bill of exchange, to present the same at but one specified place and receive the whole amount it calls for in one currency, but may present it wherever and whenever he pleases, during the time for which it is drawn, and realize on it the amount he may then need in the currency of the country where he is, thereby entirely doing away with the inconvenience and insecurity of carrying large sums of money about his person, and avoiding the frequent change from one currency to another, for which a commission in the shape of a discount on the amount paid is always charged.

LETTERS OF CREDIT.

Depending for their value, as these letters necessarily do, upon the financial standing and reputation of the issuer, whose credit to that extent has been purchased by the holder of the letter, it is of the utmost importance that these letters should only be purchased from firms of the best and widest reputation, for while a less well known firm may be equally sound financially, and the holder of its letter have no difficulty in realizing on it from the issuer's correspondents or where the issuer is known, still such a letter could not be so generally used as one issued by a better known house.

The following is the ordinary form of the first page:

Pro forma Copy.

Brothers & Co's
CIRCULAR LETTER OF CREDIT.
No. $_R^B$ 11212.   *New York,_____189*

Gentlemen.
                                              We beg to introduce to you
Mr. John Henry Jones,
to whom you will please furnish such funds as he may require up to the aggregate amount of £100, ONE HUNDRED *pounds sterling against demand drafts on Messrs.   & CO.*
LONDON, *each draft to be plainly marked as drawn under Brothers & Co's Letter of Credit No. $_R^B$ 11212.*

We engage that such drafts shall meet with due honor in London if negotiated before   , and request you to buy them at the rate at which you purchase demand drafts on London.

The amount of each draft must be inscribed on the back of this letter and to this we wish to call your special attention. This letter itself should be cancelled and attached to the final draft drawn.

Please see to it that the drafts be signed in your presence and carefully compare the signature with the one below.

We are, Gentlemen,
                                    Your obedient Servants,
                    (Signed)
                                              Brothers & Co.
To Messieurs   *The Signature of*
The Bankers mentioned on the *(Signed)*
third page of this Letter of Credit.   *John H. Jones*

NOT EXCEEDING ONE HUNDRED POUNDS.

The second page, on which the amounts paid the holder of such letter are recorded, is as follows:

Date When Paid.		By Whom Paid.	Name of Town.	Amount Paid Expressed in Words.	Amt. in Fig's.
Apr.	10	Brown, Shipley, & Co.	London.	Twenty-five pounds.	£25.
"	27	Credit Lyonnaise.	Lyons.	Ten pounds.	" 10
May	16	Munroe & Co.	Paris.	Fifty pounds.	" 50
Aug.	4	Knauth, Nachod, & Kühne.	Leipzig.	Fifteen pounds.	" 15
					£100.

Attached to these letters, either as a third page, or as a separate paper, is a list of the various correspondents or agents of the firm issuing the letter. Along with each letter goes a check book, the blank checks in which are addressed to the maker of the letter.

It will be observed by glancing at the fac-simile given above of one of these letters, that it contains the signature of the holder, which, of course, presents an easy means of identification, as he thereby has in his possession the thing by which he can always be identified. A further and safer means, and one which should be adopted, would be to imprint on each letter a photograph of the person in whose favor it is issued.

These credits are not necessarily issued only to individuals, but may be issued to several persons.

Practically all sellers of these letters will issue them upon a deposit of cash, upon guarantee of payment of amounts drawn, or upon a deposit of marketable securities. On all letters for less than £500 a commission of 1 per cent. is charged. (These letters are nearly all drawn in sterling, as that is the most generally used currency.) Letters for a sum in excess of £500 are issued against a deposit of cash, without charge, but no interest is allowed on the cash so deposited, unless the same exceed £1000.

In case the letter is issued against a deposit of securities, and the securities have to be sold to make good the payment on such letter, the usual brokerage is charged, or in case interest on the securities is collected, a charge of one fourth of one per cent. is made for such service.

Whatever part of the amount for which the letter is drawn remains to the credit of the holder is payable to him on demand either at the home office or that of any agent or correspondent.

The manner of using such letter is so simple as to require but brief explanation. The holder, when in want of funds, refers to the list of agents and correspondents attached to his letter, selects the one in the place where he may be, draws his check against the issuers of such letter on one of the blanks furnished him in the check book, presents his letter and check, and the check is cashed in the currency of the country in which it is presented, and the amount in sterling is charged on the letter.

Although it is preferable to present these letters to the correspondents of the issuer, should there be none in the place where the holder happens to be, he can procure what funds he needs thereon from almost any bank or banker.

The person or firm making advances on the letter, writes the issuers thereof, mentioning the number of the letter enclosing the check of the holder for the amount paid, together with his or their charges, and the same is remitted them.

Naturally, in the case of agents or correspondents who pay a large number of checks on different letters, and themselves draw letters on which the first house mentioned also makes advances, periodical statements are made and balances remitted.

TABLE No. 1.

1895.
Department Circular, No. 63.

TREASURY DEPARTMENT, BUREAU OF THE MINT,
WASHINGTON, D. C., April 1, 1895.

Hon. JOHN G. CARLISLE, *Secretary of the Treasury.*

SIR: In pursuance of the provisions of section 25 of the act of August 28, 1894, I present in the following table an estimate of the values of the standard coins of the nations of the world:

VALUES OF FOREIGN COINS.

Country.	Standard.	Monetary Unit.	Value in Terms of U. S. Gold Dollar.	Coins.
Argentine Republic	Gold and silver	Peso	$0.96,5	Gold: argentine ($4.82,4) and ½ argentine. Silver: peso and divisions.
Austria-Hungary	Gold	Crown	.20,3	Gold: former system—4 florins ($1.92,9), 8 florins ($3.85,8), ducat ($2.28,7) and 4 ducats ($9.15,8). Silver: 1 and 2 florins. Gold: present system—20 crowns ($4.05,2); 10 crowns ($2.02,6)
Belgium	Gold and silver	Franc	.19,3	Gold: 10 and 20 francs. Silver: 5 francs.
Bolivia	Silver	Boliviano	.44,1	Silver: boliviano and divisions.
Brazil	Gold	Milreis	.54,6	Gold: 5, 10, and 20 milreis. Silver: ½, 1, and 2 milreis.
British Possessions N. A. (except New-foundland)	Gold	Dollar	1.0	
Central Amer. States—Costa Rica, Guatemala, Honduras, Nicaragua, Salvador	Silver	Peso	.44,1	Silver: peso and divisions.
Chile	Gold and silver	Peso	.91,2	Gold: escudo ($1.82,4), doubloon ($4.56,1), and condor ($9.12,3). Silver: peso and divisions.
China	Silver	Tael { Shanghai	.65,2	
		Haikwan (Customs)	.72,6	
		Tientsin	.69,2	
		Chefoo	.68,3	

Country	Standard	Unit	Value	Coins
Colombia	Silver	Peso	.44,1	Gold: condor ($9,6,17) and double condor. Silver: peso.
Cuba	Gold and silver	Peso	.92,6	Gold: doubloon ($5.01,7). Silver: peso.
Denmark	Gold	Crown	.26,8	Gold: 10 and 20 crowns.
Ecuador	Silver	Sucre	.44,1	Gold: condor ($9.64,7) and double condor. Silver: sucre and divisions.
Egypt	Gold	Pound (100 piasters)	4.94.3	Gold: pound (100 piasters), 5, 10, 20, and 50 piasters. Silver: 1, 2, 5, 10, and 20 piasters.
Finland	Gold	Mark	.19,3	Gold: 20 marks ($3.85,9), 10 marks ($1.93).
France	Gold and silver	Franc	.19,3	Gold: 5, 10, 20, 50, and 100 francs. Silver: 5 francs.
German Empire	Gold	Mark	.23,8	Gold: 5, 10, and 20 marks.
Great Britain	Gold	Pound sterling	4.86,6½	Gold: sovereign (pound sterling) and ½ sovereign.
Greece	Gold and silver	Drachma	.19,3	Gold: 5, 10, 20, 50, and 100 drachmas. Silver: 5 drachmas.
Haiti	Gold and silver	Gourde	.96,5	Silver: gourde.
India	Silver	Rupee	.21,0	Gold: mohur ($7.10,5). Silver: rupee and divisions.
Italy	Gold and silver	Lira	.19,3	Gold: 5, 10, 20, 50, and 100 lire. Silver: 5 lire.
Japan	Gold and silver[1]	Yen	Gold .99,7 / Silver .47,6	Gold: 1, 2, 5, 10, and 20 yen. Silver: yen.
Liberia	Gold	Dollar	1.00	
Mexico	Silver	Dollar	.47,9	Gold: dollar ($0.98,3), 2½, 5, 10, and 20 dollars. Silver: dollar (or peso) and divisions,
Netherlands	Gold and silver	Florin	.40,2	Gold: 10 florins. Silver: ½, 1, and 2½ florins.
Newfoundland	Gold	Dollar	1.01,4	Gold: 2 dollars ($2.02,7).
Norway	Gold	Crown	.26,8	Gold: 10 and 20 crowns.
Persia	Silver	Kran	.08,1	Gold: ¼, 1, and 2 tomans ($3.40,9). Silver: ¼,½,1,2, and 5 krans.
Peru	Silver	Sol	.44,1	Silver: sol and divisions.
Portugal	Gold	Milreis	1.08	Gold: 1, 2, 5, and 10 milreis.
Russia	Silver[2]	Ruble	Gold .77,2 / Silver .35,3	Gold: imperial ($7.71,8), and ½ imperial[3] ($3.86). Silver: ¼, ½, and 1 ruble.
Spain	Gold and silver	Peseta	.19,3	Gold: 25 pesetas. Silver: 5 pesetas.
Sweden	Gold and silver	Crown	.26,8	Gold: 10 and 20 crowns.
Switzerland	Gold and silver	Franc	.19,3	Gold: 5, 10, 20, 50, and 100 francs. Silver: 5 francs.
Tripoli	Silver	Mahbub of 20 piasters	.39,8	
Turkey	Gold	Piaster	.04,4	Gold: 25, 50, 100, 250, and 500 piasters.
Venezuela	Gold and silver	Bolivar	.19,3	Gold: 5, 10, 20, 50, and 100 bolivars. Silver: 5 bolivars.

[1] Gold the nominal standard. Silver practically the standard.
[2] Coined since January 1, 1886. Old half-imperial = $3.98,6.
[3] Silver the nominal standard. Paper the actual currency, the depreciation of which is measured by the gold standard.

Respectfully yours,

R. E. PRESTON, Director of the Mint.

The above table is issued on the first days of January, April, July, and October in each year.

The above table, it must not be assumed fixes the interchangeable market value of coins, it is merely a statement of what the Federal Government estimates them as worth for the purpose of valuing imports.

The value of gold coin to gold bullion is unchangeable so long as the weight of pure metal in the coins remains the same, and while the value of silver coin to silver must follow the same law, the value of silver coin in gold bullion changes so rapidly and the fluctuations are so great as to necessitate a table showing the weight of pure metal in coins in order to determine their value. With the weight of pure metal known, and the gold price of silver per ounce quoted daily in the newspapers, the gold value of silver coins can be readily ascertained by dividing the portion of an ounce which a coin weighs into the quotation. The following table (No. 2, p. 266) gives the weights of both alloyed and pure metal.

In United States money the value of an ounce of pure gold is $20.67. To ascertain the value of any gold coin divide the portion of an ounce it constitutes into 20.67.

The relative value of coins to each other can be determined in the same way.

The weights both of alloyed and pure metal given in Table No. 2 are of coins as they come from the mints.

From a study of this table it will be seen that while the names of the coins which are the monetary units in different countries differ, they are in many cases of the same weight and fineness. Thus in the case of France, Belgium, Italy, Switzerland, and Greece, comprising the Latin Union, in France, Belgium and Switzerland this unit is the franc, in Italy it is the lira, and in Greece the drachma. In none of these countries, however, is the franc, the lira, or the drachma legal tender except to a limited sum. The 5-franc, 5-lira, or 5-drachma piece (silver) is the lowest denomination of coin which is legal tender.

In the case of Denmark, Norway, and Sweden, comprising the Scandinavian Union, the krone or crown is the unit, the gold coins are the 20-crown and the 10-crown piece, the silver coins are the 2-crown and 1 crown, the 50-, 40-, 25-, and 10-öre pieces.

In Bolivia, the Central American States consisting of Costa Rica, Guatemala, Honduras, Nicaragua, and Salvador, in the U. S. of Colombia (in Ecuador, called the "Sucre"), and in Peru the silver peso of 385.800 grains alloy .900 fine, or 347.220 grains pure silver, forms the monetary unit.

The weight, wherever obtainable, has been expressed in grains, but in the currencies of France, Belgium, Italy, Greece, Switzerland, constituting the Latin Union, and Denmark, Norway, and Sweden, the Scandinavian Union, the German Empire, Portugal, Spain, and Turkey it is shown in grammes.

DECIMAL GOLD AND SILVER WEIGHT TABLE.

```
                         1 Gram or 15.43235 grains
10 Grams      = 1 Dekagram  =    154.3225      "
10 Dekagrams  = 1 Hectogram =   1543.2348      "
10 Hectograms = 1 Kilogram  =  15432.34874     "
```

Taken from *The World's Metal Monetary Systems.*

TABLE No. 2.

Countries.	Monetary Unit.	Weight in Alloyed Metal.	Fineness.	Weight of Pure Metal.
Argentine Republic	Peso (S.)	385.800 grains	.900	347.220 grains
Argentine Republic	Argentine (G.)	124.451 "	.900	112.006 "
Austria-Hungary	Crown (G.)	20-Crown Piece (G.) 104.553 grs.	.900	94.097 "
Belgium (L. U.)[1]	Franc	20 Francs (G.) 6.452 grammes	.900	5.806 grammes[3]
Bolivia	Boliviano (S.)	385.800 grains	.900	347.220 grains
Brazil	Milreis (G.)	10 Milreis 138.347 "	.916⅔	126.818 "
British Possessions, N. A., except Newfoundland	Dollar (G.)	British and U. S. gold coins		metal media of exchange[4]
Central American States, Costa Rica, Guatemala Honduras, Nicaragua, Salvador	Peso (S.)	385.800 grains	.900	347.220 grains
Chile	Condor (G.)	235.384 "	.900	211.845 "
Chile	Peso (S.)	385.800 "	.900	347.220 "
China	(S.) Tael { Shanghai Haikwan Customs	564.20 " 590.35 " Canton Tael 579.84 grs.	.898	513.060 " [4]
Colombia	Peso (S.)	385.800 grains	.900	347.220 grains
Cuba	Peso (S.)	Alphonse (G.) 25 Pesetas 124.451 grains	.900	112.006[5] "
Denmark (S. U.)[2]	Crown (G.)	10-Crown Piece 4.4803 grammes	.990	4.03227 grammes
Ecuador	Sucre (S.)	385.800 grains	.900	347.220 grains
Egypt	Pound (G.)	131.172 "	.875	114.775 "
Finland	Mark (G.)	20 Markkaa 99.561 grains	.900	89.605 "
France (L. U.)	Franc (G.)	(G.) 5 Francs 1.613 grammes	.900	1.452 grammes
France (L. U.)	Franc (G.)	(S.) 1 Franc 5. "	.835	4.180 "
German Empire	Mark (G.)	5-Mark 1.99123 "	.900	1.792114 "
Great Britain	Pound (G.)	Sovereign 123.270 grains	.916⅔	113.000 grains

[1] Latin Union.   [2] Scandinavian Union.
[3] Gramme equal to 15.432 grains, 31.103496 grammes to 1 ounce Troy.
[4] While the gold dollar is the unit of value the metal circulating media is composed almost entirely of English and American coins, receivable at a fixed value.
[5] Same as Spain.

266

Countries.	Monetary Unit.	Weight in Alloyed Metal.	Fineness.	Weight of Pure Metal.
Greece (L. U.)	Drachma $\{$ (G.) (S.)	(G.) 5 Drachmas 1.613 grammes (S.) 5 " 25.000 "	.900 .900	1.452 grammes 22.500 "
Haiti	Gourde (G. and S.)	(G.) Gourde 24.890 "	.900	22.401 "
India	Rupee (S.)	180.000 grains	.916⅔	165.000 grains
Italy (L. U.)	Lira $\{$ (G.) (S.)	(G.) 5 Lire 1.613 grammes (S.) 5 " 25.000 "	.900 .900	1.452 grammes 22.500 "
Japan	Yen (S.)	416.000 grains	.900	374.400 grains
Liberia	Dollar (G.)			
Mexico	Dollar (S.)	417.790 grains	.902 $\frac{7}{10}$	377.170 "
Netherlands	Florin $\{$ (G.) (S.)	10-Florin (G.) 103.703 grains 1 " (S.)(Rixdaler, 2½ florins) 385.800 grains	.900 .945	93.332 " 364.581 " 23.545 1 "
Newfoundland	Dollar (G.)			
Norway (S. U.)	Crown (G.)	10-Crown Piece 4.4803 grammes 69.140 grains	.900 .900	4.03227 grms. 62.226 grains
Paraguay	Peso			
Persia	$\{$ Kran (S.) Toman (G.)	71.065 grains 43.981 "	.760 to .900 .900	39.583 grains 347.220 "
Peru	Sol. (S.)	385.800 "	.900	1.6257 grms.
Portugal	Milreis (G.)	1.774 grammes	.916⅔	179.219 grains
Russia	Ruble $\{$ (G.) (S.)	Imperial 10 Rubles 199.133 grs. 308.571 grains	.900 .900	277.714 " 112.006 "
Spain	Peseta	$\{$ (G.) 25 Pesetas 124.451 grains (S.) 5 " 385.800 "	.900 .900	347.220 " 62.226 "
Sweden (S. U.)	Crown (G.)	10 Crown 69.140 grains	.900	1.452 grms.
Switzerland (L. U.)	Franc (S.)	5 Francs 1.613 grammes	.900	22.500 "
Tripoli	Mohbub (S.)	5 " 25.000 "	.900	313.200 grains
Turkey	Piaster (G.)	100-Piaster (G.) called Turkish Pound 7.216 grammes	.916⅔	6.6146 grms.
United States	Dollar $\{$ (G.) (S.)	25.800 grains 412½ "	.900 .900	23.220 grains 371 $\frac{1}{4}$ "
Venezuela	Peso $\{$ (G.) (S.)	(G.) 5 Bolivars 24.890 grains (S.) 1 " 77.160 "	.900 .835	22.401 " 64.824 "

CHAPTER XVI.

Interest—Grace—Legal Holidays.

Alabama.—Legal rate of interest 8 %. Usury, penalty of, forfeiture of interest. Grace allowed. Legal holidays: Sundays, January 1st, February 22d, April 26th, July 4th, Thanksgiving day, Good-Friday, Mardi Gras, and Christmas. If any of these days, except Mardi Gras, falls on Sunday, the following Monday is the legal holiday. Paper entitled to days of grace or subject to protest falling due on a holiday becomes legally due on the next succeeding business day.

Arizona.—Legal rate of interest 7 %. Contract rate unlimited. No usury law. Protest unnecessary if suit is begun within sixty days of date when payment is due. Grace allowed on notes and bills of exchange. Legal holidays: same as New York, except first Monday in September, and Saturday half-holiday. Paper falling due on holidays or Sundays is collectible on the next business day.

Arkansas.—Legal rate 6 %. Maximum contract rate 10 %. Usurious contracts are void, both as to principal and interest, and negotiable paper tainted with usury is void in the hands of an innocent holder. Judgments bear same rate of interest as contracts on which they are recovered, except judgments against counties which bear no interest. Grace, three days. No holidays peculiar to the State. Notes and bills due on Sunday, Christmas, and July 4th must be presented the business day previous. But notice of protest need not be given until the day after such days.

California.—Legal rate 7 %. Contract rate unlimited. Judgments bear 7 % interest. No grace. Legal holidays: same as New York, except September 9th in place of first Monday in September, and no Saturday half-holiday.

Colorado.—Legal rate 8 %. Contract rate unlimited. County orders and warrants draw 8 %, State warrants 6 %. No usury laws. Legal holidays: same as New York, except no Saturday half-holiday. Same provision as in case of New York should holidays fall on Sunday, except that paper is payable the previous business day. On notes and bills of exchange three days' grace.

Connecticut.—Legal contract rate 6 %. Usury, penalty, forfeiture of interest in excess of legal rate to any one except the borrower suing within a year. Grace, three days. When either day of grace expires upon a legal holiday, the paper is collectible the business day preceding such holiday. No legal holidays peculiar to the State.

Delaware.—Legal and contract rate 6 %. Usury, penalty, forfeiture of a sum equal to the amount lent. Grace, three days on all bills payable at a future date. When third day of grace falls on a holiday or Sunday, presentation and payment to be made the preceding business day. When holiday falls on Sunday, paper maturing on Monday must be presented the previous Saturday.

District of Columbia.—Legal rate 6 %. Maximum contract rate 10 %. Usury, penalty of, recovery of whole interest paid by action brought within year after payment. Legal holidays: January 1st, February 22d, Inauguration day (every fourth year), May 30th, July 4th, first Monday in September, Thanksgiving day, and December 25th. Grace not allowed.

Florida.—Legal rate 8 %. Maximum contract rate 10 %. Contracts for more than 10 % void, interest forfeited. Double amount of interest over 10 % paid to any holder may be recovered by maker from payee. Legal holidays: January 1st, February 22d, June 3d, July 4th, first Monday in September, December 25th, Election days—Federal and State, Thanksgiving day. Negotiable paper due on holidays presentable and payable the preceding business day. Grace not allowed.

Georgia.—Legal rate 7 %. Maximum contract rate 8 %. Usury, penalty of, forfeiture of excess of interest over 8 %. Judgments bear 7 % interest on the principal recovered. No grace on sight paper. Protest unnecessary to hold endorser, except when payable at a bank or banker's office, when grace shall be allowed. Legal holidays: January 1st, January 19th, February 22d, April 26th, July 4th, December 25th, and other days appointed by the President or Governor. Paper due on holidays to be presented the preceding business day.

Idaho.—Legal rate 10 %. Maximum contract rate 18 %. Compound interest allowed. Usury, penalty of, 10 % of debt. No grace. Paper due on Sundays or holidays payable next business day. No special holidays.

Illinois.—Legal rate 5 %. Contract rate 7 %. Usury, penalty, forfeiture of interest. No grace on sight demands, three days on other instruments. Legal holidays: same as New York, except no Saturday half-holiday. Paper due on holidays payable preceding business day.

Indian Territory.—Same as Arkansas.

Indiana.—Legal rate 6 %. Maximum contract rate 8 %. Usury, when paid, can be recovered from the payee. Grace, three days, allowed on all paper. Legal holidays: same as New York, except no Saturday half-holiday. Paper due on a holiday payable preceding business day.

Iowa.—Legal rate 6 %. Maximum contract rate 8 %. Usury, penalty, forfeiture of 10 % of contract. Judgments bear rate of interest of contracts on which recovered. Grace allowed. No special holidays.

Kansas.—Legal rate 6 %. Maximum contract rate 10 %. Usury, penalty, forfeiture of double the amount of all interest over 10 %. Grace, three days. Legal holidays: Sundays, July 4th, December 25th, January 1st, Thanksgiving. Paper due on a holiday is payable the preceding business day.

Kentucky.—Legal rate 6 %. Usury, penalty, forfeiture of excess of interest over 6 %. Three days' grace. Paper due on Sundays or legal holidays payable preceding business day.

Louisiana.—Legal rate 5 %. Contract rate 8 %, although parties may agree to even a higher rate, which may be collected. After maturity of obligation any stipulation for higher rate than 8 % forfeits entire interest. Judgments bear rate of interest of the debts on which they are recovered. Grace, three days, except on sight bills, on which no grace is allowed. Paper due on a legal holiday is payable the next succeeding business day. Legal holidays: January 1st, 8th, February 22d, Mardi Gras, 4th of March in New Orleans, July 4th, December 25th, Sundays, and Good-Friday.

Maine.—Legal rate 6 %. Contract rate unlimited. Judgments bear 6 %. Grace, three days, except on demand paper. Paper, the last grace day of which is on a legal holiday, is payable the preceding business day, except where two holidays come together, the last of which constitutes the other grace day; or, if one of the other days falls on Sunday and is the second grace day, four days of grace are allowed. Legal holidays: same as New York, except Election days and Saturday half-holiday.

Maryland.—Legal and contract rate 6 %. Usury, penalty, forfeiture of excess over actual value of goods and chattels lent. Grace, three days. Legal holidays: same as New York, except that Good-Friday is observed as a legal holiday and the first Monday in September is not a legal holiday, and no Saturday half-holiday. Paper due on a legal holiday is payable preceding business day.

Massachusetts.—Legal rate 6 %. Contract rate on loans not in excess of $1000, maximum 18 %, provided contract is in writing. Corporate bonds, maximum 7 %. Three days' grace allowed on all paper in the absence of a statement to the contrary.

Michigan.—Legal rate 6 %. Maximum contract rate 8 %. Usury, penalty, forfeiture of interest. Grace, three days, on all but demand paper. Paper falling due on a legal holiday payable preceding secular day.

Minnesota.—Legal rate 7 %. Maximum contract rate (when expressed in writing) 10 %. Interest in excess of 10 % or compound interest prohibited. Usury, penalty, recovery of all interest paid in excess of 10 % with costs of action if action is brought within two years after payment. Bonds, bills, notes, assurances, conveyances, chattel mortgages, and other contracts whereby a greater sum than 10 % is charged for the loan are void. This does not apply in the case of unmatured negotiable paper. Grace allowed except where stipulated to the contrary. No grace on demand paper. Acceptances must be in writing. Legal holidays: Sundays, Thanksgiving day, Good-Friday, Christmas day, New Year's day, 22d of February, 4th of July, or the following day when any of the above named days falls on Sunday. Paper falling due on a holiday becomes payable and notice of protest should be given the preceding business day, but notice of dishonor, non-payment, or non-fulfilment may be given the business day succeeding such holiday.

Mississippi.—Legal rate 6 %. Maximum contract rate 10 %. Usury, penalty, forfeiture of interest. Notes not considered protestable paper. Bills must be protested. Legal holidays: Sundays, July 4th, Christmas day, Thanksgiving, and New Year's.

Missouri.—Legal rate 6 %. Maximum contract rate 8 %. Judgments bear rate of interest of contracts on which recovered. Open accounts bear 6 % interest from time of demand to payment. On contracts bearing usurious rate only legal rate is recoverable and defendant is allowed costs of action. No grace allowed on sight bills or orders. No written assignment of a note or bill is necessary to entitle the holder to sue. Legal holidays: January 1st, February 22d, July 4th, Thanksgiving day, general Election days, December 25th, and Sundays. Where a holiday other than a Sunday falls on Sunday, the Monday following is observed as a holiday. Paper due on holidays or Sundays is payable the succeeding business day, unless such holiday be a Sunday, when the paper becomes due the day previous.

Montana.—Legal rate 10 %, which is the rate collectible after debt is due. Contract rate unlimited. No usury law. Three days' grace allowed on bills and notes except when the last day of grace falls on a Sunday or legal holiday, in which case payment must be made the preceding business day. No grace on sight drafts or checks.

Nebraska.—Legal rate 7 %. Maximum contract rate 10 %. Judgments bear same rate of interest as contracts upon which they are recovered. Usury, penalty, forfeiture of interest. A note bearing 10 % from date to maturity and 24 % from maturity until paid not deemed usurious, the 24 % being regarded as a penalty of non-payment. Compound interest allowed upon provision to that effect in the paper. Grace, three days, on all but demand paper. Legal holidays: same as New York except no Saturday half-holiday and the addition of April 22d as a holiday. Same provision as in New York in regard to paper due on a holiday.

Nevada.—Legal rate 7 %. Contract rate unlimited. Interest allowed only on original claim. Grace not allowed.

New Hampshire.—Legal rate 6 %. Usury, penalty, forfeiture of three times excess of interest charged. Contract not invalidated by usury. Grace allowed except on sight paper. Legal holidays: same as New York, except the omission of January 1st and Saturday half-holidays. Paper due on a holiday is payable the preceding business day and must be then presented and if not paid protested.

New Jersey.—Legal rate 6 %. Usury, penalty, forfeiture of all interest and payment of costs. Grace three days. Twenty-four hours additional allowed for notice of dishonor. Legal holidays and provisions in regard to payment of paper then due same as New York.

New Mexico.—Legal rate 6 %. Maximum contract rate 12 %. Open running accounts from six months after date of last item bear 6 %. Judgments carry same rate as contracts on which they are founded. Usury, penalty of, forfeiture of double the amount of interest received, upon action brought within three years. A fine is also inflicted for usury. Grace allowed on notes same as on inland bills of exchange according to custom of merchants. Legal holidays: Sundays, January 1st, July 4th, December 25th, and all days proclaimed by the Governor as thanksgiving or fast days. Paper falling due on any holiday is payable the next succeeding business day.

New York.—Legal rate 6 %. Except bottomry and respondentia bonds and contracts, and call loans (see State Banks, page 105), all contracts or agreements bearing a higher rate of interest than 6 % are even in the hands of an innocent third party void. Corporations cannot set up usury as a defence. By the Penal Code, Sec. 378, usury is made a misdemeanor. Excess of interest over legal rate may be recovered by the borrower by action brought within a year from date of payment. Town overseers or county superintendent of the poor may bring action within three years. An equity suit may be brought by a borrower or his assignee for the benefit of creditor, but not by other assignee, agent, or devisee to discover if usury has been paid, or to declare void a usurious instrument.

State banks and private bankers are placed on the same footing in regard to interest as national banks, and forfeit double the excess of interest charged above the legal rate.

No grace.

Legal holidays: January 1st, February 22d, May 30th, July 4th, December 25th (when any of these days fall on Sunday the Monday following is made the legal holiday), the first Monday in September, any general Election day, every Saturday after 12 M., and any day appointed by the President of the United States or the Governor of the State as a day of thanksgiving or fasting.

Paper falling due on holidays or Sundays must be presented on the immediately following business day, except that paper falling due on Saturday may be presented at or before 12 noon, when if not paid, to protest the same and hold the obligors, presentation, demand, and notice of protest or dishonor may be made the first following business day.

North Carolina.—Legal rate 6 %. Maximum contract rate in writing 8 %. Judgments bear rate specified in contract on which recovered. Penalty for usury, forfeiture of interest. Payee may recover excess beyond legal rate of interest by suit brought within two years. Bonds, bills, and notes governed by custom of merchants in England. Three days' grace. Legal holidays: January 1st and 19th, February 22d, May 10th and 20th, July 4th, December 25th, and a Thanksgiving day to be fixed by the Governor. If any of said days falls on Sunday, the following Monday shall be deemed a public holiday, and paper due on such Sunday is payable on Saturday preceding, and paper which would otherwise be payable on said Monday shall be payable on Tuesday thereafter. When any of the above named holidays falls on Saturday, paper due on Sunday following is payable on Monday following. Whenever any of said holidays falls on Monday, paper otherwise payable on that day is payable on succeeding Tuesday.

North Dakota.—Legal rate 7 %. Maximum contract rate 12 %. Any rate in excess of 12 % is deemed usurious and warrants the forfeiture of all interest so taken, and the payee may recover double the amount paid. The National Bank Act provision in regard to usury obtains. Three days' grace allowed on bills of exchange or drafts and on all promissory notes. Sundays and holidays excluded in computation of days of grace.

Ohio.—Legal rate 6 %. Maximum contract rate 8 %. A higher rate than 8 % cannot be collected, and on a contract bearing such higher rate the principal sum and 6 % only can be recovered. Three days' grace except on sight paper. If third day of grace be Monday, demand must be made on the next preceding business day. Legal holidays: same as New York, except Saturday half-holiday and the first Monday in September, which for the presentation and demand of negotiable paper is not a legal holiday.

Oklahoma Territory.—Legal rate 7 %. Contract rate 12 %. Judgments bear 7 %. Grace, three days, on time paper.

Oregon.—Legal rate 8 %. Contract rate 10 %. Judgments bear rate of contract upon which they are recovered. Usury, which is charging a higher rate than 10 %, is punishable by forfeiture of principal sum and costs of action. No grace. Paper payable on a holiday due the next business day. Legal holidays: same as New York, except Saturday half-holiday.

Pennsylvania.—Legal rate 6 %. Savings banks not confined to legal rate. Commission merchants and agents may agree with parties outside of the State for 7 %. Usury, penalty of, forfeiture of interest, and when paid recovery by suit brought in six months. Grace allowed. Acceptances in excess of $20 to be in writing. A written promise on a note to pay a commission as a collection fee in case of non-payment destroys negotiability Legal holidays: January 1st, February 22d, Good Friday; May 30th, when on Sunday, Saturday preceding is the legal holiday; July 1st, the first Saturday of September, Election days, September 25th, Saturday half-holiday. When holidays, except May 30th, fall on Sunday, the Monday following becomes the legal holiday. Paper due on a legal holiday is payable the next business day. The third Tuesday of February (Spring Election day) and the first Tuesday after the first Monday of November (Fall Election day, are legal half-holidays after 12 o'clock.

Rhode Island.—Legal rate 6 %. Contract rate unlimited. Judgments bear 6 %. Debts, in the absence of a contract to the contrary, bear 6 %. Grace allowed. Paper falling due on Sunday or a legal holiday is payable the next business day. Legal holidays: July 4th, Christmas day, February 22d, May 30th (when any of these days fall on Sunday the following Monday becomes the legal holiday), the first Wednesday in April, the first Tuesday after the first Monday in November on every even year, Arbor day, and Thanksgiving and Fast days—State or National.

South Carolina.—Legal rate 7 %. The charging of a greater rate than 8 % involves the forfeiture of double the amount of interest charged. The receipt of usurious interest renders the lender further liable to an action for double the amount of interest received. This may be pleaded by way of counterclaim. Grace allowed. Legal holidays: Sundays, January 1st, February 22d, July 4th, December 25th, 26th, and 27th, first Monday in September, Thanksgiving, and all general Election days. Paper falling due on a holiday is payable the next business day.

South Dakota.—Legal rate 7 %. Contract rate 12 %. Usury, penalty, forfeiture. Also a misdemeanor punishable with a fine of $500 or six months' imprisonment or both. Interest begins to run on open account from date of last item. Judgments bear 7 %. Grace allowed. Sundays and holidays excluded in computing grace. Legal holidays: none peculiar to State.

Tennessee.—Legal rate 6 %. Usury, penalty, forfeiture of interest, also a misdemeanor. Grace except on sight paper. Paper falling due on 1st January, 4th of July, 25th of December, or any National or State Fast or Thanksgiving day, is payable the day previous, unless such day is Sunday, when it becomes payable the preceding Saturday.

Texas.—Legal rate 6 %. Maximum contract rate 10 %. Penalty of usury, forfeiture of interest. When paid, double the amount of interest may be recovered by suit brought within two years. Grace allowed. Legal holidays: January 1st, February 22d, March 2d, April 1st, July 4th, December 25th, Thanksgiving, State and National general Election days. If any of these days fall on Sunday, the Monday following is the legal holiday. Presentation of paper may be made the Saturday before.

Utah Territory.—Legal rate 8 %. Contract rate unlimited. Judgments bear rate of interest of contracts on which they are recovered. No grace allowed. Acceptances must be in writing. Legal holidays: Sundays, January 1st, February 22d, first Saturday in April, May 30th, July 4th and 24th, first Monday in September, December 25th, and Thanksgiving or Fast days. If holidays fall on Sunday, Monday following is observed.

Vermont.—Legal rate 6 %. Usury, penalty, forfeiture of excess over legal rate. Judgments bear 6 %. No grace allowed on paper made and payable in this State. Paper due on Sundays or legal holidays payable following business day.

Virginia.—Legal rate 6 %. Corporations not limited to this rate. Usury, penalty, forfeiture of all interest. When usurious interest is paid upon contract it is credited as part payment of principal. Judgments bear 6 %. Corporations cannot plead usury. Grace allowed on all save sight paper. Legal holidays: January 1st and 19th, February 22d, July 4th, first Monday in September, December 25th, Thanksgiving and Fast days. Paper due on a Sunday or legal holiday is payable the preceding business day. Holidays falling on Sunday are observed the Monday following.

Washington.—Legal rate 8 %. Contract rate unlimited. Grace, three days, allowed on all paper unless paper contains an expressed stipulation to the contrary. Where the last day of grace falls on a holiday the holiday is not counted and the paper is payable the preceding business day. Legal holidays: Sundays, July 4th, December 25th, January 1st, February 22d, Decoration day, general Election and Thanksgiving days.

West Virginia.—Legal rate 6 %. Usury may be pleaded and excess of interest over legal rate forfeited. Corporations not limited to legal rate. Judgments bear 6 %. Paper due on Sunday or a legal holiday is payable the preceding business day. Notice of protest however need not be given until the following business day. Legal holidays: January 1st, February 22d, July 4th, day of national Thanksgiving, and Christmas. Grace allowed.

Wisconsin.—Legal rate 6 %. Maximum contract rate 10 %. Contracts reserving more than 10 % valid for principal only. The payer of more than 10 % interest may recover triple the amount paid. Paper maturing on a legal holiday payable the preceding business day.

Wyoming.—Legal rate 12 %. Contract rate unlimited. Unsettled accounts bear interest after thirty days. Grace allowed. Legal holidays: January 1st, February 22d, May 13th, July 4th, Thanksgiving day, and December 25th.

In the case of paper due in a State other than the one in which the holder resides, the best course to pursue is to deposit the same in his local bank for collection, the bank forwarding the paper to the place of collection and becoming responsible to the depositor for any omission of duty on its or its agents' part whereby any obligor may be released from payment.

In the case of obligations maturing in a State not the domicile of the maker, the best course is to deposit with the local bank funds sufficient to meet the same, directing them to take up the paper.

This subject is more fully treated in various parts of this work, especially in drafts, checks, bills of exchange, and transmission of money.

GLOSSARY.

A

ABANDONEE
   The person to whom a right or thing is relinquished, surrendered, or abandoned.

ABANDONER
   One who abandons.

ABANDONMENT
   Surrender or relinquishment of a privilege, right, or possession. (Marine law) The abandonment by the master or owner of his ship and its freight to a creditor in satisfaction of a contract. (Marine insurance) The surrender to the insurers of such remaining portion of the insured property after the happening of the event insured against. This is done to hold the insurer for the total amount of the insurance. (Customs) The abandoning of dutiable goods to the government to escape payment of duties.

ABATEMENT
   Reduction. The measure of decrease. Refunding of duties. The amount deducted from the first amount of a tax bill.

ABBAS
   An Eastern weight for pearls, supposed to be 2¼ grains Troy.

ACCEPTANCE
   The obligation of the drawee to pay a draft or bill of exchange, generally evidenced by his writing the word "Accepted," and his signature on the paper the payment of which is assumed. Acceptances are "general" when unlimited by any qualifying words, "special" when payable at a specified time and place, and "qualified" when accepted for a less sum than is named on the face of the paper, "supra protest" or "for honor," when accepted by a person not the drawee to save the honor or credit of the drawer or an endorser after refusal of the drawee to accept. Also the paper accepted, or the sum named therein.

ACCOMMODATION ENDORSER
An endorser who, without consideration or protection, endorses the paper of another not payable to himself.

ACCOMMODATION PAPER
Negotiable paper drawn, accepted, or endorsed without consideration by one to enable another to obtain credit or raise money on it.

ACCOUNT
A statement of the items and amounts due by one person to another for goods, services, etc. ; a course of business dealings.

ACCOUNTABLE RECEIPT
A receipt of money or goods to be accounted for.

ACCOUNT CURRENT
(Open Account) A course of business dealings still continuing.

ACCOUNT RENDERED
A statement presented by a creditor to his debtor, showing the charges of the former against the latter.

ACCOUNT SALES
A statement rendered by a broker, factor, or agent to his principal.

ACCOUNT STATED
An account or statement which has been acknowledged as correct by the debtor, or to which he has not objected within reasonable time, showing the result of a course of transactions.

ACKNOWLEDGMENT
A written admission made before an officer empowered to take acknowledgments, such as a notary, commissioner, or judge, stating that the person making the same executed the paper for the "purposes therein stated," etc. ; generally attached to bonds, mortgages, deeds, etc.

ACT OF HONOR
An instrument executed by a person not the drawee, after protest of draft or bill of exchange, to save the honor or credit of any party thereto.

ACTUARY
An expert in the application of the doctrine of annuities, especially with reference to insurance. Commonly one of the principal officers of life insurance companies, whose duties are principally to deduce from statistics, data, mortuary tables, etc., the value of contingent assets, the amount of accruing indebtedness, the proper premium charges, and to furnish statements of the company's condition.

ADJUDICATE
To decide, to award, to settle.

ADJUDICATION
Award, decision.

ADJUST
To settle; to agree upon.

ADJUSTMENT
(In marine insurance) The ascertaining and agreeing upon the final indemnity to which the insured is entitled, also the part of such indemnity for which each insurer is liable.

ADMINISTRATOR
(Legal) One who by virtue of authority from a proper court has charge of the personal property of an intestate.

AD VALOREM DUTY
A tax calculated and imposed upon the value, and not upon the weight, numbers, or packages of dutiable articles.

ADVANCE NOTE (or Bill)
A draft or demand on the owner or agent of a ship or vessel. Wages paid to sailors by the master or agent of a vessel on the signing of articles.

ADVANCES
Payments made on consignments before sale of the merchandise consigned. Loans on bills of lading; the delivery of a value before an equivalent is received; contributions to capital or stock; increase in price.

ADVENTURE
A commercial venture or enterprise in which one or more merchants are concerned for their individual or joint account.

ADVENTURE (BILL OF)
A document issued by and bearing the signature of a merchant, shipowner, or his agent, indicating that merchandise aboard a particular vessel is at the risk of another person, the maker of such bill being liable solely for its safe delivery.

ADVICE
Information from one or more persons to others interested in a joint transaction; as notices, letters, drafts, or demands drawn, etc.

AGENCY
The office or place of business of an agent, factor, or representative also the powers or duties of such agent, factor, or representative.

AGENT
One acting in place or as the representative of another.

AGIO (also spelled AYGIO)
Premium of exchange; premium or percentage of a better sort of money when it is given in exchange for an inferior sort. The premium or discount on foreign bills of exchange is sometimes called agio (Webster). The premium on depreciated currencies is called disagio, also the depreciation in value owing to abrasion of coins.

AGIOTAGE
Rate or price of exchange; speculation in exchange, bullion, stocks, etc.

AGREEMENT (MEMORANDUM OF)
An instrument or document written or printed bearing the signatures of the parties thereto, stating the subject of their mutual contract.

AGREEMENT OF INSURANCE
A contract preliminary to the issue of the policy between the insurer and the insured, in regard to the terms and time of delivery of the policy.

ALLOWANCE
A deduction for tare, tret, breakage, etc. A limited deviation from exact conformity to the legal standard in the fineness and weight of coins.

ALLOY
v. The introduction of a baser metal into a more valuable one to decrease its value. n. The combination of a less valuable with a more valuable metal or metals.

ANNUITY
A sum payable yearly, to continue for a number of years, for life, or for ever; an annual allowance (Webster).

APPORTIONMENT
A dividing into proportions or shares.

APPRAISAL
See Appraisement.

APPRAISE
To fix a price upon, to set a value. The price or value set by appraisers named by individuals or appointed by law.

APPRAISEMENT
Act of appraising; the price set on a value or service.

ARBITER (ARBITRATOR)
: A person to whom parties have referred their differences for decision ; a referee, an umpire.

ARBITRAGE
: The agreed relative value of coin, currency, stocks, or bonds.
(Enc. Brit.)—Arbitrage proper is a separate, distinct, and well defined business, with three main branches. Two of these, viz., arbitrage or arbitration in bullion and coins, and arbitration in bills, also called the arbitration of exchanges, fall within the business of bullion dealing and banking respectively. The third, arbitrage in stocks and shares, is arbitrage properly so called, and is understood whenever the word is mentioned without qualification among business men.

ARBITRATION
: The referring for decision of a controversy or dispute to an arbitrator or arbitrators, or referee or umpire.

ARBITRATION BOND
: A bond binding a party or the parties to a dispute or controversy to accept the decision of the person or persons to whom such question is referred.

ASKING PRICE
: The price at which a value or right is offered for sale.

ASSIGN
: To surrender or transfer to another (the assignee). In matters of bankruptcy the instrument by which this transfer is effected is known as an assignment.

ASSIZEMENT
: The inspection by a person legally authorized and empowered, called an assizer, of weights and measures and the qualities of commodities.

ASSOCIATION
: A union incorporated or unincorporated of persons for a common purpose.

ASSOCIATION, ARTICLES OF
: The contract under which members of an association join together for a common purpose.

ASSURANCE (Insurance)
: A contract for the payment of a sum on the occurrence of a certain event, as loss, death, etc.

ASSURED
: The person or persons in whose favor a policy of insurance is written.

ATTORNEY
A lawyer ; a counsellor at law.

ATTORNEY IN FACT
One appointed to act in the place or stead of another.

ATTORNEY, POWER OF
The instrument by which such appointment is made.

AVERAGE
" A contribution made by all the parties concerned in a sea adventure, according to the interest of each, to make good a specific loss or expense incurred for the benefit of all, sometimes called 'general average.' A small duty paid by shippers of goods to the master of the ship over and above the freight, in consideration of his special care of the cargo, noted in bills of lading by the phrase 'With primage and *average* accustomed.' " (Wor.)

AVERAGE ADJUSTER
(Marine Insurance) A skilled accountant employed to average or ascertain the amount to be paid by each of the parties interested in the loss sustained for the general account.

AVERAGE BOND
(Marine Insurance). A bond of consignees of cargo given to the owner or master of a vessel guaranteeing when ascertained the amount of their contributions to a general average.

AVERAGE, FREE OF
A list of articles excepted from liability to particular average on the part of underwriters, which is generally attached to policies of marine insurance.

AVERAGE OF ACCOUNTS
The average date on which accounts fall or become due.

AWARD
The decision of arbitrators, referees, or umpires.

B

BALANCE
The difference between the creditor and debtor sides of an account ; the sum necessary to make the debtor and creditor sides equal.

BALANCE OF TRADE
Excess in value between exports and imports of a country.

BALLAST
Any comparatively valueless material carried in a vessel for the purpose of making it draw sufficient water to enable it to be navigated to advantage, and on which a trifling or no freight is paid.

BANCO
In some countries where banks keep their accounts in a currency other than that in common use ; the money in which such account is kept.

BANK
(P. 68) An institution for receiving and lending money.

BANK ACCOUNT
A sum deposited in a bank, which may be drawn out on the depositor's written order.

BANK BILL
A bank note, a note, bill, or draft, or demand by one bank on another.

BANK BOOK
The book in which the depositor receives credit for amounts deposited and in which his drafts or checks are charged.

BANK CREDIT
A credit extended by a bank.

BANKER
(See p. 178) The officer of a bank, or one who deals in money or credits.

BANKER'S NOTE
The note of a private banker or unincorporated bank.

BANK HOLIDAY
In Great Britain a holiday on which banks are allowed to be closed. Obligations due on this day are usually payable the next secular day.

BANK NOTE
A demand promissory note issued by a bank by authority of law (see Money of the United States, p. 60).

BANK POST BILL
A bill issued for not less than ten pounds by the Bank of England without charge.

BANKRUPT
An insolvent person ; one whose estate is being administered by a receiver or assignee for the benefit of his creditors.

BANKRUPTCY, ASSIGNEE IN
The assignee of the property of a bankrupt.

BANKRUPTCY, INVOLUNTARY
When declared on the petition of creditors, showing the bankrupt should not be continued in possession of his estate, is termed involuntary.

BANKRUPTCY, REGISTER IN
    An officer appointed by and under the control of the Court to adjudicate upon the affairs of bankrupts.

BANKRUPTCY, VOLUNTARY
    When declared on the petition of the bankrupt, asking leave to transfer or assign his estate for the benefit of creditors, is called voluntary.

BANK STOCK
    Stock issued by a bank.

BARGAIN
    A contract or agreement between two or more parties.

BARRATRY
    (Wor.) Act or offence of the master of a ship or of the marines, by which the owners or insurers are defrauded.

BARTER
    (See Barter, p. 3.)

BARTERER
    One who barters or traffics in commodities.

BAUBEE
    (Wor.) A half-penny.

BAZAAR
    A market-place.

BEAR
    (See Brokers.) One who contracts to sell stocks, provisions, or commodities, or things, not owned by him, to be delivered at a future time, for a certain price, and is consequently interested in depressing their value; one who is endeavoring to decrease the price of a stock or commodity.

BETTERMENTS
    Improvements on real property, other than ordinary repairs, which add to its value.

BID
    An offer.

BILL
    A statement of the items and amounts of articles or values furnished, or of services rendered by one person to another.

BILL OF ADVENTURE
    (See Adventure, Bill of.)

BILL OF CREDIT
A notification by one person to another to extend to the person named in the bill the credit therein stated.

BILL OF COSTS
An itemized statement of the taxable costs of a litigant.

BILL OF ENTRY
A statement, written or printed, signed by the importer, of goods entered at a custom house.

BILL OF EXCHANGE
(See page 38.)

BILL OF HEALTH
A certificate by the proper authorities as to the state of health in a vessel on leaving or arriving in port.

BILL OF LADING
A receipt given to shippers by vessels or transportation companies, setting forth the goods placed in their care for transportation.

BILL OF PARCELS
An account of goods sold given by the seller to the buyer, containing the quantities and prices of the articles, with a statement of the date and terms of credit. (Wor.)

BILL OF SALE
An instrument conveying the right, title, or interest in personal property.

BILL OF SIGHT
A form of entry at the custom house by which goods, respecting which the importer is not possessed of full information, may be provisionally landed for examination. (Wor.)

BILL OF STORES
A custom-house license permitting merchantmen to carry free of customs duties stores and provisions necessary for a voyage.

BILL OF SUFFERANCE
A coasting license permitting vessels to trade from port to port without paying customs duties, the dutiable goods being landed at sufferance wharves.

BILLS PAYABLE
The outstanding unpaid notes or acceptances made and issued by an individual or firm.

BILLS RECEIVABLE
The unpaid promissory notes or acceptances of others held by an individual or firm.

BI-METALLIC
　　A double metallic monetary system, as gold and silver.

BLANK
　　A printed form containing unfilled spaces or lines to be filled in to suit the particular occasion.

BOND
　　A written obligation under seal to do or refrain from doing a certain act or thing. When a penalty is attached for failure to perform the contract, the bond is known as a "penal bond."

BOND
　　(See Stocks, Bonds, etc., page 209.)

BONDED DEBT
　　That part of the debt of a corporation represented by its outstanding bonds.

BONDED WAREHOUSE
　　A building licensed by the customs authorities to receive and keep goods in store prior to the payment of customs or internal-revenue duties thereon.

BOND FOR LAND
　　(or bond for a deed) A bond given by the seller of land to the one agreeing to buy it, binding him to convey on receiving the agreed price.

BOND, IN
　　Goods in bond are in charge of the customs authorities, and are stored in a bonded warehouse or store.

BOND OF INDEMNITY
　　A bond conditioned to indemnify the obligee against some loss or liability.

BOOK OF ORIGINAL ENTRY
　　A book in which the first written entry of a transaction is made, such as the blotter or sales books, in which entries are or should be made at the time of the sale or transaction.

BOOKKEEPER
　　An accountant; one who keeps books.

BOOKS
　　In commerce technically means only the Ledger, Journal, Day Book, Cash Book, Bills Receivable, and Bills Payable, or books the entries in which are taken from other books or memoranda.

BOOKS OF ACCOUNT
 Books containing a record of the pecuniary dealings of a person or persons. In cases of corporations used in contradistinction to the records, or books in which a record of the meetings, resolutions, etc., of their stockholders and Board of Directors is kept.

BOTTOMRY
 Borrowing money on a pledge of the bottom of the ship as security.

BOTTOMRY BOND
 A mortgage of the ship as collateral for a loan.

BOUNTY
 A premium offered by the government to men engaged in certain industries, such as the bounty at one time paid to sugar growers. When paid to steamship companies it is generally called a subsidy.

BROKER
 (See page 182.)

BULL
 One whose aim is to raise the price of stocks or merchandise.

BULLING
 Raising or trying to increase the price of stocks, etc.

BULLION
 (See page 13.)

BUYER THREE
 A technical expression used in Wall Street, meaning the purchase must be consummated in three days.

C

CALL
 A summons or request from a superior officer of a government or corporation requiring representatives or others to assemble. An assessment on the stockholders of a corporation or joint-stock company, or members of a mutual insurance company, for the payment of assessments on insurance policies, or in the case of other corporations for the payment of instalments of their unpaid subscriptions, or for their promised, or legally liable, contributions for losses. A request to holders of bonds to present the same for payment and cancellation.

CALL LOAN
 A loan subject to payment on the call and demand of the lender.

CAPITAL
  (Page 27.) The wealth employed in carrying on a particular trade, manufacture, business, or undertaking; stock in trade; the actual estate, whether in money or property, which is owned or employed by an individual, firm, or corporation in business. In the case of a corporation it is the aggregate of the sum subscribed and paid in, or secured to be paid in, with the addition of undivided gains. Generally speaking, sums received from the sale of stock are capital, whereas those received from sales of bonds are not capital, but borrowed money.

CAPITALIST
  One who has capital; a man of large property.

CAPITALIZE
  To supply with capital.

CASH
  Ready money; money at hand or at command.

CASH CREDIT ·
  A credit to an agreed amount extended by a banker, generally on deposit of security or guarantee of repayment.

CASHIER
  One who has charge of cash.

CHANGE
  Exchange, barter. Also, an abbreviation for Exchange, a meeting-place. Coins of lower denominations. The sum of money handed the seller in excess of the price of the article sold.

CHARGE
  A demand, a claim. The price of an article, right, or service.

CHARGES, OUTWARD
  The pilotage and other charges incurred by a vessel leaving port.

CHARTER
  The instrument granted by a superior power to an inferior, defining the latter's rights and powers, as the charters granted by States to cities, towns, and corporations.

CHARTER PARTY
  A written agreement by which a ship owner lets a vessel to another.

CHATTEL
  Any movable property or goods, as money, stocks, bonds, furniture, plate, horses, etc. Everything but real estate or a freehold.

CHATTEL MORTGAGE
A mortgage on chattels.

CHECK
(See page 253.)

CHECK-BOOK
A book containing blank checks and stubs.

CLAIM
A demand. The amount of anything demanded.

CLAIMANT
One making claim or demand.

CLEAR
To free from encumbrance or detention. In the case of a vessel the furnishing and procuring the necessary customs papers, and such compliance with port regulations as will permit the vessel to "clear" or sail. In the case of goods, the payment of duties or taxes necessary to relieve them from governmental restraint.

CLEARING
The daily balance of banks' demands against each other at the Clearing House. The sailing of a vessel.

C. O. D.
Collect on delivery.

COLLECTOR
A Federal officer empowered to collect customs duties. A person employed to collect.

COLLUSION
Secret agreement for a fraudulent or harmful purpose.

COMMERCE
Barter, trade, exchange, traffic. Foreign commerce is that carried on between nations. Inland trade (commonly called "Domestic" or "Internal trade") is an exchange of commodities within the territory of one country.

COMMERCIAL PAPER
Bills of exchange, drafts, notes, etc., drawn against the purchaser of merchandise.

COMMISSION
(Wor.) A document or writing investing one with authority. The order by which one person buys or sells goods, securities, etc., for another. The percentage or compensation which an agent, factor, salesman, commission merchant, or broker charges or receives for services. Two or more persons appointed for the doing or investigating of a particular thing.

GLOSSARY.

COMMISSION AGENT
An agent who transacts business for others on commission.

COMMISSIONER
One empowered to act in some matter or business for one or more persons or a government.

COMMISSIONER OF DEEDS
A person authorized by a State or country to take acknowledgments of deeds, etc.

COMMISSION MERCHANT
One who buys or sells goods for another on commission, or who acts as agent in buying and selling, receiving for his services a commission.

COMMON CARRIER
Railroads, express companies, steamship lines, and others engaged in the business of carrying persons or freight.

COMPANY
(Page 200.)

COMPARISONS
(Stock Exchange.) The act of comparing the sellings and purchases of stock by the different sellers and buyers.

COMPLAINANT
A plaintiff, a claimant, the person who begins a suit.

COMPOSITION
An agreement between a debtor and his creditors, by which the latter accept in full payment of their claims a portion of the amounts due. The sum or rate paid or agreed to be paid in compounding with creditors.

COMPOSITION DEED
A contract between creditors and their debtor effecting a composition, usually in a manner to bind the creditors not to molest the debtor.

COMPOUND
(See Composition and Compromise.)

COMPROMISE
Mutual concession. The agreement arrived at.

CONSIGNEE
The person to whom a commodity, right, or thing is consigned.

CONSIGNMENT
The goods forwarded by a consignor.

CONSIGNOR
One who consigns or entrusts merchandise to another.

CONSOLS
A term used to denote a considerable portion of the public debt of Great Britain, more correctly known as the three per cent Consolidated Annuities.

CONSUL
An official agent of a government, accredited to a foreign power, whose office is to protect the commercial interests of the country he represents.

CONTINGENT
The interest of a particular party in a joint speculation or business venture.

COUPON
An order attached to bonds for the payment of interest.

CREDITOR
One who extends credit to another; one to whom another is indebted.

CUSTOM HOUSE
A Federal building or office where vessels and merchandise are entered, and duties upon dutiable imported goods are collected.

CUSTOM-HOUSE BROKER
A person who acts for others in the entry or clearance of ships, the entry and payment of taxes on merchandise, and the transaction of custom-house business generally.

CUSTOMS
Import duties, as distinguished from internal-revenue duties; taxes collected at a custom house.

D

DEBENTURE
(Wor.) A custom-house certificate, entitling the exporter of imported goods to a drawback of the duties paid on their importation. An instrument in some government departments by which the government is charged to pay to a creditor or to his assigns the sum found due on auditing his accounts.

DEBT
That which one person owes to another. (Wor.) A sum of money due by certain or express agreement.

DEBTEE
　　A creditor.

DEBTOR
　　(Wor.) One who owes anything to another.

DECISION
　　(Wor.) The judgment or determination given by a judicial tribunal; the report of such determination.

DECLARATION
　　A publication, statement, or formal announcement (thus declaration of dividends). The paper, message, or letter by which the declaration is made.

DECREASE
　　An allowance by the revenue officers to importers of liquors for loss by leakage while in bond, on which loss no duty is charged.

DEDUCTION
　　Taking away; abatement; the thing or amount deducted.

DEED
　　A writing authenticated by the seal of the person whose mind it purports to declare. More specifically such a writing made for the purpose of conveying real estate.

DEFAULT
　　A failure to perform within the agreed time an agreement, contract, or condition, as default in interest.

DEFAULTER
　　One who fails to properly account for or make return of values entrusted to his care.

DEFENDANT
　　In law the person against whom redress is sought; the one accused of wrong, the person attacked, the one defending.

DEFICIENCY
　　Lack of the necessary quantity or amount; the sum required to make up a given amount.

DEFORCIATION
　　A seizure of goods for the satisfaction of a lawful debt.

DEFRAUDER
　　A swindler, a cheat; one guilty of fraud.

DEFRAY
　　To compensate for, settle, pay.

DEKADRACHM
(Ten drachm.) An ancient silver coin of the value of ten drachms.

DEL CREDERE
The guarantee of a factor or agent to his principal of the credit or solvency of the persons to whom the goods of such principal are sold. Also used to indicate the reinsurance by one insurance company of its policies in another.

DEL CREDERE COMMISSION
A commission charged for guaranteeing the credit or solvency of persons to whom goods are sold.

DELEGATE
A person appointed or sent by another in his interest to perform a certain act.

DEMURRAGE
A per diem allowance granted to the owner or his agents for the detention in port of a vessel beyond the time named in the charter party.

DEPARTMENT
(Web.) Subdivision of business or official duty. One of the principal divisions of executive government.

DEPONENT
(Web.) One who deposes or testifies under oath; one who gives evidence; usually one who testifies in writing.

DEPOSIT
(Web.) To lodge, place, or put in one's hands for safe keeping; to commit to the custody of another. Also the thing deposited. Money lodged with a party as earnest or security for the performance of a duty assumed by the person depositing.

DEPOSITARY
The receiver of a thing in trust.

DEPOSITION
Written evidence taken before a duly authorized person.

DEPUTY
A substitute, a lieutenant; a representative; an assistant.

DERELICT
A thing voluntarily abandoned or cast adrift; a ship abandoned at sea. A tract of land from which the sea has receded, and fit for cultivation or use.

DERELICTION
　　The act of abandoning with intention not to reclaim. A receding of the sea whereby land is gained.

DESPATCH
　　(Marine Insurance) A certificate setting forth the value of a ship and her cargo liable to contribution in case of a loss incurred for the common benefit.

DEVIATION
　　(Marine Insurance) A wilful departure from a ship's allotted course, forfeiting insurance.

DIFFERENTIAL DUTY.
　　(Also Discriminating Duty) A higher duty levied and collected on certain merchandise when imported indirectly from the country where it is produced than when imported directly. A higher tonnage duty on vessels not owned by citizens of the importing country than on vessels owned wholly or in part by such citizens.

DIRECTOR
　　One who directs, guides, superintends, governs, or manages. One of a number of persons elected or appointed, having authority to manage and direct the affairs of a company or corporation.

DISAFFIRM
　　(Wor.) To annul or cancel, as a voidable contract.

DISCHARGE
　　The unloading or unburdening of a ship or cargo. (Wor.) The act of setting free; acquittance; the instrument by which a person is discharged from debt or obligation, or an encumbrance is cancelled.

DISHONOR
　　Refusal to pay; to repudiate.

DISPOSSESS
　　To put out of possession; to deprive; to take away.

DISTRAIN
　　(Wor.) To seize and keep as a pledge in order to compel the performance of some duty, such as the payment of rent, the performance of services, an appearance in court, etc.

DISTRICT
　　(Wor.) A civil division of a State or country for judicial or other purposes.

DIVIDEND
　　The share or sum of the estate of a bankrupt paid to creditors. In the case of stock, a sum to be distributed among the stockholders.

DIVIDENDS ON (OR OFF)
(See page 215.)

DIVIDEND, STOCK
A dividend payable in reserved or additional stock.

DIVIDEND WARRANT
A paper calling for the payment of a dividend.

TO MAKE A DIVIDEND To set apart a sum of money, or a number of shares for such dividend.

TO PASS A DIVIDEND To fail to make an expected dividend.

DOCKAGE
A charge for the use of a dock ; dock rent.

DOCUMENT
A writing, or paper.

DOMICILIATED
A note, draft, or other obligation, when payable in a different place from that in which it is drawn, is domiciliated in the place where it is payable.

DOUBLE ENTRY
A mode of bookkeeping in which two entries, one credit and one debit, are made of every transaction.

DOWER
That portion of a man's lands and tenements to which his widow is entitled after his death, to have and to hold for her natural life.

DRAUGHT
Allowance on goods sold by weight.

DRAWBACK
(Wor.) Any sum of money paid back ; an allowance made by the government to persons on the re-exportation of certain imported dutiable goods ; also a repayment or remission of a duty laid on any articles produced in a country, and suitable for the foreign market, when such article is entered for exportation.

DRAWEE
The person on whom an obligation to pay is drawn.

DRAWER
One who draws a bill of exchange, draft, or other paper ; the maker.

DUNNAGE
Material used in the stowing of cargo in a vessel to preserve the cargo from chafing or injury.

DUTY
    A tariff or tax on certain domestic and imported articles.

E

E. E.
    Errors excepted.

E. & O. E.
    Errors and omissions excepted.

EMBARGO
    A governmental detention or restraint of vessels or commerce by preventing vessels or shipping from entering or leaving its ports.

ENDORSEMENT
    The signing of one's signature on the back of any document. (See Notes.)

ENDORSER
    One who endorses.

ENDORSER FOR VALUE
    One who endorses paper drawn to his own order to obtain the value thereof, or who endorses paper payable to another, on being indemnified against loss, or who receives a consideration for his endorsement.

ENTREPOT
    A magazine; a warehouse for depositing goods (Wor.).

ENTRY
    A record. Reporting a vessel or cargo at the custom-house. Taking possession of lands or tenements.

EXCISE
    A tax upon articles of domestic production.

EXECUTION
    The seizure by legal authority of goods, chattels, or rights for the satisfaction of a judgment.

EXECUTOR
    A person appointed by a testator in his will to see that its provisions are carried out.

EXPRESS
    A regular and speedy conveyance for messages, packages, etc.

EXPRESSAGE
    The charge made by express companies for carrying.

F

FEE
   A charge; a bill.

FIRM
   A partnership; the persons composing a partnership.

F. O. B.
   Free on board. To deliver to a particular transportation company free of cartage charges.

FREE PORT
   A port where goods may be landed free from custom-house restrictions (Wor.).

FREIGHT
   Transportation charges. Articles in transit.

G

GARBLE
   The dross, dust, and refuse of drugs and spices.

GARBLER
   (In London) An officer empowered to inspect drugs and spices.

GARBLING
   Selecting the worst of any commodity.

GRACE
   The time beyond the due date in which the debtor may make payment on a note, bill of exchange, or other obligation.

GROUNDAGE
   The charge made for the ground or berth occupied by a ship while in port.

H

HUSBANDAGE
   The agent or managing owner's allowance or commission for attending to a ship's business.

I

INSOLVENT
   One who cannot pay his obligations in full.

INSURANCE
   The act of insuring or assuring against loss or damage by a contin-

gent event; a contract whereby for a stipulated consideration, called a premium, one party undertakes to indemnify or guarantee another against loss by certain specific risks (Web.).

The person who undertakes to pay in case of loss, the "insurer"; the danger against which he undertakes, the "risk"; the person protected, the "insured"; the sum which he pays for the protection, the "premium"; and the contract itself when reduced to form, the "policy."

Insurance is divided into Accident and Casualty Insurance, Endowment Insurance, Fire Insurance, Life Insurance, Marine Insurance, etc.

INSURANCE BROKER
A broker who effects insurance.

INSURANCE COMPANY
A corporation which sells insurance.

INTEREST SHORT
(Marine Insurance) The amount over-insured.

INVOICE
An account, giving particulars, marks of packages, prices, etc., of goods, furnished by a consignor to his consignee, by a seller to a purchaser, or by a shipper to a transportation company.

J

JETTISON
The use, destruction, abandoning, or casting overboard of any part of the ship's equipment, or for the sake of preserving the whole, or the running aground of the ship to prevent sinking. The owners of the cargo or property so used or destroyed, abandoned, or cast overboard, have a right to recover its value *pro rata* from the shippers whose property was saved.

JUDGMENT NOTE
A promissory note to which a confession of judgment is added, waiving necessity of lawsuit to procure judgment.

L

LETTER OF LICENSE
Creditor's permission to a debtor to manage his affairs without interference for a specified time.

LIGHTERAGE
The hire of a lighter or barge.

LINE OF DEPOSIT
The average amount, during a given period, on deposit to a dealer's credit in the bank with which he deals.

LINE OF DISCOUNT
The amount of a dealer's discounts or loans from a bank. Also the amount of credit which a bank extends a depositor.

LIQUIDATION
The act of settling or winding up.

LIVE PAPER
Unmatured promissory notes, in contradistinction to matured, dead, or protested paper.

LLOYD'S REGISTER
A book issued by the Lloyds, setting forth the name, tonnage, build, rating, and other matters pertaining to ships and shipping.

M

MANIFEST
A list or invoice, containing a description by marks, numbers, etc., of a ship's cargo. Also, in the case of transportation and express companies, a list of all goods to be delivered at a particular station.

MARGIN
(See Stock Brokers, page 186.)

MULCTS
Fines levied upon ships and their cargoes to maintain consuls, garrisons, etc.

N

NOTARY PUBLIC
A State officer empowered by commission to take acknowledgments, administer oaths, take depositions, and protest notes and other negotiable paper, within a certain county or counties as prescribed by law.

O

OVERDRAFT
Balance due on an overdrawn account. The amount of a check, note, or draft in excess of the drawer's credit with the person on whom drawn.

P

PAR
Face value.

PAR OF EXCHANGE
  The relative bullion value of the money of one country to that of another. (See Exchange, page 44.)

PERMIT
  A customs license to remove goods, after payment, of duties, from public stores.

PIERAGE
  Taxation for the maintenance of piers.

POLICIES, FLOATING
  (Fire Insurance) Policies on goods in undesignated buildings, or in two or more named buildings, where the amount of goods in each building is not specified.

POLICIES, OPEN
  (Marine Insurance) Policies in which the value of goods insured is not specified.

POLICIES, VALUED
  (Marine Insurance) A policy stating the value of the insured merchandise.

POLICY
  A contract between an insurance company and the insured.

PREMIUM
  (Insurance) The charge made by the insurer to the insured for the insurer's assumption of loss.

PREMIUM OF EXCHANGE
  (See Exchange, page 44.)

PREMIUM ON SHARES
  (See Stocks, page 209.) The price beyond the face value.

PRICE, AVERAGE
  The average money value of securities or commodities for a length of time.

PRICE CURRENT
  A current list of the market price of commodities or securities.

PRICE, MARKET
  The money measure of the value of securities or commodities.

PRIMAGE
  A percentage allowed by shippers to the owners or charterers of a vessel for the loading of goods.

PRIME EXCHANGE
Is exchange issued by houses of known solidity, whose bills are everywhere accepted.

PRINCIPAL
Capital. The sum on which interest is computed and paid.

PROCURATION.
Power or authority to act for another.

PRO FORMA
For form's sake. A fictitious transaction used to illustrate a business dealing.

PROMPT
The period of time within which payment must be made for goods purchased.

PROTEST OF NOTES
The notarial certificate required by law of the due presentation to and refusal of, a maker to pay a note.

Q

QUARANTINE
The time which a ship must remain at a given point, called "Quarantine," before entry into port. (Leg.) The right of a widow to remain in the homestead of her husband for the period of forty days after his death, without being liable for rent.

QUOTATIONS
The prices quoted or named.

R

REBATE
An allowance. A repayment by a lender to a borrower of interest from the time on which an obligation is paid to that on which it is due

RECEIPTS
Acknowledgments of delivery, payment, or satisfaction.

RECONCILE
To agree upon and correct differences in the details of an account current. To cause the balance in each to correspond.

REGISTER
An official document relating to a vessel, stating its nationality, place of building, measurement, etc.

RETIRE
　　To take up or pay before maturity a loan or note discounted.

RESPONDENTIA LOAN
　　Money lent upon the security of a cargo.

RETURNS
　　Remittances. Sales for a given time.

REVERSIONARY INTEREST
　　A right to possession of property at the termination of a precedent estate.

S

SALVAGE
　　A compensation for rescuing or preserving a vessel, its cargo, or any part thereof from entire or partial loss. The amount of such compensation.

SCRIP
　　Dividends payable in stock issued upon the capital of a company.

STOCK, PREFERRED
　　(See Stocks, page 212.)

STOCK, SECOND PREFERRED
　　(See Stocks, page 212.)

STOCK SHORT
　　(See Brokers, page 190.)

SUPERCARGO
　　An owner's agent aboard ship to superintend the sale of cargo, to procure freight, etc.

SURPLUS
　　A fund over and above the capital required to conduct a given enterprise. In banks, a fund in excess of the capital and legal reserve, and out of which dividends are paid.

SUSPENSE ACCOUNT
　　An account of unpaid notes, disputed claims, and moneys in litigation. An account of claims of dubious value.

T

TELLER
　　(See page 118.)

TIME BARGAIN
　　A contract to be performed at a future specified time, usually applied to the purchase or sale of goods or securities.

TONNAGE
   The carrying capacity of a vessel expressed in tons; also the quantity of freight a vessel is permitted to carry.

TRANSIT
   A custom-house warrant or pass.

TRUE BILL
   An indictment sanctioned by a Grand Jury.

U

UNDERWRITER
   One who underwrites or guarantees the payment of a policy of insurance; an insurer.

USANCE
   The time fixed by custom in which a bill of exchange may be paid after the due date; grace; grace as applied to foreign bills of exchange.

USURY
   An interest charge above the rate of interest prescribed by law, and applicable only to interest on debts and obligations on which the law prescribes the maximum interest charge.

V

VALUE
   (See page 4.)

VALUE, FACE
   The value expressed on the face of an instrument.

VALUE, MARKET
   The exchangeable value of a thing in open market, as distinguished from face or par value, or price.

VALUE, PAR
   The full face value.

VOUCHER
   A paper or document acknowledging that some payment has been made or other business transaction effected. A receipted bill.

W

WAREHOUSE RECEIPTS
   Receipts for merchandise issued by the warehouses in which such merchandise is stored.

WARRANT
   A draft drawn by its officers upon the treasury of a corporation, national, State, or municipal treasury.

Dictionaries :   { Web......Webster.
                 { Wor......Worcester.

INDEX.

A

Agricultural products, 81
American securities, 47
Arbitrage houses, 43
Assay Office, 67
Auxiliary industries, 9

B

Balance of trade, how settled, 46
Bank account, 129
Banks, 68, 70
  Assistant cashier, 117; Bookkeeper, 126; Cashier, 117; Check deposit, course of, 130; Check deposits not to be drawn against same day, 127; Currency deposit, 130; Deposit, course of, 129; Deposit slip, course of, 130; Directors, board of, qualifications, etc., 113; Discount, 123; Discount clerk, 123; Discount department, 122; Ledger-keeper, 126; Management of, 113; Methods of business, 110; Notes, presentation of, 128; Note teller, 126; Offering book, 125; Paper for collection, 125; Pass books, 127, 129; Runners, duties, 127; Vice-president, 116
Barter, principles of, 3, 5
Bill of lading, 243
Bills of exchange, 250
Bonds, 217
  Car trust —, 225; Collateral trust —, 222; Consolidated mortgage —, 1st, 2d, and 3d, 221; Convertible —, 222; Corporate —, 217; Debenture —, 223; First mortgage —, 220; General mortgage —, 224; Improvement and extension —, 225; Income —, 1st, 2d, and 3d, preference, 221; Redemption before maturity, 225; Remarks, 225; Second mortgage —, 220; Sinking fund —, 224
Brokers, 182
  Bear pool, 191; Bucket shops, 183; Bull pool, 190; Business routine, 184; Charges, 184, 185; Commission houses, 183; Consolidated exchange, 182; Consolidation of properties, 188; Curbstone —, 182; Information, 187; Interest charges, 186; Losses, 187; Margin, 185; Margin, speculating on, 186; Membership in exchange, 182; Pools, 190; Price of stocks, 187; Quick sale, 187; Rumors, 189; Shorts, 190; Specialists, 185; Speculation of partners forbidden, 183; Tips, 189; Traffic agreements, 188; Two-dollar —, 185
Building and Mutual Loan Associations, 167
  Amount of money invested in, 167; Accumulation, method of, 168; offering of, 179; bidding for, 176; Consolidation and merger, 173; Directors' powers, 171; Dividends, 172; Dues, 168; Funds to be put up at auction and bid for 169; Gross premium, serial plan, 169; Incorporation, certificate, what it must state, 170; certificate of, to be approved by superintendent, etc., and filed with county clerk and superintendent, 171; Incorporators, number of, 170; Interest, 176; Loans, limit of, 176; limit of amount, 171; premiums on, 169; theory of, 169; Matured shares, order of payment, 176; Method, 167, 168; Minors and wards, how held, 172; Monthly meetings, 176;

Objects, 167; Officers and creditors, liability of, 172; Old corporations may reorganize under this law, 172; Organized under State law, 167; Penalties and forfeitures, 168, 171; Shareholders, dissenting, rights of, 173; liability, 172; not exempt by reason of losses, etc., 172; Shares up to $600 exempt from execution, 172; Subscribers, 168; rights of, 169; Usury, 172

C

Cable and telegraph transfers, 244
California, discovery of gold in, 11, 16
Capital, 28
  Commercial definition, 29; — distinguished from wealth and property, 28; Insufficient capital, danger of, 31; Invested capital, available, 31; Land not capital, 29; Necessity of use, 28; Ratio of capital to business, 30; Relation of capital to property, 28, 29; Subject to decay, 28; Unemployed capital, 31
Cash, 231
Certificates of deposit, 257
Certificates of indebtedness (floating debts), 226
Checks, 253
  Cashiers' checks, 257; Course through bank, 256; Devices for protection, 255
Cheque banks, 242
Clearings, annual, 32
Clearing House (New York), 132
  Balances, how paid, 135; Clearances, average annual, 135; Clearing charge, 133; Clearing house certificates, 136; Clearings, annual, 132; Creditor banks, 135; Debtor banks, 135; Delivery and settling clerks, 134; Dues, annual, 133; England, when clearing houses first established in, 134; Government of New York Clearing House, 137; Importance of New York Clearing House, 135; London Clearing House, clearances, 136; Membership, conditions of, 133; Object, 133; Officers and committees, 133; Operation, 134; Original membership, 132; Proof clerk, 134; Sub-Treasury, 133

Clothing products, 50
Coinage a sovereign prerogative, 15
Coinage, free, 24
Coins, 15
  Government control of, 23
Commercial agencies, 234
Commercial bills, 243
Commercial houses, 230
Competition and combination, 55, 56
Comptroller of currency, 71
Co-operative Loan Associations, 173
  Accumulations, 175; Attorney, 174; By-laws, 174; Capital stock, 174; Directors, board of, 173; Dues, 174; Entrance fee, 175; Fines, 174; Objects, 173; Officers, 173; Organization, certificate of, 173; Organizers, 173; Payments, when to cease, 175; Shareholders, 175; Shares, 174; Shares, unpledged, may be retired by directors, 175; Treasurer and secretary, 175
Copper, 61
Corporations, 200
  Directors, residence of, 204; Incorporation, certificate of, 204; Objects, 200; Permits, 203; Perpetuity, 200; Privileges, 200, 204; Property owners, consent, 203; Resident attorney in fact, 204; Stock and transfer books, 204; Taxation, 202; Treasury stock, 204
Corporations—Duties of officers
  Assistant secretary, 205; Bank to be named, 206; Commissioners or committee, 205; Directors, board of, 207; General manager, 207; President, 205; Secretary, 205; Secretary and treasurer, 205; Treasurer, 205; Vice-president, 205
Coupons, 217
Credit
  Amount, 32; on what extended, 34, 35; system of country, 33; Importance of, 7, 8, 32; Money'an auxiliary to, 33; Paper money, 33; Principles of credit, 31; Credit Revenue of, to bankers, 35
Creditor banks, 135
Currency, governmental control of, 24–26
Currency, 10, 11
  — of United States, 62; — certificates, 63

INDEX. 307

D

Debtor banks, 135
Demand, 54
Disproportionate increase of commodities, 51
Distribution, 53
Diversity of industry, how created, 51
Drafts, distinction between draft and check, 248

E

Endorsements, 247
Exchange
  Arbitrage houses, 43; Buying exchange, 40; complex, 41; domestic, 41; Final balance, 47; Final debtor countries, 47; Foreign balance, 39; how calculated, 42; Gold bullion basis, 42; Par of, 44; Premium and discount, 44; Rate of, 40; Relative value of currencies, 42; constantly changing, 42; selling, 44; speculation, 40; Shipment of bullion, 47; Simple exchange, 39; World's exports and imports equal, 46
Exchange, bills of, 250
Exchanges, 104
Exports and imports equal, 46
Express companies, 238

F

Final debtor countries, 47
Food products, 50

G

Gold the universal standard of value, 13, 58
  Gold certificates, 63; coinage free, 24; money of the United States, 60; standard, 13, 58, 59
Greenbacks, 60
Gresham's law, 16

I

Interest, 35
  Current interest, 35; Discount, 35; Interest laws of States, 268; Interest warrants, 229; Legal interest, 35; Legal rate arbitrary, 35; to protect debtors, 38; Market, 36; Principal, 35; Rate, 35; by what governed, 36, 37

Import duties, 57
Individual restraints of trade, 57
Investment securities, 228

L

Labor
  Measure of productivity, 49; Measure of reward, 49; Price of, 49
Letters of credit, 258
Loans on collateral, 112

M

Margin, 185
Margin, speculating on, 186
Merchant, origin of, 7
Metals, restricted circulation, 59
Money
  A legal tender, 22, 23; Collateral restriction of use of, —20; Circulation, theory of, 20; Definition, 9; Effect on values, 9; Fiat money, 17; Government regulation of, 23; of coin, 23, 24; of paper, 24-26; How issued and distributed, 23; Inconvertible paper money, 21; objections, 21; Increase and decrease in value, 10, 11; Issuers must receive value, 25; Measure of value, 12; Metal money, 10, 15; Money a commodity, 10; Not capital of issuer, 26; Paper money, 10-12, 17; by whom issued, 18, 19; how issued and circulated, 24, 25; Proper issuers, 22; Proportion to credit, 9; Single or double measure, 12; State or national issue, 19; in what redeemable, 19; Supervision and control by government, 26
Money orders, 239
Monopoly, 56
Mortgage and debenture companies, 176

N

National banks
  Articles of association, 71; Assessment, 83; Banks and national banks, 68, 70; Bonds, comparison of, yearly, 75; exchange of, 75; held for redemption of circulating notes, 74; held in trust, 74; may be sold to pay circulation, 88; reassignment of, to bank, 76; Capital, impairment to be made

good, 82, 83; minimum, 73; not to be withdrawn, 82; Capital stock, 73; how paid in, 73; how transferable, 73; not to be received as collateral, 82; Central reserve cities, 79, 80; Certificate to be published, 74; Character of reserve and where kept, 79, 80; Circulating notes, 76; furnished by comptroller, form, dies, etc., 76; not to be hypothecated, 82; not to be used for advertising, 79; Clearing house certificates, 80; Comptroller of currency, 71; Comptroller and treasurer given access to each other's books, 75; discretion of, 89; to decide if bank is entitled to commence business, 74; Consolidation, 86; Contracts, suits, 72; Corporate life, twenty years, 71; powers, 71; Decrease of bond deposit, 74; Deposit of bonds, 74; minimum, 74; with United States Treasurer, 74; Depository of government funds, 78; Destruction of plates, dies, etc., 77; Directors, election of, qualifications, etc., 77; Directors, officers, 72; Dissolution, notice to be sent comptroller and published, 86; voluntary, 86; Dividends, 81, 82; penalty for failure to report, 84; shall not exceed net profits, 82; to be reported to comptroller, 84; Examination of plates, dies, etc., 77; ordered by comptroller on notice of protest of circulating notes, 87; Examiners' powers and fees, 85; Executors not personally liable, 78; Expense of issue, how paid, 76; Gold banks, 79, 80; Incidental powers, 72; Incorporators' organization certificate, 71; Increase of bond deposit, 75; Interest, 81; Lawful money, definition, 79; reserve, 80; Liabilities, 82; not to be increased, 80; Liquidation, 86; Maximum loan to one party, 81; May only issue notes furnished by the Federal Government, 77; National bank notes not to be used for advertising purposes, penalty, 79; National banks, functions of, 72; must receive each other's notes at par, 81; "Natural persons" defined, 71; State banks may reorganize as national banks, 79; Stock sold on failure to pay, 73; increase or decrease, 77; Surplus, 81; Taxes, 70, 84; Transfers of bonds, 74; United States first lien on assets, 87; Usury, penal, 81
National gold banks, 79, 80
Necessities of most universal value, 50
New York Stock Exchange, 196
Charges, 197; Devices, 199; Gala days, 198; Gratuity fund, 198; Membership, 198; Over-certification, 198; Seats, 198; Stock deliveries, 198; how and when paid for, 198.
Nickel, 60
Notary, 251
Note brokers, 192
Notes, indorsements of, liability of maker, how limited, 246
Notice of Protest, 252

O

Over-certification, 112

P

Papers, 243, 250
Pools, 190
Postage stamps as money, 22
Post office orders, fees charged, 240
Preservative commodities, 50
Price, 48
Competition and combination, 55, 56; Corner, 57; Demand, effective, 54; Distinction between price and value, 48; Distribution, 53; Excessive production, waste, 53; Factors of price, 52; High prices, 55; Import duties, 57; Individual restraints of trade, 57; Labor, 49; Low prices, 54; Monopoly, when possible, 56; Preservative commodities, increase in value, 58, 59; Price of wheat, 53; Production, cost of, 52; Railways, canals, steamships, 53; Restraint of trade, 56; Restricted circulation of metals, 59; Retail price, 50; Standard of value, effect on price, 57; Supply and demand, 54; Supply, available, 54; Trades unions, 55; Transportation and procurability, 52; Trusts, 55
Presentation of notes, drafts, etc., 251

INDEX. 309

Private bankers, 178
  Business of, 179; Capital of, 179; Circulating notes, 179; Financing companies, 179; Government grants, 181; Privileges of, 179; Promoting, 179; Railroads, construction, 181; Reorganization of companies, 179, 180; Right of way of railroads, 181; Securities deposited with trustee, 181; West, development of, 180.
Protest, 252; notice of, 252.

R

Railroads, construction, 181
Railways, canals, etc., effect on price, 53
Receivers' certificates, 227
Reclamations, 112
Refining gold, charge for, 23
Registered letter, 238
Restraints of trade, 56

S

Safe deposit companies, 163
  Burglars, fire, etc., safeguards against, 165; Box and safe holders, 165; Capital, maximum and minimum, 163; Corporate life fifty years, 163; Capital stock to be paid in before commencing business, 164; Consolidation, 166; Directors, number of, election, notice of, to be published, powers of, 164; Incorporators, five, 163; Location, importance of, 166; Objects, 163; Pass word, 165; President, 164; Rent of boxes, when unpaid for three years, procedure, 165; Safes and boxes, arrangement of, 165; Stockholders, liability of, and right of contribution, 164
Savings banks, 138
  Assets and liabilities to be reported to superintendent 1st January and 1st July, 148; Available fund, 145; Banks and trust companies, first lien on their assets after payment of circulating notes, 149; Books, vouchers, etc., to be examined by committee, 148; Business must be begun within a year, 141; Business, when to be commenced, 140; By-laws, rules and regulations, and amendments, copy to be sent superintendent, 141; Certificate of authorization, on what conditions granted, where filed, 140; Committees, 141; Creditors, how paid, 149; Custodians of, 138; Depositors, classification of, 147; Deposits and interest, how invested, 143-145; Deposits, amount of, limited, 143; in trust, 143; may be made by savings banks in banks and trust companies, 145; maximum, of individuals and corporations, 143; of minors, 143; Directors, number of, powers, qualifications, etc., 141; District of Columbia, 138; Dividends and interest, how declared, 148; extra, how declared, 148; unearned, trustees liable for, 148; Improved property to be insured, 146; Incorporators, number of, 138; Insolvent savings banks, 149; Interest, allowance of, how computed, 147; change of rate, posted in bank, deemed personal notice, 148; not to exceed 5 %, 147; rate regulated by trustees, 147; Liquidation, voluntary, 149; Loans, restrictions in regard to, 146; Location may be changed, 145; Organization, certificate shall state, 139; notice of intention, to be published, 139; Pass book, in case of loss, 147; to accompany check, 147; Powers, limited by banking act, 141; Quorum, seven, 141; Real estate, how held, 144; Regulations to be posted in bank and printed in pass books, 143; Restrictions, 146; Stocks and bonds, value to be determined by superintendent, 148; Superintendent, investigation as to proposed company, 140; may apply interest to defray expenses, 149; may extend time to begin business, 141; may refuse to file certificate of organization, 139; to give notice to county clerk of refusal, 140; to report to legislature, 149; Surplus, fund to be accumulated, 147; how determined, 148; Trustees, compensation of, 142; may not borrow from bank, 142; may require bonds of employees, 142; not to be interested in profits, 142; when office becomes vacant, 142

Seigniorage, 24
Sherman law, 24
Silver, 11, 14
  Coinage limited, 24, 60
Silver certificates, 63
State banks, 90
  Affidavit of officers, 94; Annual report to legislature, 97; Banks and officers, 113; Bank, definition of, 93; Banking Department, 93; "Bank," unauthorized persons prohibited from using word, penalty and exception, 109; Bills and notes must be payable on demand, 107; Bills payable in money, 108; Bonds and mortgages, 95; Call loans, 105; Capital, impairment of, 95; minimum to be paid in, 94; Capital stock, how to be paid, 103; Causes of failure of State banking systems, 90; Certificate of authorization to commence business, 94; Certificate of individual banker, 100; Certificate of organization to be filed with superintendent and county clerk, 99; to provide, 99, 100; Change from National to State bank, 105, from State to National bank, 105, 106; of certificate, 99, 100; Circulating notes, etc., 106, 107; Circulation below par not to be paid out, 107; Conditions different in 1892 from previous to 1862, 91; Consolidation of banks, 102; notice of, etc., 102; Contracts, circulating notes, how signed, etc., 104; Corporate life, 99; Creditors to receive notice, 107; Creditors or shareholders may apply for examination of securities, 96; or for receiver, 98; Directors, 105; oath, 103; qualifications, etc. (hold office for one year), 103; Dissenting stockholders, 102; Examiner, not to be appointed receiver, 93; reports to be published, 95; Foreign bank notes not to be issued, 107; Foreign banking corporations must make same deposits as State banks, 95; to secure permission to do business, and appoint superintendent their attorney, 98; instructions, 98; not to receive deposits, 108; General powers, 100; Grace, none, 108; Incorporators, five, 99; Indiana, Ohio, Louisiana, Massachusetts, and New York systems, 91, 92; Information, penalty for refusal to furnish, 96; Interest, rate of, 104; on call loans, 105; Lawful money reserve, amount, where and how held, not to be impaired, etc., 101; Loans, limit of, 97; Location, change of, 98; Losses, how charged, 97; New York State banking laws, 92; Notes payable on demand only to be issued, 107; in lawful money only to be circulated, 108; Officers not to purchase commercial paper at less than face value, 97; Plates and dies, destruction of, 106; Powers of banks, 100; President to be a director, 103; Private bankers, 100; to give information, 96; Profits, calculation of, 97; Real estate as security for circulation, 95; Real Estate, how held, 101; Receiver, appointment of, 98; Reports of examiners may be published, 95; Reports, quarterly, summary to be published, 96; penalty, 96; Residue, distribution of, 107; divided among stockholders, 107; Restrictions as to officers, 97; Securities, comparison of, yearly, 93; deposit of, 94, 95; deposited with Banking Department as guarantee of good faith, 105; kinds of, deposited with Banking Department, 94, 95; may be exchanged, 95; State Banking Department, 93; Superintendent, 93; Stockholders, definition of, 104; dissenting, to consolidation, 102; liability, 104; Transferrees of stock, 104; Uniformity in value of notes, 91; Usury, penalty of, 104
Stock brokers, 182
Stockholders, 210
Stocks or shares, 209
  Assented, 216; Assessable, 211; Common, 212; Cumulative, 212; Dividend, 215; Ex-Dividend, 215; First assessment paid, 216; Guaranteed, 216; Non-assessable, 211; Non-cumulative, 213; Preferred, 212; Promoters', 215
Sub-Treasury, New York, 64
  Balances, 66; Cost of handling money, 65; Disbursements, 66; Receipts, 66
Supply and demand (price), 54
Supply, available (price), 54

INDEX.

T

Trades unions, 55
Transmission of money, 237
  Post office orders, fees charged, 237
Transportation, 52
Transportation and procurability, 52
Transportation companies, 53, 181
Treasury notes, 62
Trust companies, 150
  Authorization, certificate of, to be filed with county clerk and superintendent, 159; Authorization may be refused by superintendent, 159; Auxiliaries to banks, 152; Banks, comparison with trust companies, 151; relation to, 150; Capital, entire amount to be paid in, 158; how invested, 159; minimum, 158; Circulating notes, not issued by trust companies, 155; Consolidation and merger of trust companies, 162; Corporate life, fifty years, 153; Depositors, character of, 152; Deposits, character of, 152; Directors, board of, how chosen, 160; election of, 161; how classified, 160; liability of, 161; qualifications, 160; Escrow, papers held in, 154; Executor, administrator, etc., when, to furnish statements, accounts, etc., 159; Financial agent, as, 162; Incorporators, number of, 158; Superintendent to ascertain as to fitness, 158; Interest, on what paid, 160; Letters testamentary, etc., 159; Loans, character of, 152; Management, 160; Organization certificate, notice to be published and sent to other trust companies before filing, 158; what it must state and where to be filed, 158; Payment of money and performance of obligations, agent for, 155; Powers and limitations, 156, 157; Registrar, 154; Reorganization, agent of, 154; Stock and bond holders, agent of, 154; Stockholders, liability of, 161; Stocks, holding of, limited, 160; Trust company, incorporated under special laws, 161; Trust funds, how invested, 160; Trustee, executor, administrator, etc., advantage of trust company, 153.
Trust company receipts, 226

U

Uniformity in value of notes, 69
United States money, table of, 64
United States notes (greenbacks), 62
United States Treasury notes, 62

V

Value, definition and principles of, 4
  Divisibility, 7; fixed by barter, 5, 17; gold the universal standard of, 13; Intermediate, 7; Intrinsic, 5; Labor measure of, 4; Limitation of quantity, 5; Measure of, 5, 12; Metals the measure of, 6; Relative, 11; Standard, 12; how fixed, 12; Standard of, effect on price, 57; where fixed, 12
Values of Foreign Coins, Table No. I., 262; Remarks as to use of table. 264

W

Warehouse receipts, 243
Weight of Unit of Foreign Currencies (Table No. II.), 266; Remarks as to use of table, 264
West, development of, 180

www.ingramcontent.com/pod-product-compliance
Lightning Source LLC
Chambersburg PA
CBHW022022240426
43667CB00042B/1053